Assessment in Early Childhood Settings

Assessment in Early Childhood Settings

Learning Stories

Margaret Carr

Los Angeles • London • New Delhi • Singapore • Washington DC

SAGE Publications Ltd
1 Oliver's Yard
55 City Road
London EC1Y 1SP

SAGE Publications Inc.
2455 Teller Road
Thousand Oaks, California 91320

SAGE Publications India Pvt Ltd
B 1/I 1 Mohan Cooperative Industrial Area
Mathura Road, New Delhi 110 044

SAGE Publications Asia-Pacific Pte Ltd
33 Pekin Street #02-01
Far East Square
Singapore 048763

British Library Cataloguing in Publication data

A catalogue record for this book is available from the British Library

ISBN 978 0 7619 6793 4
ISBN 978 0 7619 6794 1 (pbk)

Library of Congress Control Number available

Typeset by Dorwyn Ltd, Rowlands Castle
Printed in Great Britain by CPI Antony Rowe, Chippenham, Wiltshire

UNIVERSITY OF CHICHESTE

FSC
Mixed Sources
Product group from well-managed
forests and other controlled sources
Cert no. SGS-COC-2953
www.fsc.org
© 1996 Forest Stewardship Council

372.
21
CAR

Contents

To the next two generations: Merophie, David, Moses,
Polly, Robbie and Lydia

Who understand that well-being is about connecting
cognition with affect in music, dance, story and play; and
whose capacity to enjoy unscripted pathways and
uncertain outcomes I regard with esteem and admiration.

Preface

> Assessment is arguably the most powerful policy tool in education. Not only can it be used to *identify* strengths and weaknesses of individuals, institutions and indeed whole systems of education; it can also be used as a powerful source of *leverage* to bring about change. (Broadfoot, 1996a, p. 21; emphasis in the original)

In recent times, and for a number of reasons, the early childhood profession in many countries has been asked to implement assessment procedures that document children's learning and progress. This book tells about the work of a number of early childhood practitioners who have been looking for a way to do this. Many practitioners have been ill-equipped for the task. When we began this journey many of them resisted the role of assessors standing in judgement, and said that assessment took them away from what they liked doing best: working and being with young children. Most of them were sceptical about the worth of writing down and recording children's development; they saw it as an administrative task for external audit, a waste of their valuable time.

I had from 1989 to 1991 been co-directing a national early childhood curriculum development team for the Ministry of Education in New Zealand during which we consulted widely with practitioners to develop finally a curriculum that described strands of learning outcome as well-being, belonging, communication, contribution and exploration (Carr and May, 1993, 1994, 2000). This was the learning that practitioners really valued. We emphasised curriculum as being about 'reciprocal and responsive relationships with people, places and things'. But the common assessment schedules at that time were more likely to describe outcomes in terms of the children's physical, intellectual, emotional and social understandings and skills. As practitioners worked with the new curriculum, and tried to implement new requirements for assessment that followed, it appeared that 'If we want to see real curriculum reform, we must simultaneously achieve reform of assessment practices', as Sue Bredekamp and Teresa Rosegrant (1992, p. 29) have commented. Successful work with a curriculum that emphasised relationships and participation was going to require assessment that took the same view.

This curriculum project was followed by a Ministry of Education research project called Assessing Children's Experiences in Early Childhood Settings. When we began, I think the practitioners and I wanted to seize the notion of assessment, shake it around a bit, turn it upside down, and find something that was part of enjoying the company of young children. The practitioners liked the idea of starting with stories. So this journey towards a different way of doing things began. We worked in five different early childhood settings. The *childcare centre* was a non-profit childcare centre, run by a Community Trust in a small city (100,000 population) in New Zealand. The centre ran two programmes: one for 10–12 under-twos and one for 30–32 over-twos; there were ten staff. The *kindergarten* ran a sessional programme (five mornings or three afternoons) in the same city as the childcare centre and was one of 28 kindergartens under the umbrella of a local kindergarten association. Set in a suburb of low-cost housing, its catchment area also included farming communities on the outskirts of the city. The morning enrolment was 44 children, and there were three teachers. The *home-based setting* was one of about 100 home-based placements run by a childcare community trust. The same trust ran two childcare centres, one of which provided the data for the childcare setting. The group size in this setting varied during the study from three to four, and the age group from 14 months to 4:1 years. Documentation over three months was analysed for the two regular children aged around three years. *Te Kōhanga Reo* was an urban-based total immersion early childhood Māori language centre (early childhood). It was chartered to the Te Kōhanga Reo National Trust and licensed for up to 16 children to attend from 9 a.m. to 3 p.m. Children who attended were aged from babies to five years. The real names of staff and children are used, with permission. The *playcentre* was a parent cooperative, run by parents under the umbrella of the New Zealand Playcentre Association. It was a sessional programme, meeting in the mornings. Twenty-two children ranging in age from 18 months to 5 years attended, and on any one morning an average of five or six parents (during the project these were always mothers) took responsibility for the session (a system known as team supervision). The Final Report went to the Ministry in 1998 (Carr, 1998a). We made three videos of the project, and added an accompanying booklet that included four workshops and seven readings (Carr, 1998b).

Another enterprise that influenced me greatly was a research study (Carr, 1997, 2000a, 2000b, 2001) on technological practice in early childhood. In that study I had been closely observing four-year-olds making things with cardboard, glue, staples and paint over a period of time, and was wondering whether the idea of 'learning narratives' was a useful one to describe (and therefore to record) what they were learning. This book also includes data from those observations of five activities or technological practices in a kindergarten. This kindergarten was sited in a suburb of medium-income housing; its catchment area included a nearby area of low-cost housing and a farming community.

There are some housekeeping matters: a note about language, and some acknowledgements. Writers in early childhood always have to decide what label to give the adult: a teacher, an educator, a practitioner, an adult, a member of staff, a (usually home-based) carer, te kaiako, te kaiawhina. In a parent cooperative, the adults are parents; in the context of te kōhanga reo, ako means to teach (and to learn), awhi means to care, so kaiako implies more of a 'teaching' role that kaiawhina. I prefer practitioner as a general term; my students tell me they prefer educator; many writers insist on teacher. I have no strong feelings about it, and will use different labels for different situations. This is not to imply that a practitioner or a member of staff in a childcare centre does not teach; or that a teacher does not care.

The project for Assessing Children's Experiences was funded by the Ministry of Education Research Division, and I thank them for that funding and for the Ministry's continued interest and support. I want to thank the Research Division for permission to use the data from the Final Report to the Ministry for this book. Many thanks to the practitioners who contributed to the case studies: Margaret Barclay, Mere Skerrett-White, Merren Goodison, Wendy Lee, Annette Rush, Sue Zonneveld, Leigh Williams-Hobbs and Rosina Merry; to Jill Farr, Jane Barron and Kiri Gould for researcher assistance; and to the practitioners' families and children at Ferndale, Grandview, Mt Eden, Akarana, St Andrews, Insoll Avenue and Constance Colegrove kindergartens, St Marks Community Crêche, Lintott Childcare Centre, Hamilton Childcare Services Trust Home-based programme, Te Amokura Kōhanga Reo and two Playcentres (from Waikato and Bay of Plenty Associations), for their observations and Learning Stories. Able administrative assistance for the Ministry assessment project was given by Haley Stewart and Janet Mitchell; and Raewyn Oulton drew the diagrams for the technological practice project and this book. Corinne Nicholson has provided support in many many ways, including the process of communicating across the world with the very consultative and thoughtful editors at Paul Chapman and Sage. Additional data for Chapter 3 was provided by the family of two-year-old Moses. I am grateful to his parents for their collection of stories. Thank you too to Andrew Barclay, now aged thirteen, and his mother Margaret Barclay for permission to use in Chapter 2 the transcript about mathematics that Margaret taped when he was two years old. This transcript, together with the transcript of Joe and Mark trying to make sense of pirates and masters of the universe, in Chapter 1, first appeared in the *Australian Journal of Early Childhood*, Volume 19, Number 2, 1994. Darryn's mother's Parent's Voice in Chapter 9 first appeared in *R.E.A.L.* magazine, Issue 3, October/November 1999. Assessment data from early childhood centres collected since the two research projects (the one on assessment and the one on technological practice) includes, with permission, the children's and the practitioners' real names.

Learning stories from early childhood centres not involved in the original projects have been mostly collected by professional development facilitators. I am especially grateful to Wendy Lee for her assiduous and enthusiastic collections, and to the parents, children and practitioners who have given permission for these to be included in the book. Many thanks too to the University of Waikato Professional Development team who have kept me up to date on progress in their centres as well. I regret that I did not have space to include all the wonderful assessment stories that came my way. Helen May, Anne Smith, Val Podmore, Pam Cubey, Anne Hatherly, Bernadette Macartney and Bronwen Cowie have all provided ideas and support during joint projects that link to this book; at Harvard in the fall of 1995 David Perkins and Shari Tishman helped me to sharpen my ideas about dispositions. The writing of the book began in the UK in 1999, thanks to the leave programme at the University of Waikato and to the hospitality and friendship of Nomi Rowe Rakovsky, Tina Bruce, Margie Whalley, Iram Siraj-Blatchford and Guy Claxton; Guy's contribution began with our joint paper on the 'costs of calculation' in 1989 and the ideas in the book owe much to our many (southern) summers of conversations about learning. My colleagues at the University of Waikato Department of Early Childhood Studies are owed special thanks too: many of them began this journey with me on the national Early Childhood Curriculum Development team. And I warmly thank Malcolm Carr for wise counsel and superb editorial assistance.

Although working with a new curriculum highlighted the challenge of assessing it, the ideas about learning and assessment that underpin this book do not depend on any one curriculum. Hermine Marshall describes a school classroom in which the emphasis was on the challenge of learning:

> Motivation for learning (rather than ritually performing the task) was based on challenge, links to the real world, and student interest. . . . Errors were not evidence of a poor product, but a way to 'figure out what went wrong' and as a source of new learning. (1992, p. 10)

In thinking about this classroom, Marshall used the term 'learning place'. This book writes about the work of early childhood practitioners as they have tried to establish 'learning places' for young children, and to document the learning in them. The first chapter tells of my shift in understanding about learning and assessment, and sets out seven assumptions that I used to hold but now find to be problematic. In the assessment project it soon became clear that we could not proceed with the 'how' of assessment until we confronted 'what' was to be assessed (Drummond and Nutbrown, 1992). Elliot Eisner has commented that what educators say they want to accomplish and how they evaluate what students have learned are often contradictory (2000, p. 346). He adds that: 'Part of the reason for the neglect of more ambitious aspirations is that it is difficult and time-consuming to secure information relevant to their assessment.'

The second chapter and the three that follow tackle this question of 'what' to assess. Chapter 6 asks how the ambitious aspirations of the previous chapters might be assessed. The next four chapters set out the way in which the practitioners in the five case study settings, and some since then, have implemented procedures that attempt to assess the learning that the teachers, the families and the children value. It includes the difficulties and the dilemmas. The final chapter takes up the threads of the earlier chapters to answer two questions that were posed in Chapter 1 and to add another:

- How can we describe early childhood outcomes in ways that make valuable statements about learning and progress?
- How can we assess early childhood outcomes in ways that promote and protect learning?
- How were these educators assisted to make a shift in their thinking about assessment?

I hope the book will be helpful to student teachers and educators interested in assessment, and to early childhood practitioners who have ambitious aspirations for their children and are also contemplating a journey towards assessing the complex and the uncertain.

1

A Folk Model of Assessment – and an Alternative

When I was a beginning kindergarten teacher, twenty years ago, I believed that assessment was about checking to see whether the nearly-school-age children had acquired what I considered to be the requisite skills for school: the list included early writing (writing their name), self-help skills, early mathematics (counting), turn-taking, scissor-cutting. I therefore looked out for the gaps in a school-readiness repertoire, keeping a checklist, and used some direct teaching strategies to do something about them in the months before school. I did not find the process interesting or helpful to me, but I certainly saw it as linked to my reputation as a competent early childhood teacher with the children's families and with the local schools.

There are a number of assumptions about assessment here, and twenty years later I don't hold any of them. My interest has been captured by children like four-year-old Emily, an articulate and confident child, who, when her friend Laura tells her that she has done a jigsaw 'wrong', shouts angrily 'No! Don't call me wrong. If you call me wrong I won't let you stroke my mouse.' I am intrigued by processes in the kindergarten whereby Jason changes the simple activity of 'marble-painting' into a complex and difficult process, teaches Nell (who normally avoids this kind of difficulty) and then Nell teaches Jinny and Nick. In one activity in one centre I frequently hear 'good girl' from the adults but I never hear 'good boy', although boys are participating too. I pursue Myra and Molly who are practising a language that I have called *girl-friend-speak*, a language that involves reciprocal and responsive dialogue but appears to exclude Lisa. I interview Danny about what he finds difficult, and he tells me that it is drawing the triangular back windows of cars. I read a story to two-year-old Moses and he puzzles about whether the ducks have feet under the water, and what kind of feet they are. I hear Trevor advising his friend that if he finds something difficult he should just leave it.

We will meet many of these children again in this book, as I puzzle about whether there is learning going on both above and 'under the water', what kind of learning it is, how we might assess it, and whether, as early childhood educators, it is any of our business.

I have called those twenty-year-old ideas of mine about assessment my 'folk' model of assessment. David Olson and Jerome Bruner (1996) write about 'folk' pedagogy as our everyday intuitive theories about learning and teaching, about what children's minds are like and how one might help them learn. They point out that these everyday intuitive theories and models reflect deeply ingrained cultural beliefs and assumptions. In the case of my folk model of assessment, the assumptions were about: the *purpose* for assessment (to check against a short list of skills that describe 'competence' for the next stage of education), *outcomes of interest* (fragmented and context-free school-oriented skills), *focus for intervention* or attention (the deficits), *validity* of assessment data (objective observations of skills, reflected in a checklist, are best), *progress* (hierarchies of skill, especially in literacy and numeracy), *procedures* (checklists) and *value* (surveillance of me as a teacher). I developed these assumptions as I grew up, from my own experience of teachers and assessment at school and university, from my perception of the experience of my own children in early childhood settings and in school, and from the views of my family and peers. Teacher education had done nothing to shift them.

However, I held that folk model of assessment alongside a very different and more considered model of learning and teaching. Later, together with a group of practitioners who wanted to explore some alternative assessment practices, I had the opportunity to try to integrate our ideas about learning and teaching with a different set of assumptions about assessment. Table 1.1 lists the assumptions of my folk model about assessment, and sets alongside them the assumptions of an alternative model. These alternative assumptions are outlined in this chapter and form the basis for this book.

Purpose

An assumption that I was making twenty years ago was that assessment sums up the child's knowledge or skill from a predetermined list. Harry Torrance and John Pryor have described this assumption as 'convergent' assessment. The alternative is 'divergent' assessment, which emphasises the learner's understanding and is jointly accomplished by the teacher and the learner. These ideas reflect not only

Table 1.1. Assumptions in two models of assessment: a folk model and an alternative

Assumptions about	My folk model about assessment	An alternative model
Purpose	To check against a short list of skills that describe 'competence' at school entry	To enhance learning
Outcomes of interest	Fragmented and context-free school-oriented skills	Learning dispositions
Focus for intervention	Deficit, gap-filling, is foregrounded	Credit, disposition-enhancing, is foregrounded
Validity	Objective observation	Interpreted observations, discussions and agreements
Progress	Hierarchies of skills	Increasingly complex participation
Procedures	Checklists	Learning stories
Value to practitioners	Surveillance by external agencies	For communicating with four audiences: children, families, other staff and self (the practitioner)

views about assessment, but views about learning and teaching as well. I think I was holding a convergent and a divergent view of learning at the same time. In convergent mode I checked the children's achievement against a short list of skills that described 'competence' at school entry. When my checklist indicated a gap in the requisite skills, I devised ways of directly teaching them. In divergent mode I was implementing a play-based programme to enhance the learning I valued at this site, but I did not see a role for assessment or documentation in that.

I don't have any examples of those convergent assessments. However, I do have an example of my working in more divergent mode at that time. Some years after the event I wrote about the invention by one of the four-year-olds at the kindergarten of an accessible carpentry drill (Carr, 1987). I had observed one of the children wielding a G-clamp upside down to 'drill' a dent in the carpentry table. Normally a G-clamp has a cap on the end of the thread so that it doesn't mark the inside of the table when it is clamped on, but this clamp had lost the cap, and the thread had a pointed end. He called out: 'Look, Margaret, I'm drilling a hole.' We discussed how he had transformed a G-clamp into a carpentry drill, and evaluated this invention as potentially providing an extremely helpful artefact for enhancing the children's carpentry. Our drills at that time were of the egg-beater variety, where children had to keep the drill upright while they both pressed down and rotated the handle in a vertical plane. In the new 'drill', the thread maintained the pressure while the child could use both hands to turn the horizontally aligned handle at the top to drill the hole. I later persuaded a parent to weld a threaded bit onto the G-clamp, and set it into a block of wood, and it did indeed enhance the children's problem-solving and planning processes in carpentry. I wrote the story of one of the boys making a boat by drilling two 5mm holes in a block of wood, sawing and hammering in short lengths of dowel (for masts), and then floating it in the water trough (it fell to the side; later modifications to the design to get it to float the right way up were not recorded); and of one of the girls drilling holes in 'wheels' cut from an old broom handle, attaching them with flat-headed nails to the side of a piece of wood, and pulling it along as a car or cart. I had taken photos for the families, but it did not occur to me to write up either the invention or the carpentry as part of an assessment procedure. I think now that documenting that learning at the time would have given the children and the families, and me, some new insights into the goals of our early childhood programme, and of how they might be recognised and developed in other activities.

I was therefore only documenting part of the curriculum, and I was documenting it for an external audience. This may be true for many early childhood educators, and as demands for external accountability press more insistently on the profession, surveillance begins to encroach on intuitive and responsive teaching. The alternative model tries to connect external accountability and responsive teaching together: it advocates the documenting of learner outcomes and it is embedded in episodes of responsive teaching. However, it defines learner outcomes rather differently from the convergent checklist that I employed twenty years ago.

Outcomes of Interest

My folk model of documented assessment viewed learning as individual and independent of the context. Learner outcomes of interest were fragmented and context-free school-oriented skills. The alternative model says that learning always takes some of its context with it, and that, as James Wertsch has suggested, the learner is a 'learner-in-action'. This viewpoint derives mainly from Lev Vygotsky's (1978) notion of 'mediated action'. It takes a view of learning that focuses on the relationship between the learner and the environment, and seeks ways to define and document complex reciprocal and responsive relationships in that environment. Emphasising this view of learning, Barbara Rogoff (1997, 1998) has described development as the 'transformation of participation'.

A number of other writers have emphasised the context- and culture-specific nature of learning. Jerome Bruner (1990, p. 106), for instance, has described this emphasis as a 'contextual revolution' in psychology. Attention has shifted from internal structures and representations in the mind to meaning-making, intention, and relationships in the experienced world. This development is of great interest to early childhood practitioners. The traditional separation of the individual from the environment, with its focus on portable 'in-the-head' skills and knowledge as outcome, has been replaced by attaching social and cultural purpose to skills and knowledge, thereby blurring the division between the individual and the learning environment. One way to look at a range of learning outcomes is to describe them as an accumulation. Table 1.2 sets out four outcomes along an accumulated continuum of complexity.

Table 1.2. Learning outcomes along an acccumulated continuum of complexity

LEARNING OUTCOMES
(i)   Skills and knowledge
(ii)   Skills and knowledge + intent = learning strategies
(iii) Learning strategies + social partners and practices + tools = situated learning strategies
(iv) Situated learning strategies + motivation = learning dispositions

Skills and knowledge

The focus here is on skills and knowledge 'in the head', acquired by the learner. In early childhood there are a number of basic routines and low-level skills that might be, and often are, taught and tested: cutting with scissors, colouring between the lines, saying a series of numbers in the correct sequence, knowing the sounds of letters. Often complex tasks are seen as learning hierarchies with the assumption that smaller units of behaviour need to be mastered as prerequisites for more complex units later on. In B. F. Skinner's words (1954, p. 94, in Shepard, 1991): 'The whole process of becoming competent in any field must be divided into a very large number of very small steps, and reinforcement must be contingent upon the accomplishment of each step.'

Reporting on the implicit learning theories of 50 school district test directors in the USA, Lorrie Shepard noted that one persistent viewpoint seemed to be widely shared by these professionals. She called it the 'criterion-referenced-testing learning theory'. It included two key beliefs. Firstly, tests and the curriculum are synonymous. Shepard interviewed the test directors, and one of them commented (1991, p. 4): 'We have a locally developed criterion referenced testing program, and these are the skills that we have identified as being absolutely essential, and we test and retest until students show mastery.'

Secondly, learning is linear and sequential. Complex understandings can occur only by adding together simpler, prerequisite units of knowledge. Measurement-driven basic-skills instruction is based on a model of learning which holds that 'basic skills should be taught and mastered before going on to higher-order problems' (Shepard, 1991, pp. 2–3). Shepard asks (p. 7): 'What if learning is not linear and is not acquired by assembling bits of simpler learning?' Guy Claxton and I have called this model of learning 'calculated education' in which 'the intelligence of the child is decomposed into its LEGO-like ingredients, and the teacher aims to stick them together, piece by piece' (Carr and Claxton, 1989 p. 133). We pointed out that this model of learning encourages didactic adult-controlled teaching strategies which ignore the particular, the situational and the social dimensions of learning. This model does not serve us well as we try to understand the learning of Emily, Moses, Jason and Nell.

This basic skills model of learning is often used to predict children's prospects at school. The literature on 'school readiness' does not, however, persuade us that particular items of skills and knowledge, unattached to meaningful activities, predict achievement at school. Keith Crnic and Gontran Lamberty, reviewing two decades of research on 'school readiness' in 1994, commented on 'the false notion that we have a basic knowledge regarding the critical skills for school success'. They added:

> While there have been attempts to identify individual developmental or skill correlates of readiness, we currently have no theory or credible empirical base from which to judge what the most critical skills for readiness may be. In this respect, assessing a number of preacademic

cognitive, linguistic, and motor skills may be of interest but of limited assistance in determining the critical readiness issues. (p. 96)

In the same year, Kathy Sylva reviewed studies of the effects of pre-school education on children's development. She concluded that a major effect is 'learning orientation', and she quoted a meta-analysis of the effects of 11 carefully monitored US pre-school education programmes which were part of research programmes:

> (it is) hypothesized that the early education experience may change children from passive to active learners who begin to take the initiative in seeking information, help, and interaction with others. When this increased motivation to learn is met by a positive response at home and at school, long-term gains on outcome measures of cognitive development can result. (Lazar and Darlington, 1982, p. 63, quoted by Sylva, 1994, p. 138)

Of course, teachers and schools may construct a package of entry skills that, through teacher expectation effects, can become critical. But, while skills and knowledge matter a great deal, they will be fragile indeed if institutional arrangements in classrooms and early childhood settings do not embed them in motivating circumstances and imbue them with social and cultural meaning.

Skills and knowledge + intent = learning strategies

Skills that are attached to meaning and intent have been called 'learning strategies'. Similarly, funds of knowledge can be accorded meaning and intent by project approaches that connect homes and classrooms (Moll, Amanti, Neff and Gonzalez, 1992). John Nisbet and Janet Shucksmith suggested that a learning strategy is a series of skills used with a particular purpose in mind: 'Strategies are different from skills in that a strategy has a purpose' (1986, p. vii). Learning strategies are often associated with the idea that children are 'learning to learn'. Nisbet and Shucksmith described strategies like planning ahead, monitoring one's progress to identify sources of difficulty, asking questions. Research in Australia by Joy Cullen described the continuity of learning from early childhood to school in terms of learning strategies, as she observed children using the same strategies in play in their kindergarten and then in reading lessons at school: task persistence, use of (experimenting with) resources, use of peer as a resource, use of adult as a resource, seeing self as a resource for others, directing self, and directing others. She described these as 'repeated patterns of behavior and language which indicate an active, strategic approach to learning' (Cullen, 1991, pp. 45–6). Cullen noted that in the different context of the primary school classroom, however, such abilities or strategies may not be demonstrated. They will not appear if, for instance, there is little opportunity for the child to use a creative approach to choosing resources appropriate to the task in hand, or for the child to see herself as a resource for others.

Learning strategies + social partners and practices + tools = situated learning strategies

At the third level of accumulation, the purpose or intent is linked to social partners and practices, and tools. The learning strategies are *situated*. The focus is on the individual-in-action in which the action is mediated by social partners, social practices and tools (the technology and languages available). This is sometimes called a 'situative' approach, and the outcomes at this level can be called situated learning strategies. The emphasis is on learning as participation in socio-cultural activities, a central focus for this book. Mediated *action* is, as Elizabeth Graue and Daniel Walsh (1995) commented, 'located within specific cultural and historic practices and time'. Writing about qualitative research in early childhood settings they added that mediated action: 'is populated by meaning and intentions, and is tethered to particular communities and individuals (p. 148).' They compare this to a behavioural approach in which 'behavior is stripped of these local characteristics; it is mechanical description without narration'. *Mediated* action is sometimes considered to be *distributed* or 'stretched over' tools as well as social partners and practices. Writing about cognition, Gavriel Salomon comments that distributed cognition elaborates on the notion that 'People appear to think in conjunction or partnership with others and with the help of culturally provided tools and implements' (Salomon, 1993, p. xiii). David Perkins (1992) wrote about distributed cognition as the 'person-plus', and summed up the idea by saying that the surround – the immediate physical, social and symbolic resources outside the person – participates in cognition, not just as a source of input and a receiver of output but as a vehicle of thought. The surround does part of the thinking, and holds part of the learning.

   This notion of thinking or learning being distributed across social practice and partners and tools introduces the idea of learning as a product of reciprocal relations between the environment and the mind, of the learning process as a *transaction*. Individual learners engage in activities and their participation changes the activities while at the same time they are changed by those activities. Jason changes the marble-painting activity (as we will see in greater detail in Chapter 4) and becomes a tutor in the process; Myra and Molly (Chapter 5) are developing a language together, and that language will be taken up by other children; Moses (who appears again in Chapter 3) calls on adults and toys and videos not only to help him develop his fund of knowledge about animals, but to use animals as a metaphor or mechanism for making sense of and manipulating his two-year-old world.

Situated learning strategies + motivation = learning dispositions

The fourth level of accumulation adds *motivation* to situated learning strategies to form learning dispositions (Katz, 1993). A vivid way to describe this accumulation of motivation, situation and skill is to say that a learner is 'ready, willing and able' to learn. Lauren Resnick (1987, pp. 40–2, writing about critical thinking) commented that shaping the disposition is central to developing the ability, and that much of the learning to be a good thinker is learning to recognise and even search for opportunities to apply one's capacities. She added (p. 42) that 'dispositions are cultivated by participation in social communities that value thinking and independent judgement'. If we take the example of communication, or expressing one's ideas, then *being ready* is being motivated or inclined to communicate, *being willing* is recognising that the situation is an appropriate one in which to express one's ideas, and *being able* is the communication skills and understandings that will be needed for this occasion. Kathy Sylva writes about the 'will and skill to do' as a legacy of effective pre-school education (1994, p. 163); and inclination, sensitivity to occasion, and ability have been described as the three components of *thinking* dispositions by David Perkins, Eileen Jay and Shari Tishman (1993). Guy Claxton (1990, p. 164) has commented that in societies where knowledge, values and styles of relationship are undergoing rapid change: 'it can be strongly argued that schools' major responsibility must be to help young people become ready, willing and able to cope with change successfully: that is, to be powerful and effective learners.' Coping with change means coping with changing situations: social partners, social practices and tools. Learning dispositions that take account of the situation can be defined as participation repertoires from which a learner recognises, selects, edits, responds to, resists, searches for and constructs learning opportunities. In this book they will be referred to in a number of ways, as:

- learning dispositions
- being ready, willing and able
- inclination, sensitivity to occasion, and ability
- participation repertoires
- *habitus*.

Habitus is a term used by Pierre Bourdieu (habitus is a Latin word from the Greek *hexis* meaning disposition), useful here because it can also refer to participation repertoires that have become attached to a community. A term that comes from psychology (disposition) has its counterpart in sociology (habitus). It means that when we discuss a learner being *willing* to participate, of great relevance will be whether the participation repertoires that characterise the community in the early childhood setting match those of the learner. Bourdieu used the word *habitus* as 'a system of dispositions acquired by implicit or explicit learning' (1984/1993, p. 76).

> Why did I revive that old word? Because with the notion of *habitus* you can refer to something that is close to what is suggested by the idea of habit, while differing from it in one important respect. . . . Habit is spontaneously regarded as repetitive, mechanical, automatic, reproductive rather than productive. I wanted to insist on the idea that the *habitus* is something powerfully generative. (pp. 86–7)

He says that using this word we are reminded that it refers to something historically determined rather than 'essentialist', like the notion of competence. As Michael Cole has commented (1996, p. 139), a habitus constitutes a usually unexamined background set of assumptions about the world. It includes a learner's assumptions about what is expected in early childhood settings and schools, and, reciprocally, it includes the early childhood setting and school's assumptions about what is expected of a learner or a student. In this book, the terms 'dispositional milieu' and 'learning place' will also be used to refer to participation repertoires that have become attached to, privileged in, an activity or a place or a social community. They owe much to the notion of habitus, but for me they more readily allow the possibility of resistance and change. Chapter 2 discusses learning dispositions, and dispositional milieux, in more detail.

Summary of outcomes of interest

A. V. Kelly (1992) has commented (p. 4) that:

> Accuracy of assessment is related inversely to the complexity and the sophistication of what is being assessed. And, since education is a highly complex and sophisticated process, educational assessment can be regarded as measurement only in the remotest of metaphorical senses.

I have suggested here a way of analysing that complexity in terms of four levels; each level is an accumulation of the outcomes of earlier levels with the addition of another feature. At the final, fourth level, I have described learning as being ready, willing and able to participate in (and to change) learning places and activities. The four levels make up a conceptual hierarchy, not a developmental one. We can assess children's learning at any of the four levels of accumulation. However, assessment that is appropriate for level one outcomes (skills and knowledge) is not appropriate for level four outcomes (learning dispositions). As Elliot Eisner (2000, p. 346) has pointed out, 'tests are poor proxies for things that really matter'. We will have to devise something very different. On occasion, it will be appropriate to assess (perhaps to measure) narrow outcomes, but in the next chapters I will argue that if we only assess at the first three levels, then we will be taking a narrow and impoverished view of children's learning. The fourth level deserves our primary attention.

Focus for Intervention

In my folk model, assessment was designed to highlight deficits. This notion of the developing child as incomplete, a jigsaw with parts missing, means that the areas in which the child is 'unable' become the sites of greatest educational interest. Competencies that can be ticked off the checklist will attract little interest. They've been 'done'. Another option is to ignore all the inabilities, putting them down to developmental immaturity, and reassuring families that achievement is 'just around the corner'. The deficit model says either 'we'll find the missing pieces' or 'don't worry, the missing pieces will turn up in their own time'. The jigsaw model remains the same.

The alternative approach is a credit model, disposition enhancing. The relevant community decides what domains of learning disposition are important, and in a credit model the examples of successful participation that will contribute to the inclination or *being ready* are foregrounded. They are the sites of educational interest because we want their occurrence to be frequent enough to become an inclination. In the words of Lazar and Darlington, quoted earlier, events of successful participation are interpreted as increased motivation to learn and are met by a positive response at home and at school. In the background are the situations or occasions that call on this inclination and encourage the learner to *be willing*. We want these situations to be accessible and recognisable. In the background too are the skills and funds of knowledge that the child will need in order to *be able* to participate in a particular domain of learning disposition.

One of the practitioners trialling the credit model had this to say when I asked if it had been useful for getting to know the children: 'Yes. This (way of doing assessment has) turned me around from just looking at the negative stuff to focusing on the positive.' Another member of staff in the same centre said:

> A really good thing is that because I have been told I need to look more at the positive. Before, and I'm aware of that, because, it's really hard you know, it's a whole change to how you've been brought up and everything and it's actually helped me look at the kids more positively.

Deficit-based assessment is 'how you've been brought up'; a credit-based approach 'turns you around'. Here were early childhood practitioners recognising and resisting their folk models of assessment. 'Looking on the bright side', foregrounding achievement, in the ways that are outlined in this book, is not primarily a matter of encouraging self-esteem; it is a matter of strengthening learning dispositions and of encouraging a view of the self as a learner. Early childhood practitioners frequently foreground the occasion or the situation in order to evaluate their programmes, and assessment often places skills and knowledge in the foreground. Procedures for foregrounding the inclination are less familiar. They set up a credit-based framework, they channel our evaluation of the environment and the relevance of skills and funds of knowledge, and they form the basis for the alternative model of assessment outlined in this book. Foregrounding the inclination forms the *raison d'être* for turning our attention to occasion or ability.

Notions of Validity

The notion that an external 'objective' measure or standard exists for all outcomes (if only we can find it) was another feature of my folk model of assessment. I looked for performances that could be scored independently by people who had no additional knowledge about the student. In the alternative approach, however, assessment of the complex outcomes outlined above (learning dispositions, the learner-in-action and -in-relationships) is a central puzzle. To be valid, these assessments must go beyond anecdote, belief and hope. They will require interpreted observations, discussions and agreements. This process of assessment is like action research, with the teacher/researcher as part of the action. Assessment procedures in early childhood will call on interpretive and qualitative approaches for the same reasons a researcher will choose interpretive and qualitative methods for researching complex learning in a real-life early childhood setting. These reasons include an interest in the learner-in-action or -in-relationships, and an interest in motivation – in understanding the learning environment from the children's point of view. A number of people's opinions will be surveyed, including the children's, and often the assessments will be tentative. Guidelines for the assessment of complex outcomes will be developed in Chapters 3, 4, 5 and 6, and in Chapter 11 the discussion will return to validity after the details of alternative assessment procedures have been established.

Both research and assessments, in trying to 'make sense' of data and turn in a plausible story, always run the risk of over-simplification: losing the rich and often ambiguous complexity of young children's behaviour. As Ann Knupfer warns, writing about research (but her comments are equally applicable to assessment), when adults attempt to understand, to 'tell the story' of a child's learning: 'We can run the risk of not fully addressing the perplexities, the contradictions, and the conflicting perspectives if we attempt to create cohesion at the expense of complexity' (1996, p. 142). Discussions with and observations by a number of interested parties, including the child, can be a source of what Graue and Walsh have called 'thick' description, acknowledging contradiction, ambiguity, inconsistency, and situation-specific factors. Linda spends half the morning at kindergarten flitting from one activity to another, appearing anxious about whether everyone is behaving agreeably, then she sits down with Meg and they work together on a complex joint project for the best part of an hour. We observe and listen closely over long periods of time, and try to find the child's point of view. When we conjecture about progress, we will often be wrong.

Ideas about Progress

The folk model of assessment with which I began included the notion that all learning could be described as a progression through a hierarchy of skills. Piagetian stage theory, and the strong influence of the early intervention movement in early childhood, have provided a firm foundation for the viewpoint that skills and understandings have an 'early' stage and that the task of early childhood education is to ensure that specific developmental skills are taught in an orderly sequence.

A particular hierarchy or sequence implies a single *endpoint*, but views about the domains of intelligence have changed substantially since Jean Piaget's theory of a logico-mathematical endpoint to development. In 1979 the writers of an innovative Piaget-based curriculum for children (the Weikart High/Scope programme: Hohmann, Banet and Weikart) could assume that learning is about individuals acquiring knowledge and skills of an increasingly general, abstract, symbolic and logical nature: treading the path towards a much later endpoint called 'formal operations'. In more recent years, that single developmental path has given way to alternatives. Stages have in effect been tipped on their side and described as different and equally valuable modes of making sense of the world. The notion of multiple ways of thinking and knowing has challenged what Shirley Turkle and Seymour Papert (1992, p. 3) have called the 'hegemony of the abstract, formal, and logical' in particular to give renewed value to the concrete and the 'here and now', originally seen in Piagetian terms as an immature stage of development. Seymour Papert (1993) emphasised action and 'concreteness' and criticised what he called the 'perverse commitment to moving as quickly as possible from the concrete to the abstract' (p. 143) at school. He put it nicely when he suggested that 'formal methods are on tap, not on top' (p. 146). The value of Piaget's work, he maintained, is that he gave us valuable insights into the workings of a non-abstract way of thinking but (together with Lévi-Strauss):

> They failed to recognize that the concrete thinking they had discovered was not confined to the underdeveloped – neither to Lévi-Strauss's 'undeveloped' societies nor to Piaget's not yet 'developed' children. Children do it, people in Pacific and African villages do it, and so do most sophisticated people in Paris or Geneva. (p. 151)

Cross-cultural studies have also challenged beliefs in the universality of one particular endpoint, individual rationalism, indicating that any valued endpoint is a cultural construction not a developmental inevitability. Some West African communities define stages of development to full selfhood using social signposts. Children are assigned different roles at different stages of life, and progress is defined as increased authority and shared responsibility within the social community (Nsamenang and Lamb, 1998). Amongst the Yoruba in Nigeria, religion was characterised by an elaborate system of deities, each with their own duties and functions, and the culture accorded high value to the realistic plastic arts and drama. The Nupe, also of Nigeria, on the other hand, valued the decorative arts and had no similar tradition of drama; their religion centred around an 'abstract impersonal power' (Nadel, 1937, cited by Cole, 1996, p. 61). Margaret Donaldson, in *Human Minds*, has suggested two major pathways of development: the intellectual and the emotional. In the 'value-sensing' emotional pathway the imagination is central. She reminds us (p. 259) that education is about increasing what she calls the 'modal' repertoire: 'It is about suggesting new directions in which lives may go.' I agree.

The following is a transcript of two four-year-olds that illustrates two ways of knowing or making sense: the logical and the narrative. Here the discussion starts with the adult (me) trying to find out the children's definitions of pirates and 'masters of the universe', but it develops into an attempt by Mark to reassure himself, through deductive logic, that pirates (who kill people) will not come to the kindergarten. Joe, displaying an equal facility not with logic but with imaginative narrative, takes another point of view.

Me: What do pirates do, then?

Joe: They kill people.

Me: They kill people. (pause) What else do pirates do?

Joe: And they have pirate ships. Captain Pugwash has got 'Black Pig'. (laughs)

Me: That's right. It's a funny name, isn't it, for a ship.

Mark: Pirates have ships and masters [of the universe] don't have ships.

Me: Ah. . . . I see, that would be a good, that would be a good, a useful, difference.

Mark: So pirates can't come here. They have to float 'cos they can't float in New Zealand, there's no water (pause) so they can't come inside the kindy because um this isn't water outside.

Me: I see. That's right. They couldn't bring their ships right up to the door of the kindergarten, could they.

Joe: But they might be able to c . . . They might be able (pause) get a horsie (pause) come and swim through the water and get them and they can hop on their back and swim through the water again (Mark: No!) and go to the shore and race off to kindy.

> Mark: No they just (pause) um going to land on the um horse but they just but the horses just run on land (pause) and walk on land.
>
> Me: Uh huh.

Mark's logic is as follows. Premise one: All ships have to have water. Premise two: All pirates have to have ships. Premise three: There's no water here. Therefore, no water implies no ships and no ships implies no pirates. Joe introduces a narrative that includes the notion of swimming horses, an idea that is firmly rejected by Mark. They are each practising and hearing different modes or genres of persuasion.

A second challenge to the idea of progress as development through a series of cognitive stages has been the *integration* of affect with cognition, to emphasise relationships as a valued domain of knowledge. Nel Noddings, for instance, writes about an ethic of 'responsibility' and 'care' in which relations with others are a *primary* aim in education rather than a means to an end. It is interesting that at the same time as the concept 'care' was being edged out of early childhood rhetoric by the Piagetians, and 'early childhood care and education' was becoming 'early childhood education', care was re-entering educational discourse from another direction. Thus, a writer on science education in schools (Peter Taylor, in 1998) would comment that:

> an ethic of care helps to avoid self-serving relations of domination by focusing a primary concern on the need for the teacher to nurture an empathic, honest, interdependent and trustful relationship with the student. . . . In the absence of an ethic of care, which celebrates feelings, values and emotionality in communicative relationships, the threads of knowing and being are likely to be woven into a cultural fabric of ephemeral value. (pp. 1120, 1121)

A nice recognition of the duality is illustrated by Anne Smith's (1992) introduction to early childhood of the term 'educare', also taken up by others.

Therefore, new voices have suggested that responsibility, care and intuition are endpoints too. Relationships have been emphasised as central to the trajectory from early childhood experience into later learning, and these relationships may be more than mediating variables, means to cognitive ends. Reciprocal relationships and opportunities for participation, valuable in the here and now of an early childhood setting, are also pivotal to the first messages about the self as a learner that children receive in early childhood settings, messages that have an enduring effect on their capacities to learn in later years. What do they tell us about progress? Writers using ecological and socio-cultural frameworks have provided some theoretical guidelines. The theoretical perspectives that I have found useful for this question of progress are as follows. Jean Lave and Étienne Wenger described development and progress as a shift in participation from the edge (periphery) of the activities of a community to taking on a more central role. Barbara Rogoff (1997) described development as transformation of participation. Her list of features for the evaluation of learning and development from this perspective included: changing involvement and role, approaches to participation flexibly shifting from home to school, an interest in 'learning' versus an interest in protecting the status quo, and the taking of responsibility in cultural activities including 'flexibility and vision' in revising ongoing community practices. Bonnie Litowitz (1997) has also emphasised participation as responsibility and resistance (transaction and reciprocity): the child may bring a very different view from the adult to an activity or a task. Urie Bronfenbrenner (1979, pp. 60, 163, 212) has said that learning and development are facilitated by the participation of the developing person in *progressively more complex activities and patterns of reciprocal interaction*, and by *gradual 'shifts in the balance of power' between the learner and the adult*. His ecological theory also maintains that development and learning are about the learner taking on roles and relationships in an *increasing number of structurally different settings*.

We have, however, few examples of early childhood practitioners translating these ideas into assessment practice, and this book provides some. As practitioners and I worked together on assessment projects to implement some of these alternative theoretical approaches, to help the children they were working with, and to share ideas with families, five features of participation emerged. They were the following, and they are discussed further in the next four chapters:

- taking an interest in aspects of the early childhood setting that might be the same or different from home; coping with transition and changing situations;
- being involved, at an increasingly complex level;
- persistence with difficulty or uncertainty: an interest in 'learning' and a capacity to risk error or failure;
- communicating with others, expressing a point of view, an idea or an emotion;
- taking increasing responsibility in a range of ways.

The experience of the practitioners planning for progress using a participatory and dispositional framework is described in Chapter 10.

Procedures

It seems, then, that my checklist was not the only, or the best, way to document learning in early childhood. One of the advantages of a checklist is that it takes little time, whereas qualitative and interpretive methods using narrative methods – learning stories – are time-consuming. Practitioners using storied approaches of assessment, however, become part of a rich tradition of ethnographic and case study observations in early childhood. Susan Isaacs' observations in the 1930s are, in Mary Jane Drummond's words (1999, p. 4), 'transformed into a geography of learning, as she charts the children's explorations of both their inner and outer worlds'. More recently, in the UK, Andrew Pollard and Ann Filer have used case studies to analyse pupil identity and progress, while in the USA and Australia, narrative methods have frequently been used to study children becoming students, becoming literate, and (Vivian Gussin Paley, 1986) exploring 'the three Fs: fantasy, fairness and friendship'. However, although I commented earlier that a teacher is like an action researcher, assessment of ongoing learning in an early childhood centre by practitioners is rather different from observations by a visiting researcher. Staff have had to develop ways in which these more story-like methods can be manageable. The practitioners whose experience is documented in this book have had to become increasingly skilled at recognising 'critical' moments and memorising the events while jotting down the conversations, and assessment has become less likely to take them away from the 'real' action of teaching and enjoying working with children. Situated frameworks call for the adult to be included in the observations as well, and for many practitioners this is unusual and difficult. Chapters 7, 8, 9 and 10 tell the 'teachers' stories' as practitioners in early childhood settings trialled qualitative approaches to assessment that included writing learning stories about the children.

Value to Practitioners

Twenty years ago I saw documented assessment as only valuable to me when my reputation with outside agencies was at stake. It was as if in my mind I had a 'league table' of early childhood centres, and I wanted to be reassured that my children were achieving up there with the others from the early childhood centre down the road. Also, I did not want to be blamed by the school and the families for any child's low level of preparation for school. However, as I have worked together with practitioners on different ways of doing assessment that have linked more closely to curriculum implementation, a number of more valuable reasons for documented assessment have emerged. Value for practitioners has included. (i) to understand, get to know, be 'in tune' with individual children, (ii) to understand children by using the documentation as a catalyst for discussion with others, (iii) to share information with others in this setting, (iv) to reflect on practice, and (v) to plan for individuals and groups. Other values included involving the children in self-assessment, discussing the programme with families, and sharing experiences with families. These values can to a certain extent be grouped in terms of the immediate *audience*: the children, families, other staff, and the self.

Concluding Comments

This chapter has outlined a shift in my views of assessment, along seven dimensions, from a 'folk' model of twenty years ago, to my current understanding of what the much more complex parameters of an alternative model might look like. That model is elaborated in this book. I have come around to Mary Jane Drummond's definition of assessment. She says that assessment is: 'the ways in which, in our everyday practice, we observe children's learning, strive to understand it, and then put our understanding to good use' (1993, p. 13). Assessment then has four characteristics: it is about everyday practice (in this place), it is observation-based (including talking to children), it requires an interpretation, and it points the way to better learning and teaching.

It is ironic that in the latter part of the twentieth century, and at the dawn of the twenty-first, at the same time as we are becoming aware that a key feature of children's learning is that it is situated in activity and social practice, governments are requiring national curricula and universal measures of individual achievement. In many countries, this 'gaze' or surveillance (terms used by Michel Foucault and Nikolas Rose to refer to assessment of various kinds) has been focused on children in early childhood centres. Early childhood programmes are often besieged by school curricula and school entry assessments as well. At the beginning of this chapter I asked whether assessing learning in early childhood is any of our business. It has become our business as early childhood educators to respond to these demands and in doing so, in many cases, to reframe the purpose, the outcomes, the items for intervention, the definitions of validity and progress, the procedures, and the value for practitioners. Reframing the rules and redefining curriculum and achievement may simply be exchanging one form of surveillance for another. But we have a responsibility to ensure that the new communities we are constructing for children, in childcare centres and kindergartens for instance, are ethical and safe environments in which all children learn. Early childhood practitioners therefore have to make some assumptions about learning, assessment and evaluation (as well as about ethics and safety) that are informed and reflective. This book asks the following two questions:

- How can we describe early childhood outcomes in ways that make valuable statements about learning and progress?
- How can we assess early childhood outcomes in ways that promote and protect learning?

The alternative assumptions about assessment outlined in this chapter have emphasised two major views about learning outcomes that will influence the discussions of assessment in this book. The first view is that learning can be described as transformation of participation, that it is situated in social practice and activities, and includes responsibility and resistance. The second view is that learning of interest will include motivation, and that learning dispositions, that add motivation to situated learning strategies, are very complex outcomes. The next four chapters have more to say about complex learning outcomes at the fourth level: Chapter 2 develops further the concept of a learning disposition and introduces five possible domains for their description, and Chapters 3, 4 and 5 elaborate on these domains. Chapter 6 outlines how learning dispositions might be assessed. Chapters 7, 8, 9 and 10 provide details of how early childhood practitioners have tried to find ways to describe and assess complex outcomes in ways that promote and protect learning. They describe the processes that teachers went through to change their assessment procedures, and, for many of them, to shift from a folk to an alternative model.

2

Learning Dispositions

Learning dispositions were introduced in the previous chapter as situated learning strategies plus motivation – participation repertoires from which a learner recognises, selects, edits, responds to, resists, searches for and constructs learning opportunities. I also described them in terms of being ready, willing and able to participate in various ways: a combination of inclination, sensitivity to occasion, and the relevant skill and knowledge. A scaffolding metaphor of teaching – in which the teacher takes the child to the next step in a task, gives some assistance, and then gradually withdraws the assistance so that the child can perform the skill all by her- or himself – assumes, as Jacqueline Goodnow (1990) has commented, a picture not only of 'willing' teachers on the one hand but of 'eager' learners on the other. Our experience reminds us that children are not always eager (ready and willing) to learn in the domain that we are willing to teach. How can eager learning be described and encouraged? This chapter sets out, and argues for, five domains of learning dispositions. It then picks up the idea that learning dispositions can become attached to activities and places, and introduces the idea of a 'dispositional milieu' or learning place. Finally, more explanation will be given of the notion of foregrounding and backgrounding, introduced in the previous chapter.

The concept of a 'disposition' comes from developmental psychology. In everyday speech we often use it like 'temperament': we comment that someone has a 'cheerful disposition'. It is seen as a quality of an individual, something he or she was born with, or an outcome of facilitating circumstances. When motivation is situated, however, as David Hickey points out, 'context has a fundamental, rather than merely a facilitative role' (1997, p. 177). Lilian Katz made this point when she commented that: 'Dispositions are a very different type of learning from skills and knowledge. They can be thought of as habits of mind, tendencies to *respond to situations* in certain ways' (1988, p. 30, my emphasis).

In this book, learning dispositions are about responsive and reciprocal relationships between the individual and the environment. They form a repertoire of familiar and privileged processes of contribution and communication. Emphasising the contextual and socio-cultural connection, Barbara Comber called on Pierre Bourdieu's notion of *habitus* to analyse the transition from early childhood programmes to literacy lessons at school for a number of Australian children. She pointed out that the children:

> take with them to school their health and ill health and their contrastive accumulations of privileges and disadvantages or as Bourdieu (1990, 1991) puts it, their economic, cultural, social, symbolic, and linguistic *capital* and their *habitus*, sets of dispositions acquired in daily life, that incline people to act in particular ways. (2000, p. 39)

She described the successful transition to school of two children, Tessa and Mark, commenting on their 'willingness to display their knowledge and to elicit help', which meant that they often received the feedback, advice and teaching they needed at exactly the right time. Another child, for whom transition was a negative experience, appeared to 'reject his teacher's offers of pedagogical support as yet another occasion of adult surveillance' (p. 46).

Five Domains of Learning Dispositions

What domains of learning disposition are of interest? In the last chapter I signalled my interest in Emily's concern about 'being wrong', and Moses' capacity for articulating his curiosity when the topic was one for which he had a considerable fund of knowledge (animals and feet). Comber commented on Tessa and Mark's willingness to display their knowledge and to elicit help from adults and peers. Within the framework being developed in this book, learning dispositions will be about becoming a participant in a learning place and taking a critical approach to that participation. They won't be fundamentally about enhancing numeracy and literacy, a beloved topic of curriculum developers, but learning dispositions will contribute to developing understandings in a range of school curriculum areas. Writing about the concern for early literacy in school (and, I would add, an increasing feature of early childhood curriculum), Comber commented:

> I do not want to romanticise this at all, but it is interesting to think about the panic and anxiety that the demand for six-year-old, independent readers produces here in Australia, when in other countries

children do not even begin formal schooling or literacy learning until later. We need to be careful about the effects of privileging literacy at the expense of other important capabilities and explore ways that children's existing knowledges, capabilities, and interests might be used in the design of school literacies. (p. 46)

Domains of learning disposition were introduced in the section on progress in the last chapter:

- taking an interest
- being involved
- persisting with difficulty or uncertainty
- communicating with others
- taking responsibility.

The domains are analysed in Table 2.1 as three parts: being ready, being willing and being able. The table provides general descriptions, empty of context, within each table cell to illustrate the different parts. *Being ready* is a primary (foregrounded) focus of interest in this book, but it must be supported by *being willing* (an evaluation of local opportunities and a sensitivity by the learner to those local opportunities) and *being able* (funds of knowledge and abilities that support the inclination). In essence, being ready is about seeing the self as a participating learner, being willing is recognising that this place is (or is not) a place for learning, and being able is having the abilities and funds of knowledge that will contribute to being ready and being willing. In Chapter 7 the three parts will be linked to real contexts in the analysis of a project in a kindergarten, and to an episode of learning for four-year-old Chata. These particular domains have emerged from research, observations and discussions in early childhood settings in a small country in the South Pacific, New Zealand, which has a bi-cultural and socio-culturally conceived national early childhood curriculum. Learning outcomes in that curriculum are set out in five broad strands: belonging, well-being, exploration, communication and contribution. The curriculum emphasises a weaving metaphor for local programme development (New Zealand Ministry of Education, 1996a): early childhood settings 'weave' their programmes from national and local strands. This array of learning dispositions therefore derives from a particular place at a particular time. Nevertheless it serves as a case study of a framework of situated and dispositional learning outcomes and the assessment that followed. The following sections elaborate on the five domains of learning disposition.

Table 2.1.   Learning dispositions: the three parts

DOMAIN OF LEARNING DISPOSITIONS	BEING READY Children are developing:	BEING WILLING Children are developing:	BEING ABLE Children are developing:
taking an interest	interests; expectations that people, places and things can be interesting; a view of self as interested and interesting.	a preparedness to recognise, select or construct interests in this place, to make connections between artefacts, activities and social identities across places.	abilities and funds of relevant knowledge that support their interests.
being involved	readiness to be involved, pay attention, for a sustained length of time; a view of self as someone who gets involved.	informed judgements about the safety and trustworthiness of the local environment.	strategies for getting involved and remaining focused.
persisting with difficulty or uncertainty	enthusiasm for persisting with difficulty or uncertainty; assumptions about risk and the role of making a mistake in learning; a view of self as someone who persists with difficulty and uncertainty.	sensitivity to places and occasions in which it is worthwhile to tackle difficulty or uncertainty and to resist the routine.	problem-solving and problem-finding knowledge and skills; experience of making mistakes as part of solving a problem.
communicating with others	the inclination to communicate with others in one or more of '100 languages' (Edwards, Gandini and Forman, 1993), to express ideas and feelings; a view of self as a communicator.	responses to a climate in which children have their say and are listened to.	facility with one or more languages, widely defined; familiarity with a range of context-specific 'genres'; script knowledge for familiar events.

taking responsibility	a habit of taking responsibility in a range of ways, to take another point of view, to recognise justice and to resist injustice; a view of self and others as citizens with rights and responsibilities.	recognition or construction of opportunities to take responsibility.	experience of responsibility, making decisions, being consulted; an understanding of fairness and justice; strategies for taking responsibility.

Taking an interest

Taking an interest is the first domain of learning dispositions. Here is Andrew's mother talking to two-year-old Andrew while he is finishing his dinner. Margaret B. (Andrew's mother) was tape recording the occasional interaction at home for me, and she knew that I was doing some research on mathematics learning in early childhood. Note how the interest level of both Margaret and Andrew appears to shift when Margaret (perhaps) forgets her academic purpose and remembers Kylie's birthday.

Mother: How many ducks on your bib?
Andrew: A two duck.
Mother: Look and see. You tell me. One. . . .
Andrew: Free.
Mother: Two.
Andrew: Free.
Mother: Three.
Andrew: Four.
Mother: Good boy. Four. That's how old Kylie's going to be. Four. In ten days' time. She's going to have a birthday.
Andrew: I'm sick? I'm tick?
Mother: No. Daniel'll be six. You have to be a big school person to be six.
Andrew: I'm two.
Mother: That's right. You're two.
Andrew: I'm a scoo- boy . . . I'm a goo- boy?
Mother: (misunderstanding) You are a good boy, eaten all your dinner up.
Andrew: I'm a goo- boy? I'm a goo- boy?
Mother: A school boy? Oh, a school boy. No, you can't be a school boy until you're five.

Andrew: Mummy ga a Mum a coo-boy?
Mother: Mummy can't be a school boy!
Andrew: Yeah. My Da a coo-boy?
Mother: Daddy was a school boy, yes.

Margaret starts off 'scaffolding' the number sequence for counting, and Andrew politely responds. However, when her mind strays to a topic of interest to her (the need to get a birthday present for Kylie's birthday perhaps), Andrew seizes on the new topic as being of great interest to him: birthdays and becoming a school boy. In fact the conversation is still about number, but number has now been back-grounded: in the foreground is Andrew's interest in, and attempt to make sense of, the relationships in his culture between age and (school) status. Perhaps we could say that Andrew sees himself as a (nearly) school boy. It is a culturally and historically determined 'possible self' (a term used by Hazel Marcus, Paula Nurius and Susan Cross (Marcus and Nurius, 1986, Cross and Marcus, 1994) of great interest. Andrew was 'disposed' to puzzle about it. His mother picked up the new topic, and followed his lead. The interchange is not just set within a conversation between Andrew and his mother; it is set within Andrew's wider cultural world with its valued cultural goals: being five (in New Zealand children almost always start school on their fifth birthday), being at school, and being like Dad. Vivian Gussin Paley described the topics of great meaning for her three- to five-year-olds. She wrote:

> The act of teaching became a daily search for the child's point of view. . . . As I transcribed the daily tapes, several phenomena emerged. Whenever the discussion touched on fantasy, fairness, or friendship ('the three Fs' I began to call them), participation zoomed upward. . . . the phenomenon of birthday looms large. . . . 'Birthday' is a curriculum in itself. Besides being a study in numbers, age, birth, and death, it provides an ongoing opportunity to explore the three Fs. (Paley, 1986, pp. 124, 126)

Ann Haas Dyson has argued that being eager to read includes the learner 'seeing themselves as a reader'. She studied 'friends learning to write', eight focus children in a grade one classroom, and described how the process of being a writer was embedded in their social lives, and their 'feeling of belonging' to a community (1989, p. xvii). Bonnie Litowitz says that 'Reexamining what we are asking the learner to do must also include whom we are asking the learner to become' (1993, p. 191). Generally, then, the motivation to learn means that learners are eager to learn and 'see themselves as learners'. They will call on the available models of what 'learners' do, just as Dyson's children called on models of what 'readers' do.

Taking an interest can be dependent on self-categorisation and group identity, on criteria of social belonging. Carol Goodenow in 1992 described two research projects with urban high-school students. In one project, the researcher identified several different 'selves' prominent in the lives of his study participants. Other people responded to the adolescent as friend, sexual being, parent, but never as student or future worker, so there were few opportunities to gain an elaborated and realistic understanding of themselves as students or future workers. In the second project, the researchers described an 'oppositional social identity' through which children or adolescents took pride in not being like the majority or dominant group. For instance, for some minority groups this meant the perceived psychological and social necessity to disown the goals perceived as majority prerogatives, in particular open academic striving and success. Goodenow has argued that academic motivation and engagement may need to be enhanced in ways that are not perceived as compromising these important social dimensions of identity. She added that:

> research in educational psychology may benefit from exploring more explicitly the links between students' self-categorizations and group identities, on the one hand, and their behavior, motivation, and learning, on the other. (1992, p. 182)

The significance of social identity, 'possible self', social schema, and belonging to a community, has been noted by a number of writers who take a socio-cultural approach in educational matters. Ann Brown and her colleagues describe their innovative classrooms as exemplifying a 'community of learners' who are learning to learn (1993, p. 190). And in the long term, an aim for early childhood is for children to take on some of the culture's roles to do with 'being a learner'. My study of technological practice in early childhood had found that a number of social identities appeared to influence another domain of dispositions: persisting with difficulty or uncertainty. In that one centre, *being a friend* meant that you tackled difficulty in friendship development and maintenance but not necessarily technical difficulty; *being good, being a girl* and *being nearly five* meant that you avoided any risk of looking unable, and didn't tackle anything uncertain or difficult. Another identity that perhaps the children would have called 'being a maker of things' and I called *being a technologist* meant that you sought and persevered with technical difficulty. These social identities or social intents overlapped and competed with each other in complex ways. We will meet some of the children in that study – Nell, Jason, Meg and Danny – in the next three chapters.

So far in this section, I have emphasised social intent or social identity as interest. There is a growing literature on the motivational role of other aspects of 'interest' and, following the work of teachers engaged in documenting this domain of disposition, I have included *artefacts* and *activities* as well. Further examples of these three kinds of interest are in Chapter 3. An early childhood assessment format that highlights the relationship with artefacts and materials is Project Spectrum, designed at Harvard to assess learning style and domains of interest or talent based on Gardner's Multiple Intelligences (Gardner, 1983). Features of the 'play' in seven domains (with seven tasks or artefacts some of which are open-ended and some of which are structured) are observed and recorded. Of interest to the topic of domains of learning dispositions is the assessment of 'working style' to describe a child's interactions with the tasks and materials from various content areas.

> These working styles are intended to reflect the 'process' dimension of a child's work or play, rather than the type of product that results. They address indices of affect, motivation, and interaction with materials, as well as more stylistic features like tempo of work and orientation toward auditory, visual, or kinesthetic cues. (Krechevsky, 1994, p. 203)

A Working Styles checklist lists a number of 'stylistic features' of the children's approach to the tasks and materials. Sixteen of these are written as opposites: for example, playful or serious, persistent or frustrated by activity. Definitions include the following for the 'playful' child: 'delights in materials or activity; easily uses materials, frequently making spontaneous comments or playful extensions of the activity' (p. 207).

Being involved

The second domain of learning dispositions is *being involved*. Research on evaluating early childhood programmes in Belgium by Ferre Laevers, and in the UK by Chris Pascal and Tony Bertram, described 'involvement' as a central feature of a learning environment (Pascal *et al.*, 1995; Laevers, Vandenbussche, Kog and Depondt, no date; Laevers, 1994). Laevers and colleagues have developed a 'process-

oriented child monitoring system' in which they focus on two variables: involvement and well-being. They outline a number of signs of
involvement and well-being, and they say that the two are closely
linked (p. 41). By well-being they mean 'feeling at home', 'being
oneself' and/or 'feeling happy'. Involvement refers to 'the intensity of
the activity, the amount of concentration, the extent to which one is
'absorbed', and the ability to give oneself completely, to be enthusiastic, to find pleasure in exploration' (Laevers *et al.*, p. 5). Well-being is
in four 'relational fields' (with the teacher, with other children, with
the play-, class-, and school-world, and with members of the family
and close friends), and involvement is focused on activities *and* 'basic
areas of development' (self-organisation, motor development, thinking and understanding, expression, language and communication).

The role of involvement in particular activities for adolescents and
adults has been researched by Mihalyi Csikszentmihalyi and his colleagues over a number of years (e.g. Csikszentmihalyi, 1991, 1997).
This research has described the feeling of 'flow' in experiences that
one enjoys and wishes to repeat. Csikszentmihalyi and his colleagues
asked why so many people perform time-consuming, difficult and
often dangerous activities for which they receive no discernible extrinsic reward. A programme of research that involved extensive interviews with rock climbers, chess players, athletes, and artists
concluded that:

> the respondents reported a very similar subjective experience that they
> enjoyed so much that they were willing to go to great lengths to experi-
> ence it again. This we eventually called the *flow* experience, because in
> describing how it felt when the activity was going well, several used
> the metaphor of a current that carried them along. (Csikszentmihalyi
> and Rathunde, 1992, p. 58)

Experiences of 'flow' were characterised by nine features: clear goals,
immediate feedback, a balance between challenge and skills, focused
concentration on the task, awareness of the here and now, no worry of
failure, a lack of self-consciousness, little sense of time, and an activity
that is enjoyed for its own sake.

Deep involvement with a topic, even at very young ages, can provide a 'base domain' or a fund of knowledge that is useful for analogi-
cal thinking and metaphors in other domains. It provides 'hooks' for
understanding, conjecture and imagination. Kayoko Inagaki has described a number of studies in this area, including the use of analogy
by five- and six-year-olds who had been actively involved in raising

goldfish over a period of time: they produced reasonable predictions with explanations about an unfamiliar aquatic animal, the frog, by making analogies from their knowledge about goldfish. Inagaki adds that:

> These studies strongly suggest that, when children acquire intensive knowledge about some topics or domains that they have chosen as their own and thus are deeply involved in, they can go beyond the topics or domain . . . such knowledge may serve as the basis for reasoning and acquiring knowledge in related areas as well. (1992, p. 128)

In Chapter 3 we see how two-year-old Moses draws on his fund of knowledge about animals, derived from involved play, to create analogies and connections to other domains. It is an example of the combination of *taking an interest* and *being involved*.

Persisting with difficulty or uncertainty

Discussion of the domain *persisting with difficulty or uncertainty* owes much to the work of Carol Dweck and her colleagues (Dweck, 1999). In the early 1970s Carol Dweck and others in the USA identified the influence of what they called 'learned helplessness' (Dweck and Reppucci, 1973), a research theme that was to continue for more than two decades, observing children's reactions to failure and classifying them as 'helpless-' or 'mastery-oriented'. Dweck described children (including four- and five-year-olds) as having an orientation towards *'performance goals'* or *'learning goals'*. Dweck argued that: 'a deep understanding of motivation requires an understanding of the specific goals individuals are oriented toward when they behave in a particular situation' (Dweck, 1985, p. 289). When children are oriented towards *learning* goals, they strive to increase their competence, to understand or master something new. When they are oriented towards *performance* goals, they strive either to gain favourable judgements or to avoid negative judgements of their competence. Other writers have used different labels to describe similarly contrasting goals: Hermine Marshall wrote in 1992 about *learning* and *work* orientation, Carole Ames in 1992 described *mastery* and *performance* orientation. By 1994 Dweck and a colleague wrote that their research and other related studies 'suggest that by 4 or 5 years of age children have internalized an investment either in the evaluation of their achievement products or in the process of learning' (Smiley and Dweck, 1994, p. 1741). In the following transcript Susie told me that she had in the past completed a screen print 'that looked really good', but was not going to do another because it was too hard. She was quite firm that she did not want to risk making a mistake 'ever again'. She appeared to be becoming oriented towards performance goals, at least as far as screen printing was concerned.

Susie: (asked what difficult things she does here) I do some drawings, some paintings. But I don't know how to do a screen print.

Me: Don't you know how to do screen prints? (Susie shakes her head) No. Right. Are you going to have a go at that? Or not?

Susie: No.

Me: You're not going to have a go at that? (Rachel interrupts: 'I know how to do it.') Why not?

Susie: 'Cos. (Further interruption from Rachel or Wendy) . . .

Me: (brings focus back to Susie) Why, Susie? Why don't you want to have a go at screen printing?

Susie: It's too hard. I don't know how to cut out things. I don't know what to cut out.

Me: Right.

Susie: But I've done one when Alison (a teacher) was here. But I can't remember how I wanted to do it.

Me: Right.

Susie: I did a girl with two (pause) eyes. And Alison cut out the eyes. It looked really good but I don't know how to do it any more.

Me: Right. Right. So you don't want to have another go at it?

Susie: No.

Me: Mmhm.

Susie: 'Cos I might make a mis a mistake.

Me: You might make a mistake. And then what would happen?

Susie: It, um, 'cos sometimes when somebody can put the paint on I actually even put too much on. So I don't want to do that ever again.

Me: Right. So you don't want to do that ever again.

Although Susie has had a successful attempt at screen printing, there was apparently something about the experience (someone criticised the amount of paint she used perhaps) that indicated to her that she might not be competent without the help of Alison, the teacher (who has since left the centre). She does not want to risk her reputation again. Four-year-olds appear to be making quite firm decisions about whether it is appropriate to tackle difficulty and risk getting it wrong or making a mistake. On another occasion Susie told me: 'I don't do anything that's hard for me . . . If my big sister does something really hard, I won't do it.' Another of the four-year-olds, Laura, said 'I do the things I know how to do'; and Trevor advised his friend that if you make a mistake you should 'just leave it'. Hermine Marshall summed up as follows: 'In brief, these lines of research demonstrate that students enter school with goals that have potential consequences for the type of learner students become' (1992, p. 16).

This domain of learning dispositions is explored further in Chapter 4.

Communicating with others

Communicating with others is the fourth learning disposition. Research by David Weikart and his colleagues (Schweinhart and Weikart, 1993, cited by Sylva, 1994) identified a role in early childhood for 'dispositions that allowed the child to interact positively with other people' as well as with tasks. They had this to say from a longitudinal study of learners from early childhood to early adulthood:

> The essential process connecting early childhood experience to patterns of improved success in school and the community seemed to be the development of habits, traits, and dispositions that allowed the child to interact positively with other people and with tasks. This process was based neither on permanently improved intellectual performance nor on academic knowledge. (p. 4)

The work of Katherine Nelson, Gordon Wells, Jerome Bruner and many others on early language development has made it very clear that 'to communicate with others', verbally and non-verbally, takes many forms. Some of Nelson's research has centred on the growth of communication and language development within scripts for familiar events, a research direction that fits well with the view of learning as participation (she calls her view of the mechanism of change and development 'collaborative constructionism'). Children's transcripts (as well as their play) revealed their detailed event knowledge: an understanding of the sequence of an activity, its participant roles, its props, its beginning and endings. Event knowledge was used effectively to carry on discourse, to frame language structures, to learn and use new words, to engage in fantasy play, to make up stories, to remember specific happenings and to form object categorisation. Nelson adds that two sources of meaning are necessary for the establishment of linguistic meaning: the child's event knowledge and an adult's use of language referring to aspects of those events. Of great interest to the notion that documented and collaboratively shared assessment events can contribute to narratives about the self as a learner, a theme in this book, is Nelson's comment: 'Children have individual episodic memories from infancy, but it is only in the light of *social sharing* that both the enduring form of narrative organization, and the perceived value to self and others become apparent' (1997, p. 111, Nelson's emphasis).

Just as Nelson's work connects the disposition domains of *interest* (funds of knowledge, in this case event knowledge) to *communicating with others*, I can think of a good example of a connection between *communicating with others* and *persisting with difficulty* from a kindergarten I visited recently. I had asked for the parents' permission to read some of the children's assessments, and I saw several in which the children had told stories using 'story stones'. These stories seemed particularly imaginative, dramatic and lengthy. 'What are story stones?' I asked. 'Oh, that's just something we do here,' was the reply. It began one day when Shelley, one of the teachers, called on a resource she had created from stones found on holidays: a set of stones with painted symbols that represent potential characters for a story. She asked a small group of children to select a stone, and then she told a story using their name as that character. The stories, she said, sometimes have a fairly standardised format: one or more of the characters gets into trouble, frequently because of a magic spell, and the others have to come to the rescue. The stories are frequently about courage and persisting with difficulty or uncertainty. This resource has proved very popular, especially as the children began to collaborate with the teacher to decide on the details of the plot. On one occasion, the teachers noticed a group of children in a huddle, and they discovered that one child had drawn pictures and sellotaped them to some stones and was herself leading the story-telling. When Timothy left kindergarten to go to school, he used a set of story stones to tell stories to his younger sister, and when she started kindergarten, aged three and a half, she labelled her own stones and told stories to the others. This routine event had been established over time, and it had become a rich collaborative language activity that 'we do here'.

A study of 'circle' (mat or group time) routines in a classroom of three- and four-year-olds in the USA showed how the children learned to be 'conversationally appropriate' in a classroom. The authors concluded that 'these learned ways of participating have consequences for students in both present and future moments of life within schools' (Kantor, Green, Bradley and Lin, 1992). In their study, the children were learning a 'school discourse register' or *genre* that supported and constrained how they participated. Early childhood centres provide many examples of event structures that have music, dance, drama, number, writing and reading – other communication tools variously valued by the culture – embedded in them as well.

Taking responsibility

The fifth and final domain of learning dispositions is *taking responsibility*. Taking responsibility includes contributing to shared activities or episodes of joint attention. Longitudinal studies in the USA and in Sweden have indicated that early positive relationships with peers and with adults are the forerunners of positive relationships with first teachers at school and are correlated with verbal abilities at eight years (Howes, Matheson and Hamilton, 1994; Broberg, Wessels, Lamb and Hwang, 1997). Numerous studies have documented the learning potential of contexts of reciprocal and responsive relationships with others: episodes of joint attention (Moore and Dunham, 1992; Smith, 1999) where, as Bronfenbrenner put it (1979, p. 163), 'the balance of power gradually shifts in favour of the developing person', or where the balance of power was always with the learner. Barbara Rogoff and colleagues (1993) researched the way in which toddlers and their caregivers from four cultural communities collaborated in shared activities. They found that there were two aspects that occurred across all four communities: *bridging*, in which the adults and the children shared their understanding, and *structuring*, in which they each structured the other's participation in the problem-solving tasks that the researchers had set. These processes of shared responsibility enabled successful collaborative problem-solving. Participation repertoires include capacities for interdependence and joint responsibility with adults and peers. Elizabeth Jones and Gretchen Reynolds in 1992 analysed responsibility relationships between adults and children in terms of *power on, power with* and *power for*. *Power with* is characterised by negotiation, collaboration and transaction. *Power for* is characterised by scaffolding as it is usually conceived; the agenda usually belongs with the adult. *Power on* is in the nature of a tutorial. Harry Torrance and John Pryor (1998, p. 82) cite a similar distinction between *power over* and *power with*.

Children can take responsibility for assessment as well as curriculum. Timothy was an example. Over a number of days, the teachers in the story stones early childhood centre had noticed Timothy watching other children abseiling up the slide using a knotted rope attached to the climbing frame for this purpose. They wondered if he needed encouragement from them to have a go. But after a few days he began to edge his way up the slide, using the rope, firstly crawling and then a few steps at a time. Finally, one morning, he reached the top and shouted out to a nearby teacher: 'Take a photo! I've done it!' She did, and the photo and its accompanying comments took pride of place in his portfolio.

Finally, taking responsibility is about social justice and fair play, and will include children being inclined to stand up for themselves and others against biased ideas and discriminatory behaviour. Vivian Paley wrote of her attempts to make the rules of friendship problematic:

> Turning sixty, I am more aware of the voices of exclusion in the class-room. 'You can't play' suddenly seems too overbearing and harsh, resounding like a slap from wall to wall. How casually one child deter-mines the fate of another. . . . By kindergarten, . . . a structure begins to be revealed and will soon be carved in stone. Certain children will have the right to limit the social experiences of their classmates. . . . Must it be so? This year I am compelled to find out. Posting a sign that reads YOU CAN'T SAY YOU CAN'T PLAY, I announce the new order and, from the start, it is greeted with disbelief. (Paley, 1992, p. 3)

Her book *You Can't Say You Can't Play* tells the story of her attempt to shift the 'carved in stone' structure of beliefs about justice and inclu-sion. Further discussion of *communicating with others* and *taking respon-sibility* is in Chapter 5.

Learning Places and Dispositional Milieux

The discussion of domains of learning disposition has so far focused primarily on the individual learner. Learning dispositions are, however, located in activities, in places and in communities as the notions of habitus and dispositional milieu, introduced in the pre-vious chapter, implied. *Being willing* is about being sensitive to, mak-ing judgements about, responding to, dispositional structures in the environment. Learning occurs in learning places. As Margaret Do-naldson (1992) has said, education is about suggesting new directions in which lives may go, enlarging and enriching the children's particip-ation repertoires. It is, however, a complex transactional process in which 'practices should be seen as the product of an encounter be-tween a habitus and a field which are, to varying degrees, "compat-ible" or "congruent" with one another' (Thompson, 1991, p. 17, on

Bourdieu). The New Zealand early childhood curriculum describes transaction as 'the responsive and reciprocal relationships between people, places and things'. What does this mean in the real world of an early childhood setting?

Many of the examples in this book come from the 'real world' of Susie's early childhood centre. During observations in the art, craft and construction area of that centre over a period of six weeks, it appeared that there were a number of processes at work. (These are four-year-olds, and although it was the beginning of the calendar year, many of the children had been attending the same group for six months to a year; they will go to school when they are five.) Firstly, the centre was acting as a dispositional milieu, providing opportunities for interest, involvement, persistence with difficulty, communication and responsibility. Children were learning the ropes ('fitting in') and enriching and adding to their participation repertoires. Activities had developed as dispositional milieux. Secondly, the children's inclinations, together with their reading of the occasion, were changing the learning place or dispositional milieu in a number of ways. Children were selecting from and changing the dispositional milieu, and establishing what I have called 'default settings'.

The centre as a dispositional milieu

Learning the ropes
Children who attend early childhood programmes away from home are already aware that routines and rules are different in different places. Here is a friend of Susie's outlining one of the rules at 'kindy'. One of the children has just used a 'swear word' at the art table.

> You're not allowed to say swear words at all at kindy eh Sue?
> No.
> You're allowed to say 'blow'.
> Yeah.
> But not swear words. (pause) And you're allowed to say shuddup.
> I know.
> You're allowed to say shuddup.
> I know.
> But not swear words.
> I know.

They have learned the ropes in several places, and can make connections to Bronfenbrenner's three Rs – roles, rules and relationships – across settings. The scene is being set for their capacity to 'read' a new setting. Barbara Comber, describing the successful transition experience for Mark and Tessa, concluded that they were able to 'cash in' their intellectual, cultural and linguistic resources, acquired during early childhood experiences, in the classroom context, and she comments on their ability to be sensitive to occasion and context.

> At school, both Mark and Tessa indicated that they were actively reading the classroom culture, reading what their teachers valued, and altering their behaviour accordingly. They discovered quickly what counted for their teachers and their peers and how to work the classroom to get what they needed. . . . These capacities to 'read' the institutional ethos, knowing when and how to be visible and audible, were already in evidence in the preschool and home. (Comber, 2000, pp. 43, 44)

Enriching and adding to their participation repertoires
There was considerable evidence over just six weeks of observation that the children in Susie's kindergarten were trying out new ways of doing things: different interests and social intents, a different balance between performance and learning goals (persisting with difficulty), and different patterns of taking responsibility. Although three out of four of Nathan's episodes appeared to be about *being a boy* (preferring to play outside and avoid adults), in one episode he worked hard with a teacher who taught him to screen print and helped him to write his name. Peter, another of the *boys*, also worked with a teacher to draw a whale, cut it out, and turn it into a puppet, an unusual narrative for him. Martin associated difficult tasks with home and his older brothers and he usually played on his own, but twice he was involved with persisting with difficulty in an episode of joint attention (once with a peer, once with a teacher). Trevor on one occasion pursued technical difficulty (he usually settled for easy tasks). Lisa appeared to be beginning to take responsibility for evaluating and monitoring her work: she was increasingly deciding for herself what she wanted to do, completing the task, writing her own name, and then discussing her work with the teacher, occasionally asking for help for the hard parts. Joan was beginning to try out working collaboratively with peers on technical problems. Nell appears in Chapter 3: Nell unusually asking Jason for help and admitting that she didn't know how to do something. Children appeared to be seeking a balance between belonging and exploration: between displaying their membership of a collective (being good – as in well-behaved and not making mistakes – students, for instance) and risking the uncertain or the difficult.

Activities as dispositional milieux

In this centre, some activities had become dispositional milieux. The dispositional milieu that characterised an activity appeared to have developed from a combination of the physical nature of the artefacts or the task, and the social intents and responsibility patterns that had been built into it over time by cohorts of children and their teachers. At the art table, the only way Lisa communicated with peers was to comment on her actions and tell stories that the other children ignored. However, in the block area (and with boys) she could 'do friendship' by engaging with others, making suggestions, explaining (using "'cos') and holding their attention with the markers 'guess what' and 'eh'. She changed her way of participating when she shifted activity, and block-building appeared to be more favourable for her attempts to communicate with others and take responsibility. Screen printing is an art activity that affords opportunities for rendering a drawing or a shape as a silhouette and for the repetition of the same image. Observations in the kindergarten indicated, however, that the teachers emphasised the sequence of 'school-like' competencies like writing your name, cutting with scissors, waiting your turn and completing a complex sequence. Except for Danny and a few others, the children frequently retained the painted template and threw away the print.

Children selecting from and changing the dispositional milieu

The second transactional process in this learning place occurred when children selected from and changed the dispositional milieu.

Selecting from the dispositional milieu

In early childhood settings, children use dispositions to choose their own environment, in a process that has been called 'niche-building' or 'niche-picking'. Thirteen of the seventeen children for whom I had a number of observations appeared to be playing out familiar learning narratives either in the same activity or in a range of activities. For instance, Meg did not like adults to help her, so she avoided screen printing as an activity, because here the adults were always on standby to assist with difficulty. Danny, on the other hand, appeared to enjoy the tutorials associated with screen printing. Nell inclined towards friendship as a topic, tackled difficulty when friendship got into trouble, and used considerable imagination to alter activities so

that they did not involve *technical* difficulty. She used the screen printing equipment to screen paint onto collage, avoiding the tedious and
difficult preparation of a template, and she made hats for babies and
absent people, apparently to avoid the difficulty of measurement.
Linda had privileged being good and seeking adult approval, and she
avoided any activity that might display her as being unable. Emily,
also anxious not to be 'wrong', avoided the construction area and
spent most of her time in sociodramatic play, where she could be in
charge of the script. Collaborative narratives and skills developed in
dramatic or pretend play did not appear to be necessarily transferred
to construction activities. Children involved themselves in collaborative scripts in sociodramatic play, and the same children worked indi-
vidually in the construction area. Nick, whom we will meet in Chapter
5, was an exception. Many of the children chose those activities that
provided a niche for their dispositions, or altered activities to create a
match.

Changing the dispositional milieu
Dispositions provide the learner with a narrative (or a number of
narratives) about what learning is, *and ought to be*, all about. They
reflect theories about learning places (for example, Emily's apparent
theory that learning places are for avoiding being seen to be wrong or
unable), and these theories are active players in the establishment of
learning environments. Children can call on powerful dispositions to
resist, avoid or change the milieu. In Chapter 4 we will meet Danny,
whose developing skills in screen printing changed the dispositional
milieu of that activity; Meg, whose experience at the construction table
encouraged her to resist the norm and make a complicated hat with a
sun visor; and Jason, whose disposition to tackle difficulty changed an
easy activity into a difficult one for a number of children.

Default settings
I commented earlier that children appeared to be seeking a balance
between belonging and exploration. Belonging frequently wins the day.
Hermine Marshall has commented (1992, p. 16) that 'What type of
learner (children) actually become is influenced in large part by the
classroom environment' and suggested that the classroom environments that encourage learning goals will be characterised by: challenging tasks that require active involvement, use of diverse processes,
provision of options, and establishing opportunities for shared responsibility. Danny, Meg and Jason's early childhood centre had these fea-

tures; nevertheless some powerful processes on many occasions appeared to be encouraging performance goals as a 'default setting'. In Chapter 4 an episode is described in which Meg and a number of her friends, including Molly and Linda, are working on a joint enterprise: making a butterfly mural for the wall, to illustrate a current theme on caterpillars and butterflies. On two occasions, Meg tries to turn this into a more challenging activity, but her attempts are ignored. Earlier, the children had invested much of their conversational energy discussing who spilled the paint; an excerpt is as follows, ending with Ann (the teacher) coming over and reminding them that it doesn't matter and all they have to do is get a cloth and wipe it up.

> Oh naughty, what's who spilt it?
> I don't know. It spilted over itself.
> I didn't.
> I didn't either.
> I didn't.
> Somebody spilt some paint.
> I didn't.
> I didn't.
> Not me.
> Not me either.
> Not me.
> She probly knocked it over.
> Who?
> Myra.
> Yeah, you probly you probly. (giggling)
> She did it.
> Who?
> That one over there.
> You must of knocked it over.
> Yeah.
> No.
> Yeah.
> No.
> Who knocked that paint over anyway?
> Who knocked that paint over?
> Ann (teacher) arrives: Isn't the lid on properly there?

After the paint is satisfactorily wiped up, Meg then tries to turn this into a problem-solving activity, with learning goals. But the die has already been cast; no adult is present to support her, and the conversation shifts to who is going to go and play at whose house. I have called this process a 'default setting': a tendency for a group milieu to become conservative, characterised by low level performance goals, especially if there is no adult around. On another occasion, however, the same group of girls worked together in the block area making enclosures for animals; once again Meg took an initiating role, mildly upping the cognitive 'ante' by suggesting that they separate out the 'wild ones' from the others. This time the others accepted and began to develop a collaborative script:

Linda: We've still got (. . .) many more eh Meg?
Meg: Yes. Those are all the wild ones OK?
Linda: Yes.
–   Moooo. Moooo.
–   This one's the mother, this one's the baby OK?
–   Can you help me get these?
–   I will.
–   Everyone help me get them . . .
Linda: (apparently unsure about the category of one of the animals) What's this one for?
Molly: Warthog. This is for the warthog. (The 'warthog' is put into the 'wild ones'' enclosure)

Here, Meg, Molly and Linda were problem-solving and collaborating (and Molly on other occasions collaborated in friendship talk as will be apparent in Chapter 5). When they worked together on the butterfly mural, however, they did not see the task as an occasion to use these abilities. They were establishing a very different dispositional milieu. Perhaps it was because the butterfly-making episode was the teacher's idea, as Ann's initiation, below, makes clear. The block enterprise belonged, from the beginning, to the group.

Ann: And I thought the other thing we could make. Because we've got our big chrysalis. What comes out of the big chrysalis?
–   Christmas?
–   It isn't Christmas.
Ann: I thought we could make a big butterfly, 'cos this would make wonderful wings. That look right?
–   Yep.
Ann: I thought we could cut out the shape of a butterfly. Who would like to help me make the butterfly?
–   Yes.
Ann: OK. Would you like to come and draw the big wings for me? (Yes.) . . .

Ann has established the task, perhaps, as 'supporting the teacher's idea', whereas the block construction was about 'safe housing for the animals', an agenda initiated, developed and given meaning by the children. The work of Carole Ames (1992) on motivation in school classrooms identified three (overlapping) structures in a classroom that relate to adaptive or non-adaptive patterns of motivation: the tasks on offer, the nature of the assessment, and 'authority dimensions' of the classroom. The tasks on offer can take on a dispositional milieu of their own, often (like the butterfly-making episode) different from the one planned by the teacher.

Summary comments on learning places and dispositional milieux

The effects of early childhood experiences are the result of complex interactions between the learner and the learning place, between learning dispositions and a dispositional milieu. Children respond to, 'read', a new environment in various ways: in some cases to seize opportunities to enrich their current interests through involvement, challenge, communication and responsibility; at other times to try out new directions and interests; and sometimes to avoid learning. We do well to try to see or hear the child's point of view, and not to set up structures in which that viewpoint cannot be seen or heard. These observations are relevant to the assessment of learning. The activity of assessment is itself a dispositional milieu. Harry Torrance and John Pryor (1998, pp. 68–82) have given a detailed account of the base-line assessment experience of four-year-old Eloise on her second day at school. It is an eloquent analysis of an early assessment interaction between teacher and pupil in a reception class. Although the interaction was ostensibly to collect data about early literacy and numeracy, Eloise was learning that in this learning place, the 'ground rules' are in the teacher's head, activities are not expected to make sense, the teacher is in control of the direction of conversations, and she is expected to be a 'good girl'. Being a good 'person' has begun to invade the notion of being a good 'learner'. Being a good 'person' is a moral domain that is fraught with performance goals, and is integral to what Lilian Katz (1995, p. 12) has called the 'self-esteem' industry in early childhood. I would argue that being a good *learner* in most settings includes caring and being responsible, but that being a good (or less than good) *person* is not a judgement call for an early childhood centre or a school classroom. However, as the Eloise transcript illustrated, the word 'good' in the English language can mean 'competent on this occasion', 'behaving appropriately in this setting'; but it can mean 'generally morally sound, generally deserving of approval'. For young children, the meaning may be very unclear, the source of the approval unfathomable. In such cases, the teacher holds all the power.

Foregrounding and Backgrounding

In Table 2.1, I set out dispositions as three parts: being ready, being willing and being able. Earlier I commented that being ready, the inclination, is foregrounded in this book. I commented in the previous chapter that we are familiar with foregrounding the milieu in order to evaluate our programmes, and we are even more familiar with foregrounding skills and knowledge. This book argues that we should foreground the inclination, a much more unfamiliar process, and we should pay attention to the background contributing milieu, and the skills and knowledge, when they appear relevant to encouraging the inclination.

Positive experience over time in one or more of the domains of disposition makes it likely that these three parts will be in tune, but there is a sense in which on any one occasion we can describe each of the parts as being in the foreground or in the background. Three viewpoints are illustrated by Figure 2.1. The foregrounding of inclination (being ready) is illustrated by (a). Alongside that, in (b) is an interest in increasing or improving the situations in which an inclination is appropriate (being willing). Finally, we have an interest in assisting the children to strengthen or develop the abilities and funds of knowledge (being able) that will make this inclination more robust (c).

When being ready to participate is foregrounded (Figure 2.1 (a))

When being ready to participate is foregrounded, practitioners take a credit approach to what they observe, pay attention to, describe in assessments, discuss with the learner and the learner's family, document, and make public. Children are developing a view of themselves as learners in terms of the five domains of learning disposition as follows:

- interests; expectations that people, places and things can be interesting; a view of self as interested and interesting;
- readiness to be involved, pay attention, for a sustained length of time; a view of self as someone who gets involved;

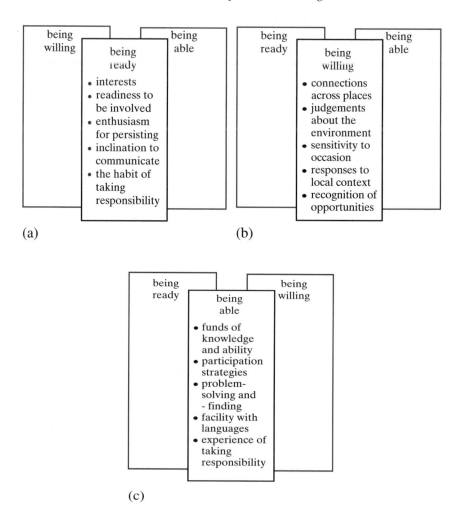

Figure 2.1.   Foregrounding and backgrounding

- enthusiasm for persisting with difficulty or uncertainty; assumptions about risk and the role of making a mistake in learning; a view of self as someone who persists with difficulty and uncertainty;
- the inclination to communicate with others in one or more of '100 languages' (Edwards, Gandini and Forman, 1993; see also Gallas, 1994), to express ideas and feelings; a view of self as a communicator;
- a habit of taking responsibility in a range of ways, to take another point of view, to recognise justice and to resist injustice; a view of self as a citizen with rights and responsibilities.

Practitioners notice those moments when Bruce (Chapter 6) takes responsibility for other children, and at the beginning those moments may be few and far between. They document the occasion (and the activity) in which Nell (Chapter 3) first tackles a difficult technological problem and admits to Jason that she 'doesn't know'. The adults contrive the re-occurrence of these 'critical moments', wanting them to become habits. Children become aware of the goals here, and can take responsibility for the detail, as Timothy did when he abseiled up the slide, valued the achievement, and knew the teachers would value it too.

When being willing, the situation, is foregrounded (Figure 2.1 (b))

The domains of disposition outlined in this chapter were: to take an interest *in*, to be involved *with*, to persist with difficulty or uncertainty (to be challenged *by*), to communicate *with*, to take responsibility *for*. They are about the learner-in-action or -in-relationships. As I have argued, the relationship goes both ways. In Table 2.1, I suggested that these actions or relationships include:

- a preparedness to recognise, select or construct interests in this place, to make connections between artefacts, activities and social identities across places;
- informed judgements about the safety and trustworthiness of the local environment;
- sensitivity to places and occasions in which it is worthwhile to tackle difficulty or uncertainty and to resist the routine: optimum challenge, open-ended and flexible activities, errors are supported as part of learning;
- responses to a climate in which children have their say and are listened to;
- recognition or construction of opportunities to take responsibility.

The exact nature of these relationships will be different in different places and for different children. When the staff at the childcare centre noticed that Robert appeared interested in the finger painting but would not become involved, they decided to change the environment in two ways. They knew that Robert was reluctant to get dirty, so they provided aprons, and the staff member who made the finger paint invited him to be involved with her in the making of the paint. He refused the aprons, but the invitation to work with an adult to make the finger paint and choose the colours was just the entry point that allowed Robert to make a judgement that this environment was safe and trustworthy. He became involved with finger-painting in a number of sustained and absorbed episodes of play. Clearly we cannot expect to find young children taking responsibility in a setting where the adults control the agenda, and one aspect of the validity of an assessment is whether the outcome (disposition) of interest is locally available. Staff can evaluate their learning place using this chapter's five-domain framework in a number of ways.[1]

When abilities and funds of knowledge are foregrounded (Figure 2.1(c))

When abilities and funds of knowledge are foregrounded, the focus is on the contributing skills and funds of knowledge. In Table 2.1, I set these out as:

- funds of relevant knowledge and ability that support their interests;
- strategies for getting involved and remaining focused;
- problem-solving and problem-finding knowledge and skills; experience of making mistakes as part of solving a problem;
- facility with one or more languages, widely defined; familiarity with a range of context-specific 'genres'; script knowledge for familiar events;
- experience of responsibility, making decisions, being consulted; an understanding of fairness and justice; strategies for taking responsibility.

These abilities and funds of knowledge develop in local contexts. In the example of the 'story stones', the teacher prompted those children who were enthusiastic participants but did not have the skills to tell a coherent story. She gave them a format ('Is the mouse going to get into trouble?'), some sequencing cues ('What happened next? How are they going to get home? Will a boat be helpful, or a helicopter perhaps?'), and reminded them of other familiar story-lines that they could copy. The view of learning as transformation of participation has many features of an apprenticeship, and that certainly includes

---

[1] Children's questions, associated with these five domains of dispositions, were the framework for a research project on evaluation that followed from the assessment project. The children's questions in that project provided a basis for the investigation of a number of ways in which practitioners could evaluate their practice. The questions were: Do you know me? Can I trust you? Do you let me fly? Do you hear me? Is this place fair for us? See Carr, May, Podmore, Cubey, Hatherly and Macartney, 2000 for more detail.

the novice watching and having a go without direct tuition; but it also includes experts teaching the novice relevant knowledge and abilities at the appropriate time.

Concluding Comment

This chapter has emphasised that, although the notion of dispositions originally comes from psychology, where it was seen as the possession of an individual, like temperament, the approach in this book is that a learning disposition is situated in and interwoven with action and activity. I have argued that learning dispositions are worthwhile outcomes for early childhood, using the definition of learning dispositions as participation repertoires from which a learner recognises, selects, edits, responds to, resists, searches for and constructs learning opportunities. Supporting this idea, Barbara Comber concluded (2000, p. 46) from her research on children going to school that: 'Our close analysis of the 20 case-study children suggested that school literacy learning in the early months of school is contingent on selective repertoires of participative practices and forms of studentship.'

I have listed five possible candidates for domains of learning disposition, drawing on my experience in early childhood settings in New Zealand, and I have suggested that in utilising a framework of learning dispositions for setting goals in early childhood, the three parts of a learning disposition – being ready, being willing, and being able – will be variously foregrounded and backgrounded. On the whole, however, we are not familiar with foregrounding the inclination through a fundamentally credit model of assessment. Chapter 6 outlines just such a model, and Chapters 7 to 10 outline how practitioners have implemented it. The next three chapters bring us back to the real experience of children, to elaborate on the five domains of disposition. I have paired the first two as *taking an interest and being involved* (Chapter 3), Chapter 4 considers *persisting with difficulty or uncertainty*, and the last two domains, *communicating with others and taking responsibility* are developed together in Chapter 5.

3

Interest and Involvement

Chapter 2 introduced the importance of interest and involvement as domains of learning disposition. This chapter considers these two domains in greater detail. They are closely connected: one definition of 'interest' is 'that which engages people in tasks', and that is involvement as well. Many studies have supported the intuitively reasonable conclusion that learning builds on interest. Vivian Paley is quoted in Chapter 2 as saying that whenever the discussion touched on topics of interest to the children in her classroom 'participation zoomed upward'. Mihaly Csikszentmihalyi has commented (1996, p. 158) that although creative people have not usually been precocious in their achievements in the early years, nevertheless 'they seem to have become committed early to the exploration and discovery of some part of their world'.

What is it that interests and involves children? Susan Isaacs, in a paper referred to by Mary Jane Drummond in 1999, wrote that children's learning depends on interest and that, in turn, interest is derived from desire, curiosity and fear. Paley and Isaacs highlighted the capacity of children to play out their fears and desires, and they focused on outcomes and processes that closely integrated emotion with cognition. In Paley's book *Bad Guys Don't Have Birthdays* (1988), Frederick's interest is his anxiety about the arrival in his family of a new baby, and Paley would, I think, see related fears about rejection as individual and universal interests. Csikszentmihalyi's book on creativity emphasises the role of interest in creativity. He too emphasises the role of emotion, and describes Linus Pauling as 'falling in love' with chemistry before he entered school, in the same way as Seymour Papert (1980) has described himself falling in love with gears as a two-year-old.

Suzanne Hidi, Ann Renninger and Andreas Krapp have written that interest plays a key role in learning and development, and they have concluded that individual interest includes high levels of stored knowledge and value relative to the other objects and events with which the individual is involved (1992, p. 434). They differentiate between individual interest and situational interest. Individual interest is often seen as a relatively enduring psychological state, almost like temperament. Situational interest, on the other hand, is elicited by interesting features in the environment.

This book's focus on learning as mediated action and concern with the question 'How will assessment enhance that learning?' implies that 'interest' will be about the mediational means and/or the action. James Wertsch, who has argued for a focus on the learner-in-action rather than the individual alone, has said that: 'The most central claim I wish to pursue is that human action typically employs 'mediational means' such as tools and language, and that these mediational means shape the action in essential ways' (1991, p. 12). Interest, when the learner is described in this way, might be described as 'mediational means'. I suggest the following three-part interest and involvement system: artefacts (objects, languages, and story-lines that cultural stories and myths have provided), activities (ways of employing the artefacts for a range of purposes; routines and practices) and social communities. It may well be that fear or grief (as in Paley's observations of Frederick, or Kathy's observations of Sally, described below) underlie these interests, but while we can observe the artefacts and activities and social communities that children pay attention to, we can only guess at their metaphorical or psychological significance. Using the three-part system, we can say that deep involvement in an interest occurs when a person, using the artefacts of the culture (such as objects, tools and stories), is engaged in an activity, and when this activity is valued and supported by a social community (see Figure 3.1). 'Interest' may initially reside in one or more of the parts of the system.

Figure 3.1. The Interest and Involvement System: artefacts, activities and social communities

This chapter elaborates on the three different kinds of interest: artefacts (Moses and Sally), a particular activity (Alan) and a social community (Nell). The observations about Moses began when he was a one-year-old and they continued until he was two years and eight months old. He attends a childcare centre two days a week. Sally is a three-year-old in nursery school in the UK; her story was told to me by Kathy Hunt. Alan is four, and attends a kindergarten session every morning. Nell is four-and-a-half, and also attends a sessional kindergarten, a different one from Alan.

Moses

Moses is a two-year-old, and his absorbed interest in animals has lasted for as long as his parents can remember. When he was one, he had a small box of zoo animals which he would carefully stand up in a number of different arrays, making the appropriate noises. He had a number of favourite books that provided him with pictures of animals that he would name or ask 'What's that?' The first observation is typical for that time.

Observation 1
Aged one year, three months.
Moses takes his small animal set (about ten animals) out of their box, and carefully sets them upright on the floor, lying flat on his tummy. He makes appropriate noises for each one.

By the age of two, his repertoire of scripts has extended, together with the list of animals that he can name. He has become familiar with three zoos, and knows where to find his favourites: antelopes and giraffes. His scripts now include acting the part.

Observation 2
Mother: Mosie, tell Pop who you saw at the supermarket.
Moses (on all fours): I'm being a goat.
Mother: Goat, tell Pop who you saw at the supermarket.
Moses: Maa maa.

Observation 3
At a children's farm enclosure set up in the middle of town, photos of Moses show him carefully investigating the animals' hooves and their bottoms, and crawling around near them with his fingers curled in a 'hoof'-like manner.

He has a particularly evocative galloping gait, and is especially fond of the sandals that he has acquired from his older cousin:

Observation 4
Moses' grandmother is reading him a story. He comments that one of the characters has 'clown shoes' and adds 'My sandals are gallopy shoes'.

He makes animals out of Duplo (a construction set), and has begun to attempt to draw them. He knows a range of animal songs that he has learned at the childcare centre, and he attempts to persuade adults within range to sing (make up) 'an antelope song?', 'a goat song?'

Observation 5
On one occasion, when given some playdough and some wooden shapes, he was absorbed for some time and then shouted 'I NEED some animals'. He transformed the rhinoceros into a camel by adding a 'hump' of dough, and made a zoo and a farm.

Observation 6
Moses and grandmother are reading *The Little Bird* (Dick Bruna); a sunflower has eyes, nose and smile drawn on it. Moses: 'Has that got a face?' 'Does it have sandals?' On another occasion they are reading *Spot at the Farm* (Eric Hill): 'That duck have hair?' and 'The duck got feet, under there, in the water?'

By the age of two-and-a-half he is grouping his animals into farm and wild animals, and putting them into enclosures: 'making a farm' he calls it. He puzzles over whether the animals have hooves, paws, trotters, or just plain 'feet'. He is also playing with words, particularly in the context of animal conversations.

Observation 7
Moses: I'm a sheep.
Mother: What's your name?
Moses: Sheepy-weepy (pause) – sleepy.

By the age of two years and eight months he continues to love books about animals, especially more technical books that label, for instance, the different kinds of horse. He now makes animals out of playdough, and draws animals (although he prefers his parents to draw them). He is absorbed for sustained periods setting up arrays of animals, often in pairs (he is very fond of Noah's Ark stories) and in lines, and has begun to build elaborate block structures to which he adds animals. These appear all over the house. He sees objects as similar to animals: a mop is like a sheep, a shadow is like a pig, a rock is like a pig; and he sees people as looking like animals (he describes one of his friend's parents as 'looks like a lion'). He does animal dances to rhythmic music, and when his father takes him to a National Equestrian Centre, he (the father) tells the following story:

Observation 8
I took Mosie to the National Equestrian Centre, and he was overwhelmed by all the horses. He went up to one horse and put his hand out slowly and patted it on the nose. He approached a man saddling up a horse and asked lots of questions, adding remarks like 'Very big hooves, aren't they'. When I commented to him about how beautifully one of the horses was galloping, he said 'It's like music'.

By now he has a repertoire of songs about animals that he has learned at the childcare centre, and is beginning to act out scenarios using his (considerable) collection of animals as actors, and providing them with different voices. The script sometimes includes exchanges like: Goat: 'Time for a sleep.' Horse: 'I don't want to have a sleep.' Goat: 'How about a rest then?' Horse: 'No. No rest.' He sets up small groups of animals to watch him sleep, dance, eat and watch TV, and his parents report that he will often take on the role of an animal in order not to listen to them (for instance, to injunctions about bedtime).

Sally

At a conference in 1999 I heard Kathy Hunt talk about Sally, a three-year-old whose mother, her sole parent, had died. At nursery school, Sally:

was in a state of complete despair and we found her pain unbearable. . . . Sally was exhibiting all the identified behaviours associated with mourning, the panic, the crying out loud, searching in places over and over again. Wandering, unable to settle, very little able to concentrate. She was unable to play, uninterested in being with other children, uninterested in mark-making or books or stories.

Kathy describes how Sally slowly began to take part in the life of the nursery, creating and calling on metaphors that expressed the meaning she intended. One of her early play actions at this time, repeated over and over, was to walk two toy polar bears, an adult and a baby, along a path around the water trough. 'Every so often she would drop the baby into the water and let it sink to the bottom then she would exclaim, with a deep intake of breath, "Oh no!" With this, the game would begin again.' Sally later became very interested in the Raymond Briggs story *The Snowman* (Briggs, 1978) and would ask for it to be read to her repeatedly. Some years later, Kathy learned that this story, although not obviously about death, was written by Briggs during a time of great personal grief. For Sally, the artefacts (toy animals and a picturebook) provided her with deeply significant and healing metaphors, the meaning of which the adults could only guess at.

Alan

Alan attends a sessional kindergarten programme which implements a project approach. The project that particularly captured Alan's imagination was when the staff and children decided to design and make a gate for a gap in the fence that divided the kindergarten playground into a front and back yard. When the builder had built the fence he had discussed with the children the need for a sturdy gate to keep the younger children safe: the back yard was difficult to supervise, and the incinerator for burning rubbish was sited there. Before the project began, Alan was a reluctant attender; once he became involved in the project, however, he began attending with enthusiasm. On one occasion after a spell at home with chicken pox, Alan decided he did not want to go to kindergarten. When his mother reminded him that this was the day when the builder was coming to consult the children about the design of the final gate, he changed his mind, and was centrally involved in the planning discussions. Observations on Alan are as follows.

15 August – 28 August
Alan drew his first simple gate plan on 15 August, a square with three diagonal lines running across it, and a small knob on the side that might have been a hinge or a latch. On 26 August Alan made his first gate in wood, following his plan. He brought hinges from home, and persevered with the difficulty of attaching them with screws: drilling a hole first. He discovered the difference between Phillips screws and ordinary screws. With adult help he drilled holes first then chose Phillips screws because he had a Phillips screwdriver. The next day he was keen to keep working: 'I want to go out and finish my gate.' He and another child, Sean, try his gate in the gap in the fence; it is clearly too narrow. Alan: 'I'll have to make three more gates.'

On 28 August he completed this first wooden model gate and in spite of its width he wanted to attach it to the fence. After discussion with a teacher he decided it was not long enough either: it won't 'reach from the top of the fence to the ground'. He said he would make a big one next 'the same size as the fence'. He tried various places inside to put his small gate up, and decided on a flat-sided log in the nature corner. 'I'll have to measure it.' He measured a gate post. 'It goes six-oh-oh.' Then he measured the log. 'No, it's not the same. It's meant to be six-oh-oh. It's not the right height.' He went outside to saw his gate post smaller. He measured and then drew a line on the gate post.

Barbara (another four-year-old) asked him 'What are you doing?' Alan: 'I've got to chop where this line is.' He nailed his gate to the log. Bev (one of the children) helped him hold it upright while he nailed. He tried shutting the gate three times, and it swung open. He pointed out to Bev. 'You have to put a lock on here Bev.' Bev fetched the level and placed it across the top of the gate. 'It's nearly in the middle' said Alan. They don't, however, make a lock.

29 August – 2 September

His second plan, 29/8, was a crisscross design and had clearly drawn hinges – 'These join onto the fence' – and round holes for screws. He indicated that a nail would be needed in the centre to hold all the pieces of wood together. This time he had measured the gap, and included the written measurements on his plan: the comment on the plan, written by the teacher, said 'Alan has measured the gap in the fence to get the right size for his gate.'

On 2 September one of the teachers suggested he make up his plan using cardboard. She observed him ten minutes later: he had cut six strips of cardboard and was sellotaping them into a square. The square was crooked. He removed the sellotape, got some masking tape and started again. Taped two parallel pieces in to support the top and the bottom. Looked at the plan, and realised it was different; said he was going to make it the same as his wooden gate. He folded small pieces of cardboard for hinges and then punched holes along one side of the gate and holes into the hinges. He taped the hinges onto the gate. Teacher: 'Did you have any problems?' Alan: 'Yes. That was sticking up (indicates where the cardboard was too long). I've got four hinges on it.' He drew it.

5–6 September

Alan describes his third plan: 'The lines on the gate go down. You need three hinges. There is a lock.' He describes the lines on the fence as going 'diagonally', and explains the measurements to the teacher: 'the numbers on the top show one metre wide' and 'it's the same high as the fence.'

The next day he made his third and largest gate: 'I'm going to build my biggest gate today.' He used very large pieces of wood to make the crisscross pieces for the centre of the gate. He didn't start with a frame and he didn't complete it: the nailing was very difficult into the hard wood, and he might have run out of long pieces of wood.

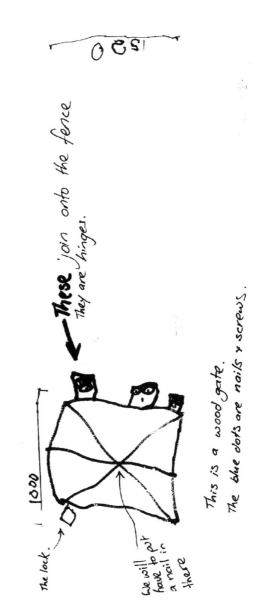

Alan 29/8

Has completed model + would like to make a big gate. This is his second plan.

Alan has measured the gap in the fence to get the right sizes for his gate (1000w x 1250 length)

These join onto the fence. They are hinges.

1000

The lock.

We will have to put a nail in there

This is a wood gate.
The blue dots are nails + screws.

1500

Figure 3.2. Alan's second plan

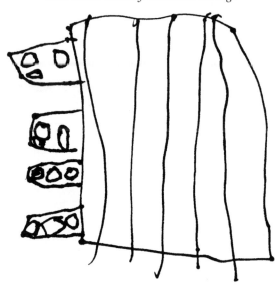

Figure 3.3. Alan's drawing of his cardboard plan

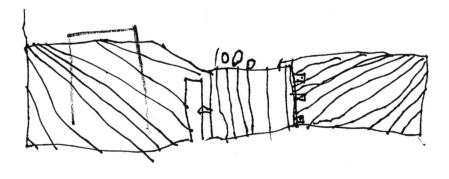

15/10

The lines on the gate go down
You need 3 hinges.
Fence "diagonally"
There is a lock.
The numbers on the top show I'm wide
"It's the same high as the fence

Figure 3.4. Alan's third plan

9 September
On 9/9 the children were looking at photos of wrought iron gates. Johnny made two models inspired by the photos: one out of wire, and one a wire and paper model. Cara made a wire and paper model 'like the one in the photo'. (Mikey turned his wire model into glasses.) Alan made a fourth model, with wire.

15 October – 22 October
On 12/9 Alan is away with chicken pox, and the kindergarten is closed for two weeks' term break from 23/9 to 7/10. His final plan is drawn on 15/10 for the builder who has come to select the final design. This model combines his first two designs: it includes three vertical supports, and two crisscross supports. On 22/10 the builder comes to build the gate. Alan helps. The final design is close to Alan's: vertical boards on the front, and a diagonal board for support across the back (not a crisscross, however). Next day he goes to school.

Alan remained interested in the project throughout, and appeared to be particularly interested in hinges and measuring. Early in the project he brought hinges from home, enough for the other children as well. When the children at mat (circle) time were discussing making a gate out of Hinuera (a local) stone he commented: 'You'll need really big hinges for a stone gate.' He used the measuring tape to read the numbers accurately and write them onto his plans.

Nell

In Nell's early childhood centre, a group of children were developing and practising a range of social and linguistic strategies which served to support her interest in making and maintaining friends: playing together and being helpful to each other, talking about being friends and about playing at each other's houses, and talk that indicated an awareness of the other's needs, understandings and beliefs (a particular prerogative of the girls). Both of the following observations are about inclusion in and exclusion from a community of friends. In the first observation, Nell (aged four) provides Lisa with a defining characteristic of a friend: 'Only friends are allowed to look at the other friends.'

Observation 1
Nell and Jinny were finger painting in the marble-painting box and Lisa was screen printing nearby, watching them carefully.
    Nell: (to Lisa) Don't watch my friend Lisa. It's rude.
    Jinny: Yeah.

Nell: But I'm allowed eh Jinny.

Jinny: Yeah, 'cos you're my friend.

Nell: Only friends are allowed to look at the other friends.

Nell interpreted threats to friendship as positive challenges to be tack-led with relish, as the second observation illustrates.

Observation 2

Emily and Laura have been establishing their friendship by excluding Nell: Laura assumes an artificial voice to admire Nell's work. Emily, as intended, perceives that this is an attempt at deception, and says to Laura in a loud whisper:

Emily: We don't like it really, eh?

Laura: Yeah, we just lying eh.

Nell: I heard that.

Laura: We love it, eh Emily?

Emily: No, we're only telling lies to each other.

This looks like trouble for Nell. However, she doesn't get upset, leave, or go and tell the teacher that Emily and Laura are being mean to her. She remains at the construction table, finding a place in the conversation where she can shift the power balance. Laura tells a story about her father during which Nell prompts her ('Did ya find some?').

Laura: Actually my Dad knows how cicadas do hatch out at night (Emily: Yeah) because if you don't see them hatching in day, they hatch in night. That's always true.

Emily: That's the you're telling the truth to us eh?

Laura: Yeah. 'Cos once, he he's already done it and I saw him do it. He did it, once he took us down.

Nell: Did ya find some?

Laura: Yes. Once we even found a live one and we letted him go . . .

Then Nell tells a story about her father falling off the trampoline. Laura says she wishes she could have a go on a trampoline, and Nell seizes her chance:

Nell: You can do it if you want 'cos we might invite you to my birthday.

Laura: Pardon.

Nell: Does your Mum know where Hauraki Downs is?

Laura: No. I don't even think she knows there.

Nell: Well you can't come to my birthday.

Laura: Well, why can't we ask your Mum.

Nell: We can.

Using a number of strategies and ending up with the time-worn offer of a birthday party, Nell has repositioned herself from the periphery to the centre and all the players appeared to enjoy the tension along the way.

Nell has revealed considerable strategies for making and maintaining friendship, and she draws on relevant funds of knowledge about conversation and story telling to add to these strategies. We will meet her again in Chapter 5 as she instructs Nick in the art of making a cardboard tray for marble painting.

Summary Comments on the Interests of Moses, Alan and Nell

Seeing 'interest' as part of a system of mediated action that has three parts – artefacts, activities and communities – allows us to analyse the way in which these children's interests have developed, the way in which they have become more complex and more involved. The development is clearest with Moses, because the observations span eighteen months. His fund of knowledge about animals has grown rapidly, and his interest has begun to encompass the whole system. His interest in artefacts (animals) has become an interest and involvement in activities associated with those artefacts (making patterns and constructions that combine animals and blocks, for instance). By age two-and-a-half his animals appear more clearly to belong to social (animal) communities: farms, zoos, participants in equestrian events; and to represent social (non-animal) communities: being a member of Moses' family and helping him to make sense of (and to resist) its routines. Alan has been integrating his interest in hinges and measuring into more accurately drawn plans and more complex constructed gates. His kindergarten programme has reminded him that this process is part of the wider 'possible self', *being a builder*, and the visiting builder has provided a model of this. Nell has extended her repertoire of conversational activities for friendship maintenance from talking about being a friend and helping others, to developing with a group of articulate friends a genre or language artefact that I have called this centre's 'girl-friend speak', and Ann Sheldon (1992) has called 'double-voice discourse'. This interest involved Nell's orientation towards her own agenda and towards the other members of the group. In Nell's case, it included telling interesting and relevant stories of just the right length, prompting the friend's story, listening to the answers – and waiting for the opportunity to offer a birthday party. For Nell and the peers who can also speak this language, developing a new artefact has enriched their membership of this particular friendship community.

When these observations were made, these four children were ready, willing and able to take a specific interest and to be involved. In every case, the interest and involvement was self-chosen and spontaneous, although Alan's interest and involvement was closely paralleled by the gate project being developed as part of the programme at his early childhood centre. Nevertheless, he made it his own, with his close attention to two aspects that had caught his attention: the measuring and the hinges. In Alan's case, the connection with *being willing* is clear: his involvement was very much along the lines of the programme. Moses and Sally chose artefacts from the environment that suited their purposes. Their learning dispositions and the learning places (home, childcare, nursery school) were compatible: Moses' family was greatly tolerant of his filling the house with animal arrays, and Sally's nursery teachers were prepared to wait until she found on her own (from a rich early childhood environment) the artefacts that provided personal meaning, solace and metaphor. This tolerance and compatibility enabled the children to develop skills and funds of knowledge: Nell's new language (which we will return to in Chapter 5, because Myra and Molly speak it too), Moses' fund of knowledge about animals that in many cases surpasses his parents' (his differentiation between types of horses, for instance), Alan's mathematical and carpentry skills and understanding, and Sally's intuitive capacity for analogy and metaphor. These interests can be interpreted in a number of ways. Alan's interest in hinges might fit the modern version of Piaget's schema developed by Chris Athey and Cathy Nutbrown and others (Athey, 1990; Nutbrown, 1994). Janet Astington and Henry Wellman would highlight Nell's apparent 'theory of mind' (Astington, 1993; Wellman, 1990). In any event, for these four children the dispositional milieux made space for their goals, although the adults could not at the outset have predicted the nature of their interest and involvement.

Assessment

These observations illuminate the definition of assessment that we have chosen: 'The ways in which, in our everyday practice, we observe children's learning, strive to understand it, and then put our understanding to good use (Drummond, 1993, p. 13).

What guidance do these examples of interest and involvement give us about assessment? They suggest the following: assessment will acknowledge the unpredictability of development, it will seek the perspective of the learner, a narrative approach will reflect the learning better than performance indicators, and collaborative interpretations of collected performances are helpful.

Assessment will acknowledge the unpredictability of development

Assessment that includes planning for progress will acknowledge that we don't always know the direction of development and learning. The examples support Katherine Nelson's comment that 'Development is an elusive underground process usually hidden from view' (1997, p. 101). Stories and narratives can capture moments of that development that come to the surface, but the direction will be difficult to predict. Case studies can describe change over time. Vivian Paley's children tell and then act out stories that have special meaning for them: often they start out from classics like Jack and the Beanstalk, or television stories, with the children adapting them and making them their own. Paley writes these told stories down, and, together with transcripts and descriptions of the children's play, they form the basis of her assessment and analysis. She says: 'I record their fantasy play because it is the main repository for secret messages, the intuitive language with which they express their imagery and logic, their pleasure and curiosity, their ominous feelings and fears' (1988, p. vii). She describes the pre-school classroom as 'the daily performance of private drama and universal theater'. Her interest is the emotional life of the children and the ways in which, for instance, they use fantasy play to illustrate to themselves that fears can be conquered. In the same way, Moses and Sally act out stories that appear to have special meaning for them, Alan focuses his attention on aspects of the environment that may be linked to a view of himself as a learner-builder, and Nell is apparently deeply involved in setting the boundaries and definitions of a social community.

Assessment will seek the perspective of the learner

Assessments of complex outcomes in which much is 'underground' will whenever possible seek out the viewpoint of the learner. In Chapter 8 we will see three-year-old Jill dictating the day's events to her mother for the home-based childcare Record Book. In many early childhood centres, tags on work in portfolios are frequently dictated by children. An example of assessment that includes the perspective of the learner is provided by the assessment of writing in a first-grade classroom in California. It has been written up by the teacher, Sarah Merritt, and a researcher (Ann Haas Dyson) in a book on assessment edited by Celia Genishi (1992). The nature of the tasks, writing stories that had meaning for the children and writing messages to each other, is an example of the assessment being part of the curriculum as well as containing the children's voices. Sarah saved the children's journals over the course of the year. Describing the writing of two of the girls, the authors comment that the journals 'reflected the girls' growing friendship as well as their developing encoding skills and the increasing complexity of their messages'. The authors illustrate how observations from three perspectives – the individual, the peer group and the classroom community – allowed the teacher to make sense of and support the children's learning. Other examples of assessments that seek the perspective of older learners include ten-year-olds keeping reflective learning logs, and an Australian study by Sue Howard and Bruce Johnson (1999) that used a 'This is Your Life' format for interviews with 9- to 12-year-olds about resilience.

A narrative approach will reflect the learning better than performance indicators

Writing about assessing authentic tasks in mathematics in the UK, Dylan Wiliam has recommended a move away from criterion- and norm-referenced assessment to the idea of 'construct-referenced' assessment, where 'the domain of assessment is holistic, rather than being defined in terms of precise objectives' (1994, p. 59). He advised (p. 54) that: 'What is required is a way of assessing authentic tasks on their own terms – in terms of what the student set out to do, but it does not seem as if any kind of explicit assessment scheme can achieve this.'

It would have been difficult to translate the involvement of the four children featured here into performance indicators, because their interests were closely situated and personal. We needed to know about the children, over time, and about the dispositional milieu. Although behavioural indicators of involvement such as the Leuven Involvement Scale (in which signs of involvement include: concentration, energy, complexity and creativity, facial expression and composure, persistence, precision and attention to detail, reaction time, verbal expression and satisfaction) may be very helpful, practitioners have accumulated a fund of stories of interest and involvement in their centre, and, knowing the children well, they are able to recognise ongoing interest and involvement.

Collaborative interpretations of collected observations will be helpful

Early childhood educators work in teams, and discussions between staff, as well as with families and children, have always been a traditional feature of early childhood practice. Sometimes called 'holistic' methods of assessment (see also Pamela Moss, 1994), these discussions include collaborative interpretations of collected observations about the children. Experience in the UK with 'agreement trials' for assessing pieces of work for GCSE English indicate that these collaborative interpretations can be made reliable (Wiliam, 1994, p. 60). In the case of Moses and Alan, for instance, the 'assessment' was an interpretation by their parents (for Moses) and the teachers (for Alan). They discussed the events with each other and with the children, remembered confirming or conflicting events in the past, and decided, often tentatively, that these were important interests and episodes of involvement for the children. In assessment terms, these are collaborative interpretations of complex and collected performances.

The next chapter provides analyses of examples of another domain of dispositions, *persisting with difficulty or uncertainty*, and as a consequence develops further guidelines for the assessment of outcomes as participation repertoires.

4

Persisting with Difficulty and Uncertainty

By now we have met a number of children's responses to difficulty or uncertainty. Timothy spent several days practising until he could manage the difficult task of abseiling up the slide, and Nell was enjoying the challenge to her rights to friendship with Emily and Laura. In Chapter 2, Susie was deciding not to tackle difficulty in screen printing 'ever again', in case she made a mistake. We can say, using Carol Dweck's terminology, that Susie appeared to be developing *performance* goals for at least some activities in the early childhood centre, whereas Timothy was developing *learning* goals. Experimental tasks were used by Dweck and her colleagues for assessing young children's learning orientation, and in 1994, she referred to 'Learning goal children' and 'Performance goal children':

> Learning goal children experienced the same roadblocks to task solutions as Performance goal children, and some of the Learning goal group lacked confidence in their future success. Nevertheless, as a group the Learning goal children remained focused on strategy and maintained an even emotional keel during the hard task; they evaluated their skills positively and persisted after failure. (Smiley and Dweck, 1994, p. 1739)

I want to integrate Dweck's ideas into a view of the learner as a learner-in-action, situated in a dispositional milieu. In one sense, of course, persisting with difficulty *should* be situated, or dependent on the context. It is not appropriate for a three-year-old to persevere with the difficulty of crossing a busy street on her own: she should be unwilling, sensitive to the occasion. In a different sense, persisting with difficulty *may* be situated: observations of Nell indicated that she 'had' learning goals when the topic appeared to be friendship, but performance goals, avoiding being seen to be unable, when technological challenge was imminent. In Chapter 2 it appeared that

Meg's friends were displaying performance goals in the butterfly-making episode, but learning goals when they worked together in the block area. In this chapter, Danny shifts from performance goals to learning goals as he begins to persevere with the difficulties of making a screen print of a favourite subject. In Danny's early childhood centre, as outlined in Chapter 2, some activities had become dispositional milieux: historically determined by cohorts of children and their teachers. However, some children appear to hold learning goals across a range of activities and domains. As we saw in the previous chapter, the situated viewpoint is helpful when it comes to appraising progress: progress will be indicated by the development of more sophisticated problem-solving strategies (like Nell's in friendship maintenance), and also when persistence with difficulty and uncertainty crosses the boundaries of artefact, activity and social community.

Jason

Jason, a nearly-five-year-old in Nell's kindergarten, was one child who appeared always to relish and persevere with difficulty, although I only met him when he was about to go to school. Here are three examples of what I perceived as Jason's perseverance in very different circumstances.

Observation 1
Marble painting.
Jason decides to do a marble painting, where the 'painting' results from the movement of a painted marble over paper in the base of a cardboard box. He elicits the help of the observer to look for the marbling box, which we can't find. Jason: 'I could just get another box!'
　　He cuts the side and then the end flap off a muesli bar box. Now he has a tray with one side cut off. He tucks some paper into one end, spoons in the painted marble, and rolls it about. The marble rolls onto the table. He controls the marble by pushing it around with the spoon, instead of tilting the box. Then he tilts the box again, catching the marble with his hand. He explains the problem to the observer: 'It needs one up there' (another side to the tray), and he curls the paper insert up to form a fourth side and a curved edge for the marble to roll up onto and back down.

Jason tries a number of strategies to solve the problem he has created by making a 'mistake' (cutting one side off the box): controlling the roll of the marble by pushing it around with the spoon, catching it in his hand,

and curling the painting paper up to form a fourth side to the box. Later
(Observation 2) he will advise Nell not to make the same mistake.

Observation 2
Marble painting.
A few minutes later Nell arrives and decides to make a marble-
painting tray just as Jason has done. She finds a cereal packet and says
to Jason 'D'you know how you can cut it? Cos I don't.' Jason replies,
pointing to parts of Nell's packet: 'You just. And this pulls out there.
You need to cut the top off. Don't cut the end off.'

Jason appears to see making an error as part of learning, and when he
tutors Nell he acknowledges that learning. This is also a significant
observation about Nell who up until this moment had never been seen
to admit that she 'didn't know' how to do something technological.
She has not been observed attempting a technical challenge that she is
unsure she can master, or asking a peer to help.

Observation 3
Writing.
This is a collaborative episode between Jason and Alison (his teacher),
in which Jason is learning how to write his friend John's second name.
Jason has already learned to write his own name, his sister's name, and
John's first name. The two participants exchange information about the
's' in each of their names; Jason sometimes asks for help ('How do you
write . . . ?') and sometimes states that he knows how to do it.

Jason: (to Alison) How do you write John's (other) name? (Alison
         writes it down for him and they go through it letter by letter as
         Jason writes) . . .
Alison: This is called an 'n'. My lips don't come together when I say
         that one.
Jason: See.
Alison: OK. Now, the very last letter of the alphabet: he has a 'z'.
Jason: Like a squiggly, like a squiggly 's'.
Alison: Yes. A very sharp one.
Jason: I've got a squiggly 's'.
Alison: I have too.
Jason: Like that.
Alison: That's right yes. It's a bit like an S but it's got much it's much
         sharper lines. (Jason: Yep) Doesn't curve. Now that one there.
Jason: I know how to do that.
Alison: Know how to do that one?

Observation 4
Giving advice on behaviour management.

Alison was teaching Jason to write John's name and they were interrupted by Rachel who complained that someone was chasing her.

Rachel: Alison.

Alison: Yep.

Rachel: Somebody want to chase us.

Alison: Ooh. What do you need to do about that?

Rachel: I don't know.

Jason: Run quickly and get away. (referring to his name writing) I done it.

Alison: Is there anything you can say to them?

Rachel: Go away!

Jason: I, I, I trip, I trip them up. I trip them up and run.

Alison: There's another, there's something else you can do instead. You can tell them. You can tell them to stop it and go away. That's another way.

Jason: Yep.

The teachers were encouraging the children to be in charge when other children were mean to them. The instruction for children was 'You say "stop it I don't like it" when someone does something you don't like.' Jason, about to leave for school, took a light-heartedly flexible view of kindergarten rules.

On another occasion, Jason made a hat that was different from everyone else's: he made a cylindrical hat (the same design as all the hats made at his early childhood centre) but he then added a fringe of perforated edges from computer paper, taking some time to attach them with sellotape so that they were evenly spaced and long enough to bounce and wave about as he ran around wearing it. Jason's disposition to persist with difficulty and to take an imaginative stance has ranged across the boundaries between artefact, activity and social community: the artefacts and activities associated with hat making, marble painting and writing, and his taking on the role of a kindergarten adviser on behaviour management.

Meg

Another four-year-old, Meg, also illustrates this capacity to persist with (and to choose) difficulty, but on the first occasion it is swamped by a more conservative and non-challenging dispositional milieu. I have already, in Chapter 2, commented on the possibility that this conservatism is a 'default setting' in group enterprises which are designed and initiated by the teacher and not sufficiently taken on as an interest by the children.

Observation 1

A group of children are working on a large collage/painting of a butterfly. In this observation, Meg twice tries to shift the topic to tackling difficulty, suggesting that they make the model a more accurate one by constructing antennae on the wall hanging of the butterfly. Meg's 'upping the ante' of the activity is italicised in the following. Both initiatives are buried by a 'whose friend is whose' discourse.

–   That's the middle. That's the butterfly's middle.
–   Yeah. Body.

Meg: *You forgot about those you forgot you forgot the things what go up like that.*

Linda: Meg I'm going to your place today.

Meg: I know. (takes on a funny voice) My friend's going to my place today. (ordinary voice) That's my friend.

Linda: She always does that when I go to her place.

Meg: *Now two more things what stick up. Those things what stick up.* (Amy, a teacher, and a child came past, saying 'beep beep' (excuse me)).

Valerie: Do you know what, did you tell your mother I'm coming over?

To take up the challenge would mean tackling and persisting with a difficulty. Performance goals, displaying whose friend is whose, took over, and making antennae was never attempted. Meg is vulnerable to performance goals, as the following transcript may indicate:

Penny is finger painting in the marble-painting tray. Meg and Linda focus the attention of the teacher on Penny's behaviour because it might not be allowed.

Meg: Look at hers. (Penny is finger painting in the marble tray)

Linda: Are you allowed to do that?

Penny: (. . .) to do.

Linda: What? . . . Oh, gross. Did the teacher said you could do that? Wow, look at her.

Meg: (to teacher) She's doing it wiv her hands.
            (Teacher says that this is allowed)

Linda: You're allowed doing that.

Penny: Yes.

But the second observation illustrates the circumstances in which Meg can pursue a difficult enterprise, making an imaginative hat that was possibly inspired by an artefact, blue cellophane, and a popular activity, making hats.

Observation 2
Making a hat.

(10.22 a.m.) Meg is stapling two strips together to make a longer strip. Tries to measure her own head. (10.30) Meg has made her hat but it's too big, she takes a pleat out of the back and staples it. It is still too big. Helps Linda by gluing her templates to a sheet of paper. (10.35) Cuts three blue sheets of A4 sized paper in half lengthwise, staples three of them into a strip, tries it around her head. Not long enough. (N.B. Linda copies the use of blue paper, cuts strips widthwise, goes on to make a paper chain; Peter copies Linda's loops, makes handcuffs.) Staples two more strips together, and then sellotapes and staples them all together in one long strip. She tries it on again, it slips around and she can't hold it in position to staple when it comes off her head. (10.43) Takes her cardigan off and takes it to her locker. Returns, tries again, then goes off with the strip and a stapler (presumably to ask an adult). Returns with it stapled. Sellotapes a circle of blue cellophane on. Puts the hat on, adjusting it so that the cellophane hangs down in front of one eye. Takes hat off and goes to look in the decorative paper box for more cellophane. Finds another piece of cellophane, cuts it to a similar size and shape, and by a process of sellotaping and putting hat on to adjust it, attaches the second piece of cellophane to eye level. (10.49) Distracted by Emily talking about birthday party in the family corner. Returns to sellotape blue lids onto the hat, in 'ear' positions. Meg and Linda distracted by Emily screeching in the family corner. Amy calls out for her to be quiet. They stop work for this. Then they resume. Meg draws down the centre ('nose' position) and then paints across the back. She hangs it up to dry. (10.55 a.m.)

This hat with built-in sun visor may have had its beginnings eight days earlier when she and Linda made telescopes by sellotaping coloured cellophane across the ends of cardboard tubes (they may have been alerted to the qualities of cellophane during the group butterfly mural construction on the same day).

Danny

Danny is very interested in small animals: in particular, bugs, spiders, ants, butterflies and rabbits. At home he draws them frequently, enjoys books on the topic, and is becoming very knowledgeable about them. At kindergarten he is introduced to screen printing, and a series of observations document his increasing expertise at this expressive medium. Although most children only made one screen print, and frequently kept the painted template and threw away the print (as Danny did at first), over a period of six weeks there were five episodes when he made screen prints, and by the fourth and fifth he was beginning to exploit the silhouetting opportunity of this medium. The sequence is described as follows:

Observation 1
In the first episode, on the first day of term, Alison (one of the teachers) taught Danny how to fold and cut his face shape so that 'we can see the eyes and the mouth. There's a trick. I'll show you the trick. You fold the piece of paper in half, I'll show you something you can do. When you draw a mouth, and some eyes, and you want the screen print to show it. You see what's going to happen. It comes out that way. Shall we do the eyes? Now we'll have to fold it a different way, this time, oh no. Fold it this way . . . Like that . . . . Like that. That's one eye. Fold the piece of paper and cut it just where you drew. Look. You can start to see the face, and that's what it's going to look like on the screen print.'

In the second episode, he discussed with me (a researcher) which way up his cut-out drawing should go, and did not appear to be convinced when I said it didn't matter. He put his pictures of 'ants' drawing side up, and was much more interested in the template than in the print:

Observation 2
Danny has drawn and cut around two figures: one big and one small, and is making a screen print of them. Which side up? he asks, doesn't like my suggestion that the drawn side goes down, puts them face up, and makes a print. But is more interested in preserving the cut-out figures and we later protect them on a sheet of card. I ask him if they are people. 'They're ants,' he says. This one is the Tennis Ant (?). He throws away the print and hangs up the cut-out figures to dry.
    The researcher rescues it: 'I'll hang this one up. Danny, shall I hang this one up for you? That's the actual print.'
Danny: Right.

Observation 3
In the third episode, he drew and cut out a whale. This was not his choice of subject, and the initiative to make a screen print was the teacher's. Danny and Bridget were together and Amy (one of the teachers) said 'Do you want to make something to take home today? Danny. Danny and Bridget. What about a screen print Bridget?' She suggested a screen print of a whale (a topic introduced at mat time) and when Bridget said 'I don't know how to' she said 'Well I can help you.' They got the book, and Danny joined in too. Amy reminded him that if he didn't cut out the eye it wouldn't appear on the screen.
Amy: 'Hey, look at this. He's beautiful. Good cutting Danny. Well done. You stuck it out and you finished it. Excellent. Cut the eyes out, 'cos that's all you're going to see, you see. Oh he's beautiful. So you

fold it over. And you just cut in here. Like that. So you can see it the eyes on the screen print. Isn't that neat Bridget. There, see there's one eye. You may need to do the same the other . . . now. It's coming to the inside. There you go. Let's have a look. Oh. That's what you're going to see on the screen. He's beautiful. (Raises her voice) Have a look at this whale everybody. Look at Danny's whale.' She hangs up his print to dry.

Although it was not initially his choice of occupation and topic, and Danny did not need the public praise (as Observation 4 indicates), he was learning more of the craft of screen printing.

Observation 4
In the fourth episode, with no teacher present, he put his drawing upside down on the screen, and indicated that he was exploiting the silhouette-forming affordance (potential) of a screen print. His friend Joan notes that he put the drawing upside down onto the screen.
Joan: You putted that on the wrong way.
Danny: Going to do the shadow of it. Oooaah.
He hangs up the print to dry.

Observation 5
In the fifth episode, assisted by a teacher, he also did the 'shadow of it', a screen print of a rabbit. He carefully ensures that the paint covers the paper beyond the template, saves the print, and hangs it up to dry.

Danny had become a screen printer, exploiting screen printing's capacity to provide a silhouette, and adding it to his modes of representing one of his favourite topics, small animals.

Summary Comments on Jason, Meg and Danny

Persisting with difficulty was operating at the three levels of artefact, activity and social community. At the first two levels, it might be expected that artefacts and activities that are obviously challenging will encourage persistence with difficulty. However, the children often introduced the challenge. Making a cylindrical hat from strips of card was a moderately unchallenging activity, except for the process of making it fit. Many of the children avoided even that difficulty by making hats for un-measurable people at home, babies or even cats. But Meg turned it into a challenge. Marble painting is normally easy, but Jason made it difficult. What these examples illustrate, however, is not (just) perseverance over time (Timothy and Moses have provided examples of this), but a capacity to *resist* what had become the normative run of events in this social community. Jason suggested an alternative to the clearly established rule: 'use your words'. And when the marble painting box was lost, he didn't go off to do something else, he turned his hand to making a new one, and thereby radically changed the dispositional milieu of marble painting. As a result, box construction became for other children a new and challenging part of the hitherto boring and easy marble-painting activity. Meg makes a complex hat, for a complex purpose, whereas most of the hats produced were cylindrical 'birthday' hats with paint or collage added. Danny appeared to come, finally, to screen printing with an artist's (rather than a kindergartener's) agenda. He announced to Joan that he was 'going to do the shadow of it. Oooaah.' These events also illustrate a playfulness that appears to have followed from a period of involvement and play with the artefacts or the activities. Meg had made several traditional hats, and in (at least) two activities discovered the qualities of blue cellophane. Danny had made a succession of screen prints. I had not observed Jason marble paint before, but he had experimented with paint in a number of ways. Nearly at school, he was an 'old hand' with the routines and rules in the kindergarten, confident enough in his expertise to risk censure and take a playful stance.

In what sense were the children ready, willing and able? The observations are testimony to the value of documenting children's learning over a period of time, and in all cases they are a selection from a number of observations. The children's inclination to risk error and to persist with difficulty was a consistent theme, and appeared to be especially in evidence in those examples where they were resisting the normal routine way of doing things. Their early childhood centre provided plenty of time and space and materials for child-initiated enterprises, setting the scene for the children's willingness to explore and to persevere. Meg had previously experimented with hat-making and with cellophane: in the hat-making episode described here, she put these two activities together in an unusual way. Jason cheekily suggested that when someone is chasing you it's a good idea to 'trip them up and run', when he knew that this was unacceptable; and his teacher's mild response 'There's something else you can do instead' suggested that she appreciated his playfulness if not his advice. Many of these episodes included others as participants, even if the enterprises were not themselves always collaborative (Jason teaching Nell, being taught how to write John's name by the teacher, giving advice to Rachel; Meg makes her hat at a busy art table, interrupts her work to help others, and seeks an adult for help with the stapling). The skills and funds of knowledge that the children called on and developed to support their persistence were diverse, and in three cases they received and accepted adult help of just the right sort: Jason with writing, Meg with stapling and Danny with screen printing. The children appeared to see themselves as experts: Jason is writing a name for John, and he teaches Nell how to make a marble-painting box; Meg tries to direct the butterfly-making task, and during the hat making she assists and is copied by Linda, Danny explains the screen printing purpose to Joan.

Another perspective on the children's persistence with difficulty was gained when I interviewed Danny and 37 other four-year-olds to try to find out their viewpoint about tackling 'difficulty' (Carr, 2000a). Danny seldom drew pictures at the early childhood centre, but I knew that he was a talented artist. When I asked him what he found difficult, he replied 'drawing cars, like Jack, my big brother'. When prompted (What's the difficult aspect of drawing cars?) he replied:

> Um. The um the windows. (Me: The windows.) 'Cos um you have to do the triangle ones (Me: Yes) and the for the um for the back windows and then those, you know those um triangle windows?

Interviewing young children is a notoriously difficult task. I tried to overcome some of the difficulties by writing a picture book that mirrored the pattern of activities in the early childhood centre, and seeking the children's response to this. I wove into the story-line of the book my interest in whether the children thought it was a 'good' idea to tackle difficulty and to risk failure at the centre, and gave the book an incomplete ending. I asked their advice about how to end the story, and also added some open-ended questions about what they thought was difficult, and what they were looking forward to being able to do that they could not do now. Some of the findings were instructive. Only nine of the 38 children advised the hero or heroine to tackle a difficult task and risk failure. Twenty-three children gave 36 responses to supplementary questions about 'what is difficult?' and it was interesting that 22 of the 36 responses referred to difficult skills or activities that the children perceived they were learning or practising at sites *away from* the early childhood centre. Ten of the 23 children located difficulty elsewhere only. Almost half of these children did not, apparently, see the early childhood centre as the place where they tackled and persisted with difficulty – but they were able to give me a list of difficult activities that they valued elsewhere. The interview also revealed that these four-year-olds cited difficulty in diverse fields of artefact, activity and social community. Mastering the cultural artefact of writing was mentioned several times (writing 'a' and 'e', said one of the children; writing my name, said another); Samuel said he liked doing hard 100-piece jigsaw puzzles. Many of the children cited jumping, doing handstands, forward flips and cartwheels as difficult activities, and one child told me he was learning to whistle ('Dad is teaching me'); Freda told me that she was finding it difficult to draw noses. In the social field, Matt said he was looking forward to being old enough to 'go up the street and get the eggs, by myself', Rita said she wanted to be able to 'do the vacuum', and Laura said that she found it difficult to tell Emily that she didn't want to play with her.

Assessment

The previous chapter set out four guidelines for assessment from the examples about interest and involvement. The examples in this chapter suggest two further guidelines for informal feedback and formal, documented assessment: many tasks will provide their own assessment, and assessment will itself contribute to the children's learning dispositions.

Many tasks will provide their own assessment

Authentic tasks that engage the learner in problem-finding and problem-solving will provide assessment sites in which tackling and persisting with difficulty provides its own assessment or reward. The literature describes a positive relationship between intrinsically interesting tasks and on-task work; by contrast, Carole Ames (1992, p. 265) commented on a study in which extrinsic rewards were common: 'the first-year teachers . . . were found to use the amount of recess time, stickers, and privileges as incentives to induce children to complete their work or to behave in a certain manner'.

Torrance and Pryor (1998, p. 86) cite research that suggests that extrinsic reward systems have 'detrimental effects on intrinsic motivation, especially when initial interest is high'. They add that: 'children who become used to extrinsic rewards tend in future not to choose activities where these incentives are not attainable, and also favour less demanding activities' (pp. 86–7).

This guideline means that in many cases the assessment will be an authentic product of the learning task or activity. In early childhood, the materials themselves often provide the feedback. For instance, Montessori equipment frequently has its own built-in feedback, and jigsaws always do. Examples of *learning* as opposed to *performance* goals at younger ages are frequently cited in activities with clear goals. Writing is a good example.

Jinny (four years old, writing a card): IIow do you write 'love'?
Alison (teacher): If I say the letters, can you write them down? Do you know them if I say them? If I say 'L'?
Jinny: Yep. There's an L in Nell's name.
Alison: (to Nathan: Look at that) Yes Nell's got an 'L'. (to Nathan: OK Can you hang that up Nathan?) L.O. (Jinny: O, yeah) V. Yes. E. (*Video notes: she writes the letters in the air*) That's it. Do you want to do the word 'from'?
Jinny: Yeah.

The teacher did not add praise. Later, someone in her family will read this back to Jinny and this will provide for Jinny the assessment of successful achievement. It was often those activities in which children could readily perceive success (and failure) which provided practitioners with stories of persistence with difficulty: mastering tools like scissors and carpentry equipment, riding a bike, completing a jigsaw, writing a name.

Assessment will itself contribute to the children's learning dispositions

In the case of persisting with difficulty and uncertainty, the assessment will emphasise that errors are part of learning. More generally, the assessment will itself contribute to the children's dispositions to take an interest, be involved, persist with difficulty and uncertainty, communicate with others, and take responsibility in a range of ways. Assessment will take a fundamentally 'credit' approach, on the assumption that a disposition, being a habit of mind, emerges in a climate of positive learning experiences that are recognised and highlighted. It will minimise negative social comparison; planning from the assessment will be designed to enhance the outcomes assessed. The difference in approach of Jason from Emily ('Don't call me wrong' in Chapter 1) and Susie (in Chapter 2) alerted me to this guideline, and other writers have made similar observations. Carole Ames commented that:

The impact of social comparison on children *when they compare unfavorably* can be seen in their evaluations of their ability, avoidance of risk taking, use of less effective or superficial learning strategies, and negative affect directed toward the self. (1992, p. 264) (my emphasis)

The portfolios prepared for individual children at the Pen Green Early Childhood Centre in the UK are of particular interest. These portfolios celebrate the children's learning, including photos (often sequences of pictures from video recording) and children's drawings, with a focus on patterns of (usually) kinaesthetic and motor 'schemas'; examples include work and interests that suggest a trajectory, enclosure, or enveloping pattern. The portfolio of one of the children, described as 'an enveloper', was shaped like an envelope. The text of the portfolios carefully annotates the drawings and the photos in terms of schemas; they include learning episodes that illustrate the schemas, and they include 'PLODs', Possible Lines Of Development. Margy Whalley has described the process in her book *Learning to be Strong* (1994). Some of the examples in the portfolio may come from home, because many of the families keep a journal and borrow the video camera. Parent meetings at the centre indicate that the celebratory and interesting nature of the record (reflecting the philosophy at Pen Green) has positive consequences for relationships with the children at home as well as at the centre. In a similar way to the assessments documented later in this book, the assessment practice contributes to children's dispositions to learn.

The next chapter provides examples of *communicating with others* and *taking responsibility*, and suggests one more guideline for assessment.

5
Communicating with Others and Taking Responsibility

Chapter 2 set out five domains of learning disposition, and the previous two chapters have provided examples of the first three of these in action. The final two domains are *communicating with others* and *taking responsibility*. They have been combined together to illustrate episodes of joint attention, where children express a point of view or a feeling, and take on the point of view of others. These episodes are examples of reciprocal and responsive relationships with people that weave together the affective, the cognitive and the social into rich fabrics of learning. In each case the children have been able to find or construct places in which the tasks of interest work best within responsive and reciprocal relationships. The stories of Rosie, Kiriwaitutu, Nick, Myra and Molly are told and analysed, followed by an implication for assessment from these examples.

Rosie

The routines and props at Rosie's childcare centre allow plenty of time and opportunity for elaborated sociodramatic play, and the centre provides a programme where events and plans are as often as possible negotiated, and reasons for rules given. Rosie is a four-year-old with an apparent interest in the ambiguous territory between the binaries of scary–friendly, good–mean and real–pretend (concerns and interests also the subject of commentary by Vivian Paley and Kieran Egan). Rosie has a number of fantasy story-lines which she negotiates and adapts, and she structures the participation of others in enterprises that elaborate on the topics she finds to be of interest. These processes of shared responsibility enable successful collaborative problem-solving. Her strategies of 'bridging' (sharing understanding) and 'structuring' (directing or negotiating each other's participation) include: directing the sequence of events, offering alternatives, giving reasons, negotiating the story-line, acknowledging another's interest to try to persuade, persevering towards a negotiated settlement, communicating her ideas to an adult when she discusses her drawing, and having a conversation.

Observation 1
Directing the sequence of events, offering an alternative and *giving a reason.* Rosie and Anna are inside at the childcare centre, 'fishing' with sticks and ribbons. They have a box of 'bait' (pieces of jigsaw from the table nearby) beside them. It is 9.20 a.m. Rosie resists Anna's attempt to negotiate the story-line, giving a reason. She also has a light-hearted negotiation with Dan (If you're my friend. . . only if you're mean). Later during this episode the adult too offers an alternative and gives a reason.

Rosie: We can fish from our home 'cos our home is by the river.
Anna: We're going home now.
Rosie: No, our home is here.
        (Dan comes over and treads on the fishing lines, and Anna shouts at him)
Rosie (to Dan): If you're my friend I'll let you come to my house and play with my cat Cato.
Dan: He might scratch me.
Rosie: Only if you're mean to him.

The adult asks Rosie to return the jigsaw pieces they have put into a cardboard box as 'bait' and explains that the other children cannot complete their jigsaws. She suggests shells as an alternative, and they replace the jigsaw pieces with shells.

Observation 2
Directing the sequence of events. Rosie is playing inside at the childcare centre; Rosie has devised a 'Going to Pizza Hut' script. She has made one of the staff a pretend pizza and poured her some pretend lemonade. Louise arrives and attempts to take on a leading role: the Mum, and then the cashier. Both are rejected by Rosie, on each occasion using as rationale a re-statement (or rapid reconstruction) of her script.

Louise (who has just arrived): I'll be the Mum OK?
Rosie: No, we're at the Pizza Hut. (Gives adult an empty plate) Want chocolate on this? We took our pizzas home eh?
Adult: Did we remember to pay for our pizzas? (Rosie nods) How much was it?
Louise: Two dollars.
Adult: That was cheap, two dollars each.

Louise: You have to give me two dollars.

Rosie: No. Let me say something. We took the pizza home to our place. Do you know. We took the pizza to our place and the ice cream too and guess what I say to you. We're not at the Pizza Hut, we're at home.

Observation 3

Negotiating the story-line. The 'dress-ups' have been taken outside; at the beginning of the play Rosie is Dad and Anna is a puppy. Rosie finally gives way on the sequence of events, and once again a staff member (a different staff member from in Observation 1 or 2) gives explanations.

Rosie: Thanks Puppy. I'm the Dad.
(They hang up the camera on the clothes hangers that are part of outside equipment for dress-up play)
I'm going to take a photo of you.
(Anna asks staff member to make the swings available. Adult explains why she can't:)

Adult: There aren't enough adults at the moment. I know it's really hard to understand, but if the swings are down I have to watch them, and I need to watch the whole area.

Anna: (to Rosie) That's my camera. (They argue about whose camera it is)

Rosie: I buyed it.

Anna: No, you didn't buy it. I'll take this away if you didn't buy it. (She snatches an item of clothing that Rosie has been taking on and off)

Rosie: OK. I didn't buy it.

Observation 4

Acknowledging another's interest to try to persuade. Rosie is playing Captain Hook and Peter Pan, and Louise arrives. Louise's favourite role is a mermaid. Rosie tries to persuade Louise to join in on her Peter Pan script.

Rosie: There are mermaids in it.

Louise: No there aren't.

Rosie: Yes there are.

Louise: No there aren't.

Rosie: (putting her face up close to Louise's) Yes there are. 'Cos I got the video and I saw mermaids on it.

Louise: I didn't see it.
(Louise is not convinced and sets herself up as a mermaid in a nearby enclosure. Rosie takes up a role in both her own and in Louise's stories, alternately moving from one place to the other.)

Observation 5

Negotiating the story-line. In this episode, Rosie and Anna are playing outside. Anna has some say in the story-line and the allocation of roles, and Rosie tries to script Anna's thoughts ('You say to yourself, I love Belle eh?'), seeing these as central to the story-line. She tries to get Anna to elaborate on the Beast's planned behaviour ('Who're you gonna kill?'). Even Jeanie, who is not yet four, is willing to negotiate a turn with the doll.

Anna: You be Belle and I'll be the Beast.

Rosie: You say to yourself, I love Belle, eh?

       (A toddler comes over to tell Rosie about a helicopter overhead)

Rosie: Go away.

       (Anna makes beast-like noises and talks about killing)

Rosie: Who're you gonna kill? (Anna doesn't reply)

       (Jeanie comes over and wants the doll baby that Rosie has. Rosie won't give it to her)

Jeanie: When you go home, you give it to me OK? (No reply from Rosie)

Observation 6

Persevering towards a negotiated settlement. The children are outside, riding around on tricycles. Rosie doesn't have one. Another child fends off negotiation (or makes it difficult) by using an ambiguous but powerful timing mechanism for sharing (holding up her fingers: 'this many minutes'); the same child later arranges the environment so things are fair for everyone. Rosie perseveres.

Rosie (to Amy): Please can I have one of those?

Amy: I haven't finished. (Rosie follows her around) This much minutes (she holds up the fingers on both hands) when I've finished.

Rosie: Can I have the bike soon, can I have it when you've finished please?

Amy: Yes.

Rosie (turning it into a story): OK. 'Bye.

       . . . (a few minutes later)

Rosie (tearful, to adult): She said this many minutes (holds up her fingers).

Amy: But I'm not getting off.

       (The adult assists Rosie onto a rather too big trike)

       . . . (a few minutes later)

Amy to Gina (who is tall): You have the big bike.

       (Gina gets onto the biggest trike, Amy then gets onto Gina's trike, and Rosie onto Amy's. They ride around, following a chalk line drawn on the concrete by the adult).

Observation 7

Communicating ideas to an adult. An example in which the activity is not sociodramatic or social play, but drawing. Rosie draws her family at the zoo, with animals that are either friendly or scary. She talks to an adult about her drawing as she draws: Mum, 'me', Dad, a friendly dinosaur ('even though that spiky bit is sharp'), a friendly lion, a scary tiger, a coconut, a 'little kitty' (shall I do the claws? Yes), the grass, a flower ('the stalk, the circle, the pollen, and the petals') and the sun.

Observation 8

Having a conversation. Rosie is sitting having morning tea and chatting to me about what she likes doing, and what she will be able to do when she's older (drink tea and eat fish) and what she likes doing now that's really difficult (head rolls, and hopping).

Me: What about your drawing? What do you draw that's difficult?
Rosie: Dragons.
Me: Mmm. Is it the tongue and the eyes that's difficult?
Rosie: Dragons look like this (mimes a dragon face) and they have prickles down their back and claws on their feet. And you know the cupboard where the television is (gestures, whispers) there's a dragon in there, behind the television.
Me: Oh, no. And does it peep out?
Rosie: (whispering) Oh no. It's not a good one. It eats you.
Me: (whispering) Eats children and grown-ups?
Rosie: Yep. Eats children and grown-ups.
Me: What colour is it?
Rosie: Green and orange. It has an orange tongue and green skin.
        (A toddler comes over)
Me: Mm hm.
        (Rosie and adult nod to each other in tacit agreement not to frighten the little ones)

Rosie struggles with language skills at the top end of her range: she strings sequential ideas, provides reasons, describes imaginative events, and discusses thought. Her pretend play, her drawing, and her conversations all reflect these increasingly elaborated topics or story-lines. At singing time, one of Rosie's favourite song routines is 'We're going on a Bear Hunt, I'm not scared', which she joins in with great gusto, helps decide on the script, and jumps into the adult's lap in mock terror. On another occasion, she announces that she is a cowboy. An adult asks if she is not a cowgirl? She replies that she is a cowboy, mean to monsters and nice to people.

Kiriwaitutu

A good example of the close connection between these two dispositional domains – communication and taking responsibility – and the
mediational means (artefacts, activities and social community) comes
from a total immersion Māori language early childhood centre or
kōhanga reo (the literal meaning is language nest). Kiriwaitutu is a
four-year-old who attends an urban Māori language centre, and the
observations here come from the write-up of the children's learning
by their kaiako (teacher), Mere Skerrett-White. The observations focus
on Kiriwaitutu's language experiences in context. Mere refers to
Rogoff's work when she reminds us (Rogoff, 1990, p. 79) that context
is 'an interwoven web of relations which form the "fabric of meaning".' Reflecting the culture of the centre, these examples include a
number of ways in which Kiriwaitutu communicates with and takes
responsibility for the other children: turning painting into a joint conversational activity, using a different language genre for the younger
children, and correcting an adult who uses the wrong name; as well,
she is using increasingly complex and precise linguistic functions.

Observation 1
Turning painting into a joint conversational activity. Kiriwaitutu and another, younger, child are both painting alongside each other. The two
children discuss what Kiriwaitutu is going to be painting on her page.
  Kiriwaitutu says 'Ka pēnei . . .' (Like this . . .), demonstrating her
technique. They both carry on working for a while looking at one
another's work and discussing what they are doing. Kiriwaitutu is
painting vertical strokes with black paint. Her companion is painting
horizontal strokes with green paint. He checks to see what stage
Kiriwaitutu is at. He then looks around for some more black paint,
returns and adds some black vertical strokes to his painting. They
continue their conversation about the work. Their paintings are in a
sense another conversation, exchanging design and colour.

Observation 2
Using a different language genre for the younger children. Kiriwaitutu and
four other children are all playing in the sandpit. The children work
together on a construction. Meanwhile one of the babies has come over
to 'help' with the construction. Kiriwaitutu says, in a sing-song (baby)
voice:
'Kao . . . kao. I te mahi mātou ēnei – a-a-a i-o-u.'
'No . . . no. We all (excluding you) have created this.' She finishes with
a little vowel ditty.

Observation 3
Correcting an adult who uses the wrong name, using increasingly complex and precise linguistic functions. Kiriwaitutu has taken on the responsibility of assisting a newly arrived adult who is having difficulty with a name. Some of the children were working at the collage table when they were approached by an adult on her first day in the centre. Whilst working with one of the children, the adult uses the wrong name, Kiriwaitutu, who is looking on, corrects her, and supplies the correct name (K . . .)
Kiriwaitutu: 'Ko K . . . tēnā, ko K . . .'
              (This is K . . .)

Mere comments on the linguistics, in particular:

> Firstly her use of 'ko' as a particle designating a proper noun, and secondly the correct use of 'tēnā', (as opposed to tēnei or tērā) as a locative denoting a case of 'the person there next to you'. This latter is a concept that many adults have difficulty with when learning Māori as a second language.

The observations of Kiriwaitutu reflect some aspects of participation repertoires at this centre, in particular the strong culture of mutual support and caring; even painting, on this occasion, was a joint, conversational, activity. The example of using a different language genre for the younger children was typical of the older children. The children have a number of languages that are sensitive to the occasion. Mere's observation and comments in the third episode also clearly illustrate the different kind of foregrounding of analysis: on the one hand highlighting the inclination and the willingness to communicate with and to take responsibility for others, and at the same time highlighting the developing language skills and expertise that underpin that inclination.

Nick

Communicating with others and *taking responsibility* have been combined together in this chapter to illustrate episodes of joint attention. Rosie and Kiriwaitutu provided examples of these reciprocal interchanges, in sociodramatic play (Rosie), and in the general running of the programme and caring for others (Kiriwaitutu). The following are further examples of peer collaboration (in an art activity and in sociodramatic play) that involve four-year-old Nick. The children are bridging and structuring. The first episode is primarily about *bridging*, in which the children share their understanding of the task at hand:

they are giving instructions, explaining what's going on, asking questions, and reminding of difficulty in a reciprocal and responsive fashion. The second episode is an example of some skilful *structuring* of the others' participation by Nick. In the first observation, two familiar characters appear again here: Nell and Jason. It is a marble painting episode in which Nell instructs Jinny; then Nick asks Jinny about the process; then Nick takes on some of the responsibility, spooning marbles in for Jinny.

Observation 1

Giving instructions, explaining what's going on, asking questions and *reminding of difficulty.* Nell (who has recently been instructed by Jason on how to make a marble-painting tray) instructs Jinny (and Jason repeats his reminder to cut the sides of the boxes 'only off the tops').

Nell: I (you?) can't do one yet, Jinny, 'cos you've got to make a box. You've got to get some of these scissors. Go and get a box. As big as this prob'ly or like that. And then you can cut it.
Jason: Ah, only off the tops, not these.
Nell: No, not the sides.
Nick: Where did you get that box from?
Nell: I don't know. On the shelf.
Nick: Is there two balls in there?
Nell: Yep.
Nick: What are those, do those, balls do that
Nell: Marbles. (same time)
Nick: painting? (same time)
Nell: Yeah. They make it. (sound of marbles rolling about)
Jinny: Green in there.
Jason: Is it windy outside Trevor? (Trevor?: Mm) (Jason has earlier made a kite)
Nell: And put some of that colour into the green. (sound of marbles rolling about)
Nick: Is it easy?
Nell: It is easy.
Nick: Can I've a turn now? . . .
Nick: Do I put a bit of this in? . . .
Nick: Shall I put the ball in . . .
Nick: Shall I put a bit more paint in . . .
Alison (teacher): (sound of marble dropping)
         Ooh that went high.
Nick: Well. It landed in the box.
Alison: Uh huh.

All 18 of the initiating comments by the children (out of 27 comments in total) were collaborative bridging comments: giving instructions, explaining what's going on, asking questions, and reminding of difficulty. Nell took the lead giving Jinny an explanation about why she could not do a marble painting straight away (she has to make a box), and then gave her four instructions. Jason warned of possible difficulty ('only off the tops'), a warning confirmed by Nell. Nick then shared the responsibility by asking questions about the process (do those balls do that painting? and, Is it easy?), asks if he can have a turn, then did some of the work for Jinny (checking with her that it is all right). The field notes record that 'Nick now does one, absorbed by it. He asks Alison (the teacher) to look at it, and they talk about the tracks the marbles have made, where they have turned a corner.'

Observation 2
Structuring the others' participation. Nick negotiates a compromise that is satisfactory to all parties. He is in the 'family' corner with Rachel and Tony. Nick and Rachel are getting ready to go to a party. Rachel tells Tony he's not playing. When Tony doesn't go away she gets (mildly) cross and reiterates that he's 'not coming to our party'; Nick combines the two viewpoints by suggesting that when they prepare the party food they prepare something for his (Tony's) dinner: Tony can be part of the play, although he cannot go to the party.

Nick: . . . some yummy meat balls for the party tonight.
Tony: And I'm making some.
Rachel: No, you're not playing this game with us.
Tony: Uh?
Nick: 'Cos these are just for us for the party.
Tony: I'm making something as well for the party.
Rachel: No, you're not coming to our party.
Nick: No, he's just making something for us to take eh?
Tony: And I'm coming as well, eh?
Nick: No.
Rachel: No.
Nick: You're just making something for us to take. And you can. And we can cut a bit in half for you to have for dinner tonight, OK?
Tony: Because I'm.
Nick: Because you won't have any dinner left, will he Rachel?
Rachel: No.
Nick: So we we're going to cut him a bit.
Tony: I'm cutting.
Nick: 'K. Now go and put that bit in the fridge. That bit. That bit of pizza. It's a bit of pizza. OK?

Molly and Myra

One of the observations of Kiriwaitutu illustrated the complexity of language genre that young children are developing, to match the social communities to which they belong or aspire to belong. Molly and Myra are four-year-olds in the same early childhood centre as Nick, Nell and Jason. They were experts at a genre of language that I have called 'girl-friend-speak' because in this early childhood centre it appeared to be the prerogative of the girls. An example was provided in Chapter 3 when we met Emily attempting to deceive Nell but not to deceive Laura by pretending to admire Nell's work. In this centre a number of the girls were setting up some subtle conversational rules, and many of them called on what has been called a 'theory of mind', or a theory about other people's minds: an understanding of the influence on action of another person's beliefs, attitudes and feelings. Nell has a conversation with Emily about Emily's brother's name: 'Margie [Nell's sister] thinks your brother's Bobby.' Laura tells a story about her brother who made a wish for a pirate suit and a sword and a pirate ship and he was 'expecting it to float down our creek (stream).' Four-year-olds that I have observed often comment on others 'not knowing' something: Myra says to Molly 'You didn't know that I went to day care'; Linda is in a bad mood with Meg and says 'Anyway, you don't know what my other name is.' In my observations 'girl-friend-speak' involved:

- talk about the *needs* of others:

   Rachel (to Wendy about materials or tools for decorating her hat): That's what you've done so you need that . . . (to Wendy about hanging up her collaged hat to dry) Can you reach it? (Wendy: Yep. Easy to).

- talk about *desires* of others:

   Myra (to Molly who, she knows, likes painting with yellow; the marble for the yellow paint had been temporarily lost but was found by the teacher): Now you'll be able to do the yellow won't you Molly?

- talk about *knowledge* of others:

   (i) Linda (to Meg): You don't know how my name goes. You don't know how my name goes either.
   Meg: You don't know how *my* name goes.
   (ii) Bridget: This is Meg. My g. My other friend . . . She doesn't know where I live though.

- talk about *beliefs* of others:

  Emily: We don't like it really eh?
  Laura (loud whisper): Yeah, we just lying eh? . . .
  Laura (telling a story about her brother): And then he was expecting it to float down our creek.

- associated discourse strategies for keeping the conversation going, indicating that the speaker is listening to the other, or wants the other to participate: prompting for a coherent story-line, giving advice or assistance (perceiving or assuming a need on the part of the other), demanding and holding each other's attention, asking for support or praise, explaining what's going on, giving instructions, questioning.

Here are two examples of Molly and Myra talking together. In the first the conversation is about who knows what. The second observation is an example of Molly and Myra using strategies for keeping the conversation going. The third observation, like the first observation about Nick, is an example of bridging and structuring understanding and participation.

Observation 1
Talk about the knowledge of others (You didn't know that I went to day care) and *prompting for a coherent story-line* (Did she? When?):
Myra: D'you know what Molly?
Molly: What?
Myra: I knew that girl and her name was Penny.
Molly: I knew her too.
Myra: I know her 'cos she played with me um at day care but now I go to kindy.
Molly: Did she?
Myra: You didn't know that I went to day care.
Molly: When?
Myra: Um. The other year. But I'm here now.

Observation 2
Demanding and holding each other's attention (using each other's names, the use of 'isn't it?', more direct: 'watch this', 'look at this'), *giving advice or assistance perceiving or assuming a need on the part of the other* ('you should have a golden light . . .') and *asking for support and praise* (Mine's pretty isn't it?).

   This second example is tape-recorded while Molly and Myra are making 'flashing lights' hats: cylindrical hats which they have decorated with material, adding a 'light' on the front.
Myra: Molly, this thing is the flashing light. (Molly: Yes) Look at my lovely thing. And I've got a lovely light. That shines golden.

> Gonna turn the shining light on. Look at the shiny light Molly. Look at that gold in the middle.

Molly: Mine's even prettier 'n yours Myra. Got more stuff on it. This little bit's going to be the light.

Myra: Look at the golden light flashing on. The golden light goes on so I can see in the night. You should have a golden light to see in the night. Here's your flashing light. I'll get a little flashing.

Myra (to another child): You can make a hat if you like. I'm making. What are you making? (Molly: I'm making a princess hat) I'm not. I'm making my Dad, a hat for George.

Molly: Mine's pretty isn't it?

Another child: Where are you going to stick that though?

When Molly said 'Mine's pretty isn't it?' Myra did not reply, perhaps because Molly had already said that hers was 'even prettier 'n yours'; this transcript had a competitive edge, but the children still helped each other, and Myra later saved some of her precious gold paper for Molly.

Observation 3

Explaining the process (The ball's making me do that. See the squiggles that it made? Purple and yellow), *giving instructions* (perhaps to herself: then we put it back. Show me), *questioning* (Where's yours? Where? Why're you doing it again?). Myra had just completed a marble painting and Molly was in the middle of making one. When Myra made her marble painting the marble for the yellow paint was lost, and she had to make do with the purple only. Alison (the teacher) then found the yellow marble, and Molly then made a painting with the two marbles and two colours.

Molly: Yuk. Hey the ball's making me do that. (laughs) Now. Now we take it out and put some more paint, then we put it back.

Myra: Mine is purple as the.

Molly: Where's yours?

Myra: Just in there.

Molly: Where? Show me.

Myra: (from a distance) Here.

Molly: Oh yeah. Come on ball. Ah see. (laughs) . . .

Myra: Why're you doing it again Molly?

Molly: 'Cos I want to.

Myra: Now you'll be able to do the yellow, won't you Molly?

Molly: (to Myra and Alison, a teacher) See what squiggles that made?

Alison (teacher): Oh, look at that.

Molly: There. Purple and yellow (explanation of process).

Alison: Oh, what's it (. . .).

Molly: Look. Colour (explanation of process).

Some of the ingredients of girl-friend-speak are apparent here: keeping the attention by using names (twice, from Myra) for instance. Myra's comment 'Now you'll be able to do the yellow, won't you Molly?' refers to her knowledge that yellow is Molly's favourite colour.

Summary Comments on Rosie, Kiriwaitutu, Nick, Molly and Myra

These examples of communicating with others and taking responsibility are, not surprisingly, mostly at the level of the social community. They describe ways in which the children establish their membership of a community (through particular language genres), and the strategies with which they keep the conversation going or the group together for the task at hand. These included *bridging* strategies for mutual understanding, and *structuring* strategies for maintaining the participation of all the players, in order to get the task done or the story played out. Symmetrical and collaborative patterns of interaction were often to be found in sociodramatic play, where the outcome is clearly a joint one and frequently the scripts are similar. The examples provide illustrations of *power with*, introduced in Chapter 2: relationships between adults and children, and between children, characterised by negotiation, collaboration and transaction.

These were examples of children being ready, willing and able to communicate with others and to take responsibility in group settings. The relevance of the socio-cultural context was very much in evidence. These early childhood communities have encouraged the children's inclination to communicate and take responsibility in ways that were appropriate to their setting. The dispositional milieu of the Māori language centre is one of mutual support, caring, collaboration and conversation across all areas (including painting). But in both the childcare centre and the kindergarten there were at least some activities which commonly featured reciprocal bridging and structuring, and mutual support. Rosie's disposition to communicate her ideas and to listen to others in episodes of joint attention had found a match in responsive and reciprocal environments in her childcare centre. The adults were modelling the same bridging and structuring strategies that Rosie was striving to make work for her. Collaborative scripts in sociodramatic play are common in early childhood settings, but the collaborative scripts in other areas (the marble painting in Nick's kindergarten was an example) are often less familiar. The communication (in this case almost entirely oral language) strategies and understandings that the children were developing in order to support their group orientation were clearly in evidence in these examples.

Assessment

The learning *place*, the dispositional milieu, was central to the learning disposition exemplified in this chapter. These examples provide a further assessment guideline: assessment will protect and enhance the early childhood setting as a learning community.

Assessment will protect and enhance the early childhood setting as a learning community

We assess the learner-in-action-with-mediational-means in terms of the mediational means that are locally available. The literature provides examples of early childhood settings and classrooms that have been described as learning communities. The early childhood programmes in the Reggio Emilia region of northern Italy have deliberately attempted to incorporate community participation by including resident artists and craftspeople, by taking their projects out into the local community, and by taking community projects into the early childhood centres. The documentation of learning in Reggio Emilia programmes provides an example of assessment that reflects a learning community (Dahlberg, Moss and Pence, 1999). In one of the Reggio programmes, a project described as 'an amusement park for birds' was documented in detail in a 1995 video with that title by George Forman and Leila Gandini. The children, three- to five-year-olds, designed and built an amusement park for birds. Activities included observing, drawing, modelling and constructing fountains and water wheels. Adults documented the process of 'emergent curriculum' with wall charts, videos and photos. The project, the participation and the individual were not separated out. Assessment of the learners and evaluation of the project were the same process.

In another example of assessment that highlights the dispositional milieu, Ann Filer (1993) has outlined the assessments of speaking and listening (an attainment target for education in the UK) for four-year-old Peter in Year 1 and then later in Year 2 of his primary school. She has added her own (the researcher's) observations of Peter's speaking and listening. The Year 1 teacher assessed Peter's vocabulary as limited and commented that although he appeared to listen he failed to understand what he heard. She recommended a return to reception class. The Year 2 teacher assessed him as having a good background general knowledge, contributing to discussions, and being 'good in groups'. Her conclusion was that there was 'nothing wrong'. The researcher's analysis concluded that the differences in assessment were not the result of a developmental leap, because she had had many conversations with Peter during Year 1 in which he had always 'talked freely and expanded on the topic of conversation'. She categorised the two classroom environments in terms of the teacher's coping strategies and the framing of educational knowledge. She described classroom 1 as 'routinised', based on work cards and highly visible grading levels of achievement, with few unstructured exploratory/play activities and in which the framing of educational knowledge was within formal communication. Discussions of home life from children's perspectives and child culture appeared to be excluded from the classroom. The teacher maintained a position as the holder of the knowledge. In the Year 2 classroom, however, the teacher was more mobile and interacted with pupils in a much greater variety of situations; there was a more overt 'affective tone', class discussions arose out of children's interests and discussions were more unpredictable and conversational rather than the question and answer format characteristic of the Year 1 classroom. Filer concluded that Year 1 and Year 2 classrooms were very different teacher-created language environments. She sees the classroom as 'a social and cultural context that would act *differentially* upon children' (p. 208):

> It is clear that the preoccupation with the *content* of assessment – the ticked boxes or their equivalent – relating to many and various Statements of Attainment – is obscuring what we know about *process*. . . . The difficulty of standardised presentation, of separating dispositional attributes and social-class expectations from cognitive attributes and the working out of self-fulfilling prophecies are some of the factors that have been shown to complicate assessment procedures. (Filer adds a number of references that have not been included here.)

The message for assessment from the observations of Rosie, Kiriwaitutu, Nick, Myra and Molly, the example of Reggio Emilia, and the research by Filer, is that assessment will reflect the learning community. In the framework outlined in the last four chapters, this requires a milieu characterised by interest, involvement, persistence with difficulty and uncertainty, communication with others, and responsibility. The next chapter gathers together the messages and guidelines of the previous four chapters to explore how we might carry out this assessment.

6

Learning Stories

Assessing Learning Dispositions

The previous three chapters provided examples of domains of learning disposition, and focused on the children and their learning. Those chapters also developed some guidelines for the assessment of that learning. This chapter turns more directly to the process of assessment, and the focus of the book now shifts from the child as a learner, to the teacher as an assessor. They are, of course, closely connected, and the frame of reference is still one of a 'disposed' learner in a dispositional milieu, but the major players are now, primarily, the adults. I set out the guidelines for assessment that have been developed so far, add two more, and then outline an assessment procedure that a group of practitioners have been putting into practice: Learning Stories.

The following were the guidelines for assessment that emerged from examples of children taking an interest and being involved, persisting with difficulty and uncertainty, communicating with others and taking responsibility. They are guidelines for the assessment of participation repertoires that are an accumulation of skills + knowledge + intent + social partners and practices + tools + motivation.

- *Assessment will acknowledge the unpredictability of development*
  Assessment that recognises the unpredictability of development will not insist on a 'staircase' model in which one step follows from another in orderly fashion. To use a botanical metaphor, development and learning is like a network of underground stems or rhizomes, every now and then revealing a flower (lily of the valley, or flag iris) on the surface (Patti Lather, 1993, has written, for instance, about 'rhizomatic' validity). Case studies, over time, will be appropriate.
- *Assessment will seek the perspective of the learner*
  Seeking the perspective of the learner is neither easy nor always possible, but if the 'underground' and motivational nature of

learning is to be accessed in some way, then children will need to have a say. In the assessment of writing in a first grade classroom in California, described by Sarah Merritt and Ann Haas Dyson (1992), the children's journals reflected their friendships as well as their developing encoding skills and the increasing complexity of their communication.

- *A narrative approach will reflect the learning better than performance indicators*

The observations in the previous three chapters were set out as stories, often a series of stories over time. Stories include the surround, and stories over time provide data for interpretation. Jerome Bruner (1996, p. 94) wrote that narrative is a mode of thought *and* a vehicle of meaning-making. By using a narrative approach, a learning disposition will be protected from too much fragmentation, although skills and knowledge may well be foregrounded at times.

- *Collaborative interpretations of collected observations will be helpful*

Assessment will draw on exemplars rather than performance indicators, and teachers will determine constructs ('Is this an example of tackling difficulty for Alan?') and participation patterns by agreement. In Chapter 3, agreement trials for exemplars of complex understandings in school curriculum assessments provided an example.

- *Many tasks will provide their own assessment*

For most of the time, the adult will not be the assessor: the artefacts, activities and the social community itself will provide for the learner their own indicators of achievement or success; the learner will judge for him- or herself how things are going. Those artefacts, activities and membership rites in which the goals are clear to, or constructed by, the child will provide their own intrinsic rewards. They include jigsaws, writing a name, building a building, being included in the play.

- *Assessment will itself contribute to the children's dispositions*

Dispositions are combinations of being ready, being willing and being able that emerge from learning experiences which occur often and which are supported, recognised and highlighted. Credit models of assessment will be foregrounded, and a deficit focus on the skills and knowledge that the learner might 'need' will be occasional. Although the assessment will be specific and local, we will nevertheless look towards robust dispositions that will provide a participation repertoire for learning in other places. In the portfolios prepared for children and families at the Pen Green Early Childhood Centre in the UK positive achievements are recorded and celebrated.

- *Assessment will protect and enhance the early childhood setting as a learning community*
  Assessment will protect and enhance the centre as a learning community in whatever way the community defines learning and provides for it. Assessment will be about participation: it will be of the learner-in-action-with-mediational-means in terms of mediational means that are locally available. The documentation in Reggio Emilia programmes provides an example in which the evaluation of the progress of projects and the evaluation of the progress of the children's participation in those projects is the same process.

Many of the examples for these guidelines come from special programmes in which practitioners are given a great deal of time for documentation, or from research in which the observer is a researcher with no other responsibilities in the centre. These examples are instructive because they illustrate important guidelines and principles, but they will almost always need to be adapted for real early childhood education settings. This reality check on assessment acknowledges the perspective of the assessing adult. Two more guidelines are important here:

- *Assessment processes will be possible for busy practitioners*
  I remember some years ago beginning a workshop on assessment in early childhood for about fifty practitioners by explaining that academics always like to teach new and unfamiliar words. 'Here is one that I would like you to become familiar with,' I said, and I wrote the word 'lunch-hour' on the whiteboard. The idea was greeted with laughter and a buzz of mutually sympathetic talk. One of the difficulties with interpretive methods of assessment is that they appear to involve the writing of lengthy observations which take up time that early childhood staff feel would be better spent working with the children (or having lunch). This perception means that in the eyes of the early childhood practitioner, the time spent on assessment is not time well spent – and in many cases this may well be so. Management and external agencies frequently make heavy demands on practitioners for documentation. One option is to minimise the time this takes by using numerical scales and checklists. However, if assessment is to assist the children with their learning, the other guidelines have indicated that this option is a problem. A balance needs to be struck where the time and effort required by more elaborated processes is manageable and practicable and the assessments are interesting and enjoyable.

- *The assessment will be useful to practitioners*

  To use another botanical metaphor and quote Gray's elegy in an unusual context: many an assessment is 'born to blush unseen and waste its sweetness on the desert air'. Unanalysed and unused observations and running records lie unseen in countless portfolios, record books and cupboards. We want assessments that will be *formative*: they will inform and form the ongoing teaching and learning process, and be useful to practitioners.

Learning Stories

In the last three chapters, when I wanted to illustrate the domains of learning disposition in action, I called on *stories* about a number of children. The stories included the context, they often included the relationship with adults and peers, they highlighted the activity or task at hand, and they included an interpretation from a story-teller who knew the child well and focused on evidence of new or sustained interest, involvement, challenge, communication and responsibility. In some cases the evidence could be listed: the examples of taking responsibility in an episode of joint attention, for instance, had many common features of bridging and structuring. In some cases the interpretation was much more to do with knowing the child very well, and of acknowledging the 'underground' and unknowable nature of the development: Sally coping with grief was an example. Many of these stories were part of a sequence over time, and in many of them a number of story-tellers had collaborated with the author in the interpretation (Moses' parents, the staff in Rosie's childcare centre and Alan's teachers, for example). Stories can capture the complexity of situated learning strategies plus motivation. The research on children's relationships by Judy Dunn (1993) highlights the way in which stories integrate the social with the cognitive and the affective. And stories can incorporate the child's voice, as the work of Sue Lyle (2000) has illustrated. They emphasise participation and culture, and their use as a framework for understanding learning owes much to the discussions of narrative in the work of Jerome Bruner. Mary Beattie quotes the poem 'Among School Children' by W. B. Yeats (from a 1958 collection, p. 242) to highlight the connectedness of a story approach:

> O chestnut-tree, great-rooted blossomer,
> Are you the leaf, the blossom or the bole?
> O body swayed to music, O brightening glance,
> How can we know the dancer from the dance?

What are learning stories?

The capacities of stories to highlight the outcomes that we were interested in led me and a number of early childhood practitioners to trial, develop and adapt an alternative method of assessment. We call it the Learning Story approach. Learning Stories are similar to the narrative-style observations set out in the previous three chapters, but they are much more structured. They are observations in everyday settings, designed to provide a cumulative series of qualitative 'snapshots' or written vignettes of individual children displaying one or more of the five target domains of learning disposition. The five domains of disposition are translated into actions: taking an interest, being involved, persisting with difficulty or uncertainty, expressing an idea or a feeling, and taking responsibility or taking another point of view. This framework developed over several years from 1995 as part of the research project 'Assessing Children's Experiences in Early Childhood'. Staff in each of the five different settings debated the criteria for each of these actions in relation to individual children and to their programme. Practitioners collected 'critical incidents' (Gettinger and Stoiber, 1998) that highlighted one or more of these actions. A series of Learning Stories over time, for a particular child, were collected together and scanned for narrative pattern. Children's stories were kept in a folder or a portfolio, and they often included photographs, photocopies of children's work, and children's comments.

The following is an example of a Learning Story for Sean, who is four years old. He attended the same kindergarten as Alan (who appeared in Chapter 3) and was part of the gate project. His portfolio included a polaroid photo of him using the carpentry drill. Attached to the photo is the following short Learning Story, written by Annette, one of the teachers. It describes a situation in which Sean perseveres with a difficult task, even when it gets 'stuck'. Comment included:

> 'The bit's too small Annette, get a bigger one.' We do, drill a hole and then use a drill to put in the screw. 'What screwdriver do we need?' 'The flat one.' Sean chooses the correct one and tries to use it. 'It's stuck.' He kept trying even when it was difficult.

There is just enough detail in the text and the photograph for this to provide a discussion point for Sean and the teacher next day. The story is filed with others that tell of similar occasions when Sean has completed a difficult task of his own choosing. In most centres, there is a specially devised Learning Story form for this purpose. The teachers regularly review the stories, and plan for progress in a number of ways. In Sean's kindergarten, for instance, examples of persisting with difficulty included: following a plan (and adapting the plan), persevering with (choosing, persisting with, and perhaps completing) a difficult or complex task, acknowledging an error or problem (and planning to solve it, or actually solving it).

Many of the Learning Stories began with a primary focus on one domain of learning disposition, such as persisting with difficulty for Sean. However, two processes integrate the five domains of learning disposition: overlapping and sequencing. *Overlapping* is the process in which related domains work together. Interest and involvement frequently occur at the same time (although one can have an interest without the involvement), and creative problem-solving is frequently (but not always) a common factor in both involvement and the tackling of difficulty. Children who have the motivation to tackle and persist with difficulty often express their ideas or feelings in the process. Episodes of joint attention include expressing one's ideas or feelings and taking the point of view of others (taking responsibility). Emily's capacity for taking on the viewpoint of others may have been associated with her concern for being seen to be right and her anxiety about making a mistake: a negative correlation between taking on another point of view and persisting with difficulty. Research (Yair, 2000, p. 205) has shown that choice and agency (having responsibility) raises students' interest and sense of accomplishment. *Sequencing* views this integration of domains of learning disposition as a sequence of actions. Danny's persistence with challenge followed from his interest and involvement. Rosie's negotiations in sociodramatic play were an accumulation of interest, involvement, perseverance, expressing her ideas and taking on the viewpoints of others. The sequence of actions is set out in Figure 6.1.

Shifting from Deficit to Credit: An Example of Learning Stories in Action

Bruce is a four-year-old at the childcare centre. Before the centre introduced the Learning Story approach to assessment, they were using a checklist where skills were ticked or crossed and dated, and the items with a cross alongside were discussed. Intervention was planned as part of a skills- and deficit-based assessment system. Bruce's schedule always had crosses alongside the social skills. He was frequently aggressive, the other children were afraid of him, and he was often unhappy. The staff were also using a behavioural programme that

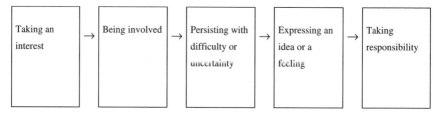

Figure 6.1   A Learning Story sequence

assessed the surround to the aggressive and angry behaviour: they looked for the antecedents and the payoff (the consequences). Practitioners know just how a Bruce in their programme can dominate the attention of the adults and the children. Staff now began to use the categories in the Learning Story framework to document those occasions when Bruce was interested and involved, when he persevered with difficulty, expressed his point of view in acceptable ways and took on responsibility. They still had to handle the aggression, but the following stories began to appear. The Learning Stories document and encourage Bruce's emerging readiness, willingness and ability to communicate with others in acceptable ways and to take responsibility in negotiations and relationships.

> *Learning Story 1*
> Louise and Bruce have laid out mattresses on the hill in the sun, and have had discussions about which one they will each lie on.
> Bruce to Louise: I'll be the Dad.
> Louise: No, Jeanie's the Dad.
> Bruce approaches Jeanie, with his face close to hers.
> Jeanie: I'm the Daddy.
> Bruce: There can be two Daddies.
> Jeanie: No.
> Bruce: I'll be the mate eh?
> This appears to be acceptable to Jeanie and Louise (they don't say 'No'), and they play together amicably for some time.

Apart from the fact that Louise and Jeanie have now learned to say 'No' to Bruce, this Story highlights Bruce's capacity for negotiation ('There can be two Daddies' and 'I'll be the mate eh?'). At first this is confined to stories about sociodramatic play that include Louise, but the staff are optimistic that this capacity will develop in other settings. Previously he has normally expressed his point of view by pushing and punching.

> *Learning Story 2*
> Bruce believes (perhaps accurately) that Amy has scratched him: he tells her he doesn't like it, chases her, and explains to Milly (a teacher)

that he didn't hit her (Amy). [Both Milly and another teacher gave positive feedback.]

This was one of the first times that Bruce appeared to be deliberately taking control of his own behaviour: taking on the kind of responsibility expected of him here. Teacher feedback included a comment on their recognition of this.

> *Learning Story 3*
> Bruce asks Annie to look after his block and animal construction, and she attempts to do so. At one stage he says: 'Annie, it's okay, it looked after itself!'
> Bruce is beginning to call out or goes to an adult to demand attention instead of creating an unacceptable incident.

> *Learning Story 4*
> This morning Bruce announces: 'I'm a good pirate.' 'And I save people.'

Although the adults were still spending a lot of time protecting other children from disruption and disturbance, and paying attention to Bruce, they now notice the stories in which he communicates with others in acceptable ways and takes responsibility for his actions. They discuss these at staff meetings and plan to try to maximise these occasions by encouraging play with Louise (monitoring her comfort with this, and adding extra players where possible), and by continuing to help him to reframe his pirate stories (saving people and finding treasure, rather than killing and taking hostages at the point of a sword). On especially flexible days, adults are on hand to give him a cuddle when he retreats into baby-like behaviour. They also remind him that indeed he is big: he shows Vera (one of the teachers) his sand construction: Hey Kimi made a little one and I made a big one. [Vera: well, she's little and you're big.]

Adults explain clearly why they cannot always guard his constructions, incorporating their respect for him with their responsibility to be with other children: i.e. this is a place where everyone takes responsibility for everyone else. Interestingly, other children share some of the responsibility for Bruce's curriculum. Rosie tells me (a visitor) to 'Say don't do that Bruce. I don't like it' when Bruce hits me on the cheek with a piece of jigsaw. Andy takes on the role of encouraging Bruce's sociable behaviour. Andy to adult, with Bruce listening: 'Lucky (that) Bruce shifted the truck (to let me make the road).' Adult: 'Yes, lucky that Bruce shifted the truck.' (Mind you, later when Bruce jumps on Gina and makes her cry, Andy says 'That was funny, Bruce.') Later Andy moves little Paul away from Bruce's vigorous sand throwing: 'Look out Paulie in case you get sand in your eyes.'

At a staff meeting the comment is made that Bruce's stories and explorations appear to reflect his interests in being powerful and being noticed. They are often to do with territory. He claims the climber as 'his' horse, and the area of the sand pit as 'his', where only a few can go (even when he's not there). Pirates is a popular script, for obvious reasons. And he is often keen to join sociodramatic play as the Dad, although other children are wary of this unless an adult is also part of the play and can protect them. Stories in which an adult takes a secondary role to Bruce are also enjoyable, in particular because they keep an adult in tow and listening, but Snow White and the Seven Dwarfs is also a particular favourite, for unknown reasons. A long spell of enjoyable play occurred when he built an enclosure around an adult and some children in the family corner: it began with Bruce as a tiger, and later developed as Bruce protecting and enclosing the tigers (the tigers were involved in kitchen play, but fortunately this did not concern the director). Earlier in the day he had built an enclosure around toy wild animals in the block corner.

Learning Story 5
Bruce in the block corner.
He builds an enclosure around the wild animals.
Very involved.

Learning Story 6
In the family corner, Bruce starts off being a tiger. I (teacher) suggest that I am a tiger as well, and I encourage him to make a larger enclosure around us all (I noticed that he had made an enclosure around wild animals this morning). Other children are playing a domestic kitchen 'making breakfast' game, and take no notice of Bruce. He makes an enclosure around us all.

Adults help him to elaborate these stories, negotiate peaceably, and take responsibility for the safety of others. They facilitate and document positive stories, and re-tell them to each other, to Bruce, and to his family.

The Four Ds of Learning Stories

Bruce was making a number of implicit judgements about whether and how to participate in this learning environment. There were a number of activities (enclosing animals and people and building safe areas) and social communities (with Louise, and with the adults) that were of interest to him, as well as the traditional stories that he enjoyed playing out for reasons we could only guess at. He appeared to be coming to view the environment as safe enough to get involved in and to talk about his feelings. He was starting to see that he could take responsibility in group settings in the childcare centre in acceptable and satisfying ways. The Learning Stories were focusing the staff's attention, providing a basis for teaching, contributing to Bruce's learning and highlighting these actions for Bruce and his family. In doing that assessment, the staff were interpreting the learning in four ways. They were *describing* Bruce's interest, involvement, challenge, communication and responsibility in terms of the local opportunities to learn as well as in terms specific to Bruce. They were *documenting* some of his actions, but not all, and during *discussions* at staff meetings they were reminding each other of other relevant – congruent and alternative – stories. The Learning Stories were providing guidance for their interactions: they were both formally and informally *deciding* what to do next. These are judgements by the adults (although the children will be included in as many of them as possible). I have called these the 'four Ds' of assessment: Describing, Documenting, Discussing and Deciding.

Describing and deciding

Learning Stories have been sufficiently wide-ranging in their focus to acknowledge the unpredictability of development and to both map *and* enhance participation repertoires. Chapters 7 and 10 provide details of the practitioners using Learning Stories to describe the learning, and to decide what to do next (plan for further learning). They illustrate ways in which Learning Stories can:

- acknowledge the unpredictability of development;
- contribute to the children's learning dispositions;
- protect and enhance the early childhood setting as a learning community;
- reflect the learning better than performance indicators.

Learning Stories are a pedagogical tool for: the transformation of participation (encouraging further and deeper learning), the prevention of the narrowing of learning, the transmission of the classroom culture to the participants, and the reframing of incoming narratives.

The transformation of participation
Transformation of participation, or development, can be encouraged in four ways through the writing of Learning Stories (Chapter 10

provides examples of practitioners planning for this development). The four ways involve analysing for: frequency, length, depth and width. Firstly, *similar episodes become more frequent*; they have a pattern to them. Occasional actions are becoming inclinations. Secondly, *stories get longer* in the sense that the episode covers more of the actions outlined in Figure 6.1. When Jason, whose actions have been characterised by involvement and perseverance, begins to teach others then the sequence of the stories is extended. Thirdly, *stories get deeper*. The learning appears more complex. In the case of Sean's centre, for many of the children, persisting with difficulty extended from making a plan to following and adapting increasingly complex plans. Fourthly, *stories get wider*. Nell, who has been so adept at tackling difficulty in social domains and in avoiding them when technology was involved, begins to tackle difficulty in constructing a box for marble painting. With implicit reference to learning as *participation*, Caroline Gipps (1999) has indicated that within the framework of socio-cultural theory, 'rather than an external and formalised activity, assessment is integral to the teaching process, and embedded in the social and cultural life of the classroom' (p. 378). She refers to the work of Vygotsky to suggest that it is consistent with his notion of the zone of proximal development for assessment to be of *best* performance: assisted by other people and tools. She outlined three kinds of assessment procedure that can embed assessment in the social and cultural life of the classroom. The first is to use portfolios that reflect the process of learning over time, in a range of well-documented actions and activities. The second is to assess students in collaborative group enterprises, observing the relationships and interactions and perhaps devising ways in which the students have to take responsibility to develop ideas and solutions to problems collaboratively. The third is to include the learners' views on their learning and to give them a role in negotiating assessment and in self-assessment. Gipps added that 'much of the work in this field is still at the level of research'. Learning Stories are nudging that work out of the research field and into the field of everyday practice; in turn we need to make sure that research continues to explore the connections with assessment goals and guidelines. Much of this research will now be, and is being, carried out by the teachers themselves.

The prevention of narrowing of learning

If we find the case a compelling one for 'broadening the basis of assessment to prevent the narrowing of learning' (as Mary James and

Caroline Gipps (1998) argue, referring to higher-order skills and 'deep learning'), then we should explore more complex ways to do assessment. Learning Stories is one of these ways. I commented in Chapter 1 that assessment procedures in early childhood will call on interpretive and qualitative approaches for the same reasons as a researcher will choose interpretive and qualitative methods for researching complex learning in a real-life early childhood setting: an interest in the wider frame of the learner-in-action or -in-relationship, and an interest in an accumulation of outcome that includes motivation.

Transmission of the classroom culture to the participants
Learning Stories document the learning culture in this place: this is what we do here, this is what we value here. Narrative in education usually refers to teachers' stories and stories about teachers (see, for instance, the work of Jean Clandinin and Michael Connelly, Mary Beattie, and the teachers' stories told by Sue Middleton and Helen May). They reflect an interest in the classroom or the early childhood centre as culture and community. Sigrun Gudmundsdottir (1991) writes about narrative structures in curriculum and describes narratives as 'vehicles for teaching' (p. 212). Jean Lave and Etienne Wenger (1991) include examples of the role of story-telling in the transmission of a community of practice: Yucatec Mayan girls in Mexico who will eventually become midwives will hear stories of 'difficult cases, of miraculous outcomes, and the like' (p. 68).

Reframing incoming narratives
Learning Stories can reframe pessimistic narratives that take a deficit approach, as the example of Bruce illustrated. The use of the term *narrative* to describe recursive cycles has become part of the counselling literature (Monk, Winslade, Crocket and Epston, 1997). In a 'narrative therapy' approach to counselling, the counsellor is not the expert, fixing up the problem. Instead, the therapist and client together 'story' the client's experience. Because this is a therapy context, the narrative usually begins as a constraint and the client wants to change it. The therapist and the client search for glimmers of an alternative narrative, for what they call 'sparkling moments'. A narrative about helplessness and despair becomes a narrative about competence and optimism. Problems are interpreted as social constructions that can be changed. These optimistic stories have often not had an audience before, and the influence of a valued audience is a key element in the reconstruction of life stories.

Discussing and documenting

Learning Stories have been transparent and accessible to four audiences: the staff, the children, the families and external reviewers. Chapters 8 and 9 provide details of the practitioners using Learning Stories to share the assessment by discussing and documenting it in a range of ways. They illustrate ways in which Learning Stories can:

- seek the perspective of the learner;
- include collaborative interpretations of collected observations;
- allow tasks to provide their own assessment.

One example of the impact of discussing learning with children has already been cited in Chapter 2. In Harry Torrance and John Pryor's (1998) account of a teacher's base-line assessment discussion with four-year-old Eloise on the day after she joined the reception class, Eloise was picking up some clear messages about the power structure in the classroom and the learning that was valued there. Rhona Weinstein (1989) has argued that children are well-tuned to pick up these messages – verbal and non-verbal – about adult expectations, and that the expectations of teachers are a critical variable in the development of children's expectations for their own learning (Chapter 9 discusses teacher expectation effects in greater detail). Torrance and Prior also commented (p. 81), with reference to the teacher's assessment of Eloise's progress some months later, that the nature of those early interactions can frame up continuing and future interactions as well. The interaction with Eloise was an example of *power on* (introduced in Chapter 2). Some months later the teacher was still primarily interested in Eloise's ability to conform, and not in her academic progress. The three guidelines that introduce this section are about power sharing. Learning Stories have illustrated a way in which assessment can be part of a *power for* and *power with* framework of learning and teaching, seeking the perspective of the learner, including other interpreters, and mirroring a dispositional milieu in which the artefacts, activities and social communities provide their own reward. They are designed to be part of dispositional milieux in which learners take responsibility.

Concluding Comment

This chapter has picked up the theoretical analysis of learning from the earlier chapters and has begun to answer the question about assessment practice in Chapter 1: How can we assess early childhood outcomes in ways that promote and protect learning? Chapters 3, 4 and 5 had proposed seven guidelines for assessment which supported the development of complex learning outcomes. Two further guidelines have been added to acknowledge the voice of practitioners: assessment should be possible and useful. All these guidelines will weave their way through the next chapters. This chapter called on these guidelines to argue for an assessment framework called Learning Stories. The next four chapters are about practice. They provide an account of how the Learning Story framework has been implemented in a number of different settings and they discuss the changes that have been made to adapt it to local opportunities and learning places. The four Ds of assessment procedure form the topics for the next chapters: Describing, Discussing, Documenting and Deciding.

7

Describing

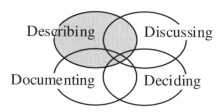

The next four chapters are informed primarily by the experience of practitioners in five early childhood settings as they explored the Learning Story approach to assessment. Examples and comments also come from centres which have implemented Learning Stories since that assessment project.[2] As the practitioners confronted this alternative approach many of their firmly held views about learning and assessment were challenged; they were going through exactly the same process of questioning assumptions that I wrote about in Chapter 1. At the same time they were investigating ways in which this new procedure might work for them. The implementation of Learning Story assessments is considered with reference to four processes: Describing (this chapter), Discussing (Chapter 8), Documenting (Chapter 9) and Deciding (Chapter 10). Describing is about defining the learning, developing and

---

[2] Early childhood settings in New Zealand that receive government funding are required to document some assessment. In 1996 the Revised Statement of Desirable Objectives and Practices (DOPs) included the following, relevant to assessment: (i) Educators should demonstrate knowledge and understanding of the learning and development of each child, identify learning goals for individual children, and use this information as a basis for planning, evaluating and improving curriculum programmes. (ii) Educators should implement curriculum and assessment practices which: (a) reflect the holistic way that children learn, (b) reflect the reciprocal relationships between the child, people and the learning environment, (c) involve parents/guardians and, where appropriate, whānau [extended family], and (d) enhance children's sense of themselves as capable people and competent learners. (iii) Educators should provide opportunities for parents/guardians and, where appropriate whānau to . . . discuss, both formally and informally, their child's progress, interests, abilities and areas for development on a regular basis, sharing specific observation-based evidence (New Zealand Ministry of Education, 1996b). These DOPs became mandatory in 1998.

applying constructs that are relevant to local learning opportunities. Discussing is about talking with other staff, the children and the families in order to develop, confirm or question an interpretation. Documenting is about recording the assessment in some way: using text, picture and/or collected work. Deciding is about deciding what to do next: spontaneous responding, and informal or formal planning. These assessment processes do not necessarily occur in sequence. An adult might describe the learning ('This is an example of taking responsibility') and then, without discussion or documentation, decide how to respond. Much assessment is not documented, and not all of it will be discussed with others. An observation might be documented, and this might be a catalyst for discussion. The four processes also overlap considerably as the diagram that introduces this chapter implies: discussing is frequently about describing the learning or deciding what to do next, documenting provides a topic for discussing, documenting in which families add their say is very like discussing.

This chapter is about practitioners *describing* the children's learning, applying the framework of domains of learning disposition in their setting, and building up a wealth of exemplars in the process. Features of this *describing* that most challenged their assumptions and excited their interest were:

- moving to a focus on giving credit for what the children were doing and away from reference to what they were not doing;
- developing structured observations that reflected local opportunities and programmes;
- foregrounding and backgrounding being ready, being willing and being able.

Focusing on credit

Learning Stories describe episodes of achievement: taking an interest, being involved, persisting with difficulty and uncertainty, expressing an idea or a feeling, and taking responsibility. I have already commented that a credit focus is appropriate for formative assessment of domains of disposition because the framework has foregrounded inclinations, or *being ready*. An inclination becomes part of the child's participation repertoires, integrated into the way they see themselves as learners. By the time he went to school, Jason's view of himself as a learner was as a competent problem-solver (persisting with and relishing difficulty) who tutored others in his fields of expertise. As more and more centres trialled Learning Stories as an assessment procedure, it appears to me that the first feature that they found attractive when they described the learning was the *credit* nature of the observation categories which connected with a view of their role in early childhood care and education: not judging children and finding them wanting. On the other hand, they occasionally expressed some anxiety about the possibility that the assessment schedule was asking practitioners to ignore bad behaviour. At that point, they needed to understand the dispositional nature of the categories.

Early conversations with practitioners in one setting reflected these quandaries about what to describe as learning, and the assumption that assessment means describing need and deficit. A related assumption was that this assessment would then have to be followed by teaching (assumed to be didactic) to redress the deficit. This early view appeared to be that therefore it was not appropriate to do any assessment.

> 'Excuse me, because . . . (we) don't evaluate children. Actual children.'
> 'No, not as individuals.'
> 'No, so it's [the assessment project] not useful. Well, I mean, it's not useful to the centre or anything.'
> 'Our aim isn't to have the children achieve anything in particular, so, in that sense they're not useful to keep.'
> Researcher: 'You do some evaluation of what, of your programme? What do you evaluate?'
> 'The evaluation we do . . . is on whether we're effectively maintaining and covering areas of play that are in our policy. That . . . '
> 'All the children are involved.'
> 'All the children are involved and have the opportunity to try . . . the activity they can choose . . . '
> 'Because we don't have any specific goals.'
> 'Yeah, but because we don't want, we're not trying to get any particular children achieving any particular skills or goals, just learning whatever . . . they possibly can.'
> 'Yes. So that (the) only planning that (we) could do from these is to provide opportunities where children could go through all these (and) get to the stages for themselves.'

The notion of describing learning in terms of achievements or goals (that the children might have failed) was rejected as a role for the adults, and this was for some adults central to the definition of assessment. Later, however, the conversation shifted to the 'credit' nature of the learning descriptions:

> 'It doesn't say "he can", "he can't", "he can, can't".'

Researcher: 'That's what you want to get away from?'
'Yeah. It's not actually an evaluation really.'
Researcher: 'No.'
'It's just an observation . . . and you rethink and you evaluate.'

Staff in the childcare centre liked the idea that the Learning Stories did not fragment the children's experiences, and paying attention to the positive rather than using a deficit model was an early focus of interest.

> Lara: I definitely like that (Learning Story) way of observing (better) than the other way. Because I was, or maybe it was just my ignorance, I just got totally lost when we had those other sheets.
> Jane: But, I think there was too much information and unless you really worked at it, it's just so easy to fall into that deficit, that negative, way of observing. . . .

Pat referred back to her own experience as a parent to reinforce her point that this focus was important: 'I've got a real passion for it because (at school) T. really needed that encouragement to work from her strengths rather than from a deficit, and they almost always work from a deficit at school.' Their experience with Bruce (summarised in the previous chapter) reinforced this.

By the end of the assessment project, many of the practitioners had put together the attractive idea of credit (rather than deficit) with the more complex notion of a developing disposition. The latter had given strength to the former, and the value of a credit focus became a key feature of the practitioners' arguments for Learning Stories.

Structured Observations that Reflect Local Opportunities and Programmes

If the first phase for practitioners was enthusiasm over permission to record and share *positive* experiences, the second phase was to structure those observations, drawing on the specifics of local opportunities and programmes. This was an altogether more difficult process. Many practitioners were either used to summarising with stock phrases like 'has good social skills', 'a cheerful learner who concentrates well', or they had typically written detailed 'running records' which were unstructured and unanalysed. They were not familiar with this process of providing a trail of specific evidence of learning. One of the practitioners commented that:

> you're looking at a child painting and (with a running record) you say, 'well that child picked up the paintbrush in his left hand and moved it

sideways or round in a circle' and I found that, with the same sort of thing (with a Learning Story) you might think to yourself, well that child hasn't done very many circles in the past, it's just done up and down, you could just say 'well look, you know, this child is starting to move it in circles, realising that the paint can go in different ways.' Yeah, it's quite good . . . the concentration too.

The learning began to be described with reference to the local opportunities to learn. The childcare centre is a good example of this. The childcare centre staff began with a Learning Story template that included two very closely related categories: engaging with challenge *and* persisting when difficulties arise. The other categories were: finding something of interest here, being involved, and taking another point of view. After three months' trial they decided to change the title of 'taking another point of view' to 'taking responsibility' and to put 'engaging with challenge' and 'persisting when difficulties arise' together. Describing the children expressing their ideas or feelings in a range of ways was another important aspect of learning that they wanted to feature in the assessment processes. The project adopted these ideas. The childcare centre staff also widened the description of 'taking responsibility' to include not only looking out for and listening to each other, but also taking responsibility for the programme in various ways: choosing a song or a story, deciding on what activities should be available. Taking responsibility for the well-being of others was highly valued by both staff and children, and numerous Learning Stories documented this. When the childcare centre staff described 'taking an interest' and 'being involved', they emphasised settling in and coping with change. This reflected the special features of the programme here: full day childcare, transitions from the under-twos to the over-twos, and from home to centre. An analysis of how the childcare staff described each category of participation for their setting follows.

Finding an interest

Some children moved rapidly from one activity to another, or watched but were reluctant to move to the next step: involvement. At this point staff were trying to detect topics or activities (including people) of interest. They looked for:

● *Things of interest.* Five Learning Stories all indicated that James was particularly interested in trucks and trailers, attaching trailers, and filling trucks, trailers and trolleys.

- *Topics of interest.* One child was particularly interested in stories about Ranginui (Sky Father) and Papatuanuku (Earth Mother). One of the teachers brought a number of books in and read them over several days; she wrote down his comments and particular interests. At a staff meeting she said 'I was amazed at his memory.'
- *Cues about individual differences.* Robert was interested in messy play but reluctant to have dirty or possibly wet clothes. The staff discussed how they might get him involved. They decided to reduce the uncertainty of messy play for Robert by involving him in the preparation of the (warm) fingerpaint, a plan that worked well.
- *Activity.* Shelley had just moved into the over-twos programme and appeared to be 'flitting' from one place to another. Staff wanted to document her shift from interest to involvement. They timed her length of stay at a number of activities. Over a few days, her longest stay was in water play.

In Chapter 3 I analysed interest in terms of artefacts, activities and social communities. In the assessment project, interest was less likely to be explicitly described as social intents or social identities; the interests that came more readily to the practitioners' attention were associated with artefacts or activities.

Being involved

These early categories (taking an interest and being involved), frequently part of settling in, were often a feature of describing the children's experience when they first arrived in either the under-twos or the over-twos programme. 'When they're new they stand back and don't want to get involved,' commented one of the staff. Even some of the 'old hands' needed frequent reassurance that the environment could be trusted, and children recently promoted to the over-twos were frequently invited back into the familiar environment of the under-twos. Staff looked for:

- *Constraints to involvement.* Both Robert and Rangi appeared interested in messy play, but reluctant to get messy.
- *Special clothes or toys or rituals that signified safety.* Terry, nearly two, had to wear his raincoat or have it nearby to feel safe. Learning Stories documented his increasing ability to manage without it. Ada, one of the staff, commented that 'if someone even touched his coat, he's got a thing about his little raincoat, he's either got to wear it or he tucks it under his arm . . . and if anybody touches it he

screams. . . . But he's even got kind of, you know, he's even not too bad about things like that now. So, I mean, it's showing that he feels safe enough to (indistinct) . . . and he nearly doesn't worry.'

- *The characteristics of those activities where children appeared to be most involved.* Shelley's involvement at water play – was it the water, was it a familiar adult nearby, was it a special friend? Some children did not enjoy large groups. Discussing the Learning Stories on Ray, one of the staff said: 'So, I think big groups aren't a very good thing. . . . That's like adults. I mean adults don't like it (being in big groups) do they? So.'

- *Challenges that keep children going* (the transition to the next step of the Learning Story). Robert is prepared to be involved in the challenge of cutting with scissors: it is a 'transparent' activity in which success is readily apparent. Billy will remain involved for long periods in technical activities (carving and carpentry) that are a little bit 'dangerous'.

- *Special people.* Tania may have needed the reassurance of Fern (a staff member) nearby to encourage her sustained involvement with bicycle play. The following Learning Story, written by Fern, covers all five domains of disposition the sequence of *Taking an interest →Being involved→Persisting with difficulty→Expressing her ideas →Taking responsibility.*

Tania

Tania is playing outside with older children on bikes. She sees a bike that is unused and runs to get it. Before she gets to it another child gets on and rides off. Tania looks at me, wanting me to get it for her. I tell her to wait and soon it will be her turn and to find another bike. She gets on another bike and follows the other child closely, watching her every move. The other child finally stops and gets off. Tania hops off her bike and gets on the other bike. She looks at me and smiles and rides away.

Persisting with difficulty

Persisting with difficulty or uncertainty was described in a range of ways. Often those activities in which children and adults could readily perceive success were a feature of the description: the paper is cut, the nail stands up, the jigsaw is complete, the ball goes through the basketball hoop. Staff looked for:

- *The characteristics of uncertainty or difficulty* for each child, and (as for their descriptions of involvement) the nature of the context that made it 'OK' to make a mistake or risk error.

- *Ways to assist with the challenge.* In a carpentry episode, Robert and Jodie assumed that any lack of competence was the fault of the tool, not the technician.
- *Ways to insert challenge or difficulty or uncertainty* into the child's programme (drawing on information already gained about interesting and involving contexts).

Expressing an idea or a point of view

One of the features of the childcare centre staff's description of learning in this domain was their enjoyment of it. At one of the staff meetings a Learning Story was told about one child who was absorbed in pretend play with two teddy bears, his 'twins'. Someone asked him where they had come from and he answered 'You can't just buy them at the sale you know' (laughter). Staff looked for:

- *The 'hundred languages'* (a concept developed in Reggio Emilia: Edwards, Gandini and Forman, 1993) that children use to communicate ideas or feelings: words and rhyming, pattern, gesture, song, number, art, literature. Lyn writes the following story about Kate: 'Five children sitting on the bench . . . "There are three girls two boys" (correct) said Kate.'
- *Sequences of difficulty within these languages.* The staff brainstormed new ideas for rhymes and rhyming books for A. and listened carefully to the way his interest in rhymes developed.
- *Stories that revealed thoughtful and creative approaches* to language and communication, confirming the creative and imaginative nature of the early childhood years.

The Learning Stories about Kenny and Maria describe both persisting with difficulty and expressing their ideas:

Persisting with difficulty→Expressing his ideas
Kenny
Kenny was found sitting on Pat's chair in her office.
'Kenny,' I said 'Please come out of here, this is Pat's office and her chair is too big for you.' . . . (Later) I noticed Pat's office door was open again. I looked in and there was Kenny standing on a small chair (which he had obviously used to open the door) playing with the hole punch at Pat's desk. Pat's chair [the 'too big' chair] had been pushed right over to the window.
Persisting with difficulty→Expressing her ideas (pattern)
Maria

Gets out half-circle blocks, puts two together to make a circle. Gets out longer curved block and tries to add it, then tries to add small half circle. Later returns, puts two half circles together, claps her hands. Piles up small blocks, laughs when they fall. Later, building, carefully fits blocks into a rectangular pattern.

Taking responsibility

In the childcare centre this domain was extended to include not only episodes of joint attention and shared responsibility, but also episodes where children took responsibility as part of belonging to the childcare community. There were few Learning Stories of joint adult–child enterprises from this centre, some discussion of peer collaboration episodes (a discussion about Joseph at a staff meeting included the comment 'He doesn't have the skills to negotiate with anybody about how he's going to [get a turn] and a lot . . . of the other two-year-olds know how to do it'), and many occasions when children took responsibility for each other's well-being and comfort. Staff described 'taking responsibility' in the following way, and they looked for the contexts that encouraged these Learning Stories:

- *Adult–child collaboration on joint tasks.*
- *Peer collaboration on joint tasks.* Examples included: Kate and James are jointly 'driver' in a bus that they have jointly constructed out of chairs, cooperation in the sandpit, pushing each other on the swing, examining a ladybird together.
- *Children taking responsibility for other children's well-being.* Shari takes Billy off to get him a plaster for his sore finger, he in turn explains the importance of washing the wound to her; Freddie helps Mike with his lunch; sensitive understanding of a friend who has been away and whose mother has been ill; helping the littlies; comforting sad children.

  Shari
  Concerned about Billy screaming, she asks him: 'Did Cameron hit you with the hammer?' I explained: No, he had hurt himself with the saw. She said 'I'll get Billy a plaster.' They walk off together, Billy explaining to her that he would need to wash it first and then put the plaster on.

- *Children taking responsibility for the programme.* Shari introduces children to visitors, children take responsibility for their own toileting, Flora organises a painting activity, Erica gets a team together to water the plants, Kate runs an exercise session.

Descriptions in other settings

The domains were often described differently in the other settings. In the kindergarten, for instance, the focus was on participation in the gate project, the project in which Alan had become involved and in which the staff and children planned to make a gate for a gap in the fence that divided the playground into a front and back yard. Interest was indicated by children attempting to draw a plan for a gate, or spending some time observing the work at the carpentry or planning table. The teachers felt that the plans the children were drawing enhanced their involvement and thought. In May the teachers are discussing how the project encouraged Jenny to work creatively: one of the teachers suggests that it 'set her in motion.' Another said: 'I think that maybe the planning has got quite a lot to do with it too.'

> Researcher: Tell me a bit about that.
> Teacher: Well, we never got children to plan what they were going to do before, sitting down and thinking about what they were going to do. If you read the comments on the plans, they're really thinking. You say to them, 'Now what do you think this piece is?' 'Oh, that's to put your head on.' And I'm sure they weren't just trying to find an answer for us. . . . They've learned to really think about what they're doing and become more precise. . . . Carpentry also . . . they go into the shed, they look for the pieces of wood that they want and they actually think about what they're going to do, whereas before it was just putting two pieces together except for anyone who was particularly good in that area. [Team meeting 16/5]

One aspect of the project was that the children were solving the same or similar problems (designing a gate that would fit the gap in the fence). The children were therefore often looking to each other for ideas, and one way to analyse the project is as a collaborative web of joint attention, collaborative problem-solving, and discussion. As in the childcare centre, the description of *taking responsibility*, taking another point of view, shifted because of the nature of the early childhood programme.

In the parent cooperative, 'persisting' was described as 'having another go'. At one of the parents' meetings a parent told the following story:

> Everyone was dancing . . . she was having a go . . . trying hard. She (had) reached beyond the stage of just watching and (was) having a try

now. . . . And there was a group of them and they were holding their waists . . . and she was just watching them for ages and then all of a sudden she actually (got) closer to them . . . she got the courage to go over right by them . . . and she actually hopped in a circle with them and started clapping her hands, because they were clapping. . . . Having another go, that's persisting isn't it?

And there was considerable discussion about the difference between problems and challenges, whether 'difficulties' and 'problems' were, perhaps, something to be avoided. Discussing a Learning Story about a child working with clay, someone said:

> 'Difficulty is a strong word for this. . . . It wasn't a problem more than a challenge.'
> Researcher: 'So it's not necessarily a problem as we might define a problem?'
> 'As in something bad happening.'
> 'It is a problem, but, we often classify in our mind a problem as something bad.'

This reminded me of the description of learning in a small primary school in Hertfordshire, the subject of an Occasional Paper by Mary Jane Drummond (1999). The teacher, Annabelle, structures much of her teaching around what she calls 'tool-words'.

> The first of these words to become important in her pedagogy was 'problem', when she realised, some years ago, that without this word in their working vocabularies, children did not appreciate what was happening to them when they met a problem. . . . Once her pupils had grasped that a problem (a disagreement with a friend, a technical difficulty in a construction project with the blocks, a puzzling observation of the natural world) could be understood as a challenge to their inventiveness and ingenuity, could be relished, explored and finally resolved, they were much less likely to walk away from problems, to abandon their projects, or to refer their disputes to adult authority. (p. 11)

One of the purposes of the Learning Story framework was to introduce children, and adults, to what Annabelle would call 'tool-words': interest, involvement, difficulty, uncertainty, responsibility.

In the home-based setting, one of the requirements of the umbrella Childcare Services Trust that managed the network was for the home-based carer to make daily entries in a Child Record Book. This is described as 'for parent/guardian and carer information sharing', and it must accompany the child between home and home-based setting each day. Required entries for children older than babies are (i) medical information and accidents (these records are also kept in a Record of Medication and a Carer's Record of Accidents), (ii) day-to-day information: (a) a brief record of food and drink taken during the period of care, (b) a record of sleep time and duration, if appropriate, and (c) any activities or events that happened during the day that would interest parents/guardians. This last requirement was of interest to the assessment project. Georgie, the home-based caregiver in the case study setting, wrote up activities each day; the following are excerpts from entries in their Record Books for Matthew (aged 3 years 10 months at the beginning of the study) and Jill (aged 2 years 11 months at the beginning of the study). In this home-based setting, persisting with difficulty was described in terms of activities where the goals were clear, and it was also illustrated by stories about the children that referred to:

- *Puzzling about things*: asking a lot of questions.

> Matthew 16/5
> (At the Rose Gardens) he asked me a lot of questions about the Little Bull statue, 'how was it made?', 'did they put the concrete down first?', he was intrigued by it and spent a lot of time at it.
> Matthew 20/5
> Matthew asked, 'How old will Dad be when I am 40?' '77' 'How old will Jill be when I'm 40?' With discussion he worked it out, 39.
> Matthew 27/5
> Driving out to Riverlea – 'Why did the dinosaurs die Georgie?' Completely out of the blue – Help! I replied 'It got too cold – there was no food for them.' Jill: 'So they won't come back again.' 'No. Only in pictures and videos and movies.'

- *Puzzling*: predicting, figuring it out, using one story or episode as an analogy for answering an adult's questions.

> Jill 11/8
> After lunch cuddled on the couch for some stories – new books from the library, one about waiting for a baby. 'My Auntie she's got a tummy like that and the baby will be . . . (couldn't find the right word).' So we went through 'boy' 'no' 'girl' 'no' 'You know Georgie. It's Lara's baby but my . . . ' 'Oh, cousin,' I managed. 'Yes. Yes.' She is doing well with her relationships – nearly got 'Who's nana's son and daughter?' Once I said 'twins,' she replied: 'My Dad.'

- *Coping with uncertainty*: there are a number of stories about Matthew starting kindergarten, and the settling-in process; the following two stories are about Jill and her concerns.

Jill 28/5

Lovely puppet show everyone had a go at leading – just lovely. Jill wore the mouse mask, amazing for a girl who was very scared of it up until a month or so ago – would look at it but as soon as it was put on her anxiety level rose quickly.

Jill 19/5

[Jill puzzles over an uncertain situation when she meets a baby with the same name] Took baby (8-week-old) Jill her hat we knitted. Our Jill [nearly three] has been very mystified 'It's not me is it?' 'Will she get big like me?' 'Does she have a Mum and Dad like me – but not mine are she?'

In the parent cooperative there was some discussion about how to describe 'expressing a point of view' for younger children whose expression was mostly non-verbal. Facial expressions which convey messages were acknowledged as relevant. 'When they have discovered something their faces just light up, they smile and they, you know, they know. They look at you as if to say "oh". You know, it's all in their face.' Gina: 'Some of them (the children that don't communicate as much) have come out in the open since last term and I've found it really nice. I've written a few stories about them and their speech. . . . I thought well after doing a few stories on the older children, I'll try some of the younger ones and I did two stories on the younger ones . . . And some of their expressions and the way they express themselves, it is a learning curve.'

In the home-based setting, the description of expressing their ideas and taking responsibility was often set in imaginary and sociodramatic activity, a feature of the play here of Matthew, Jill and Sarah (Georgie's daughter, aged two).

13/5

An amazing session of imaginary play. I just puddled in the sewing cupboard, no adult was needed. There was cooperation. Moved from one theme to the next – Doctors, Easter Bunny, Mothers and Fathers, baking, birthdays, shopping, video watching, all pretend. No one was leader.

27/6

Peter Pan the thread for most of the play – We read Matthew's Peter Pan books, flew here and there – dined at a restaurant with Chef P/Pan and Tinkerbell (S.) and Wendy (J.) and Captain Hook (me) the lucky eaters – gelato – pizza and cappuccinos – the best in town – then Captain Hook was admitted to hospital.

29/7

Matthew and Adam (another child) were playing ten pin bowling – Jill left her baby for me to look after while she went to work. Her work is watching the bowling. 'How much do you get paid?' J.: '$7 a minute.'

In the home-based setting, *taking responsibility* also meant establishing the network of family and friends; Georgie always included the names and connections of people met or visited during the day.

> 26/5
> Note from mother: Busy weekend . . . Helped G. squash leaves on the trailer at the flats. Response from M.: heard about the rakes to sweep the leaves up and lots about 'cute little Joe'. I thought it was a child she was talking about until 'He went outside to go toilet on the lawn.' – 'Harry and Barbie we sometimes go and visit them by the lamb.' Note from mother explaining who 'Harry and Barbie' are, where they work, where the lamb lives, and that Joe is a pug dog.
> 11/4
> Saw a poodle go by. 'That's just like Mitty, by Grandad's place,' said Matthew.

In the Māori language centre, one of the Learning Stories highlighted their observations that expressive language often developed within familiar events and routines:

> On this particular day the children of the centre were on a special outing – a trip to the teachers college to work with clay in a new environment alongside an expert in the field. Because the morning was extremely busy, one of our usual routines, and a very important one for the children, had been overlooked – morning tea. It was late in the morning when one of the younger children, only 20 months old, found some spoons, approached me holding up the spoon and said 'E tō mātou mātua' which is the first line of the karakia kai (food blessing) 'to the creator'. We promptly realised that morning tea was still sitting untouched. Her actions were interpreted to mean 'Well, perhaps if I start karakia kai then food will appear because I am hungry.' For us adults we realised the importance of routinised language (the language expressed in real-life, meaningful recurring contexts) and its part in the development of the child.

Finally, in another centre which introduced Learning Stories much later, stories are appearing about things being fair. The following story is abridged:

> At one point this afternoon Davie was very upset. I asked 'What's wrong Davie? Why are you upset?' He told me he was sad because someone told him he couldn't play in the pirate ship. . . . Victoria also says she was excluded too. I said 'Well, that ship needs some more sails – who wants to help me make some more sails?' (The teacher and the two children worked together, stapling fabric to poles and decorating them, joined by some more children. They then as a group went together to

erect the new sails in the pirate ships and put up a sign: 'Everyone is allowed on the pirate ship.') The next day the teacher writes: I noticed today there were fewer episodes of exclusion – and none involving Davie that I am aware of. Davie played happily on the ship.

Foregrounding and Backgrounding

Describing the learning involves the process of foregrounding and backgrounding introduced in Chapter 2. This process is illustrated here with reference to the kindergarten programme. The gate project in the kindergarten developed when the teachers were changing their programme to highlight three particular outcomes for the children: (a) questioning and perseverance with difficulty and uncertainty, (b) experience and expertise with a wide range of media for representing ideas (expressing their ideas), and (c) collaboration (taking responsibility). The teachers were interested in all three dimensions of a disposition: being ready (the inclination), being willing (linking to the programme, in this case the gate project) and being able (the funds of knowledge and the skills that the children were acquiring). An analysis of the project using this framework is set out in Table 7.1 at the end of this chapter.

One of the children's projects might serve to illustrate this analysis:

> One morning, four-year-old Chata drew a plan for what came to be called the 'party gate'. This design included a number of vertical lines, a cross bar at the top, and a series of happy faces drawn along the cross bar. She then worked with three other four-year-olds (her sister was one of them) to make this gate out of cardboard tubes. They joined the tubes into a grid, using masking tape, then adding faces made from shells and feathers. When Jenny joined the group Chata included her, saying, 'I'm your friend now eh.' A teacher and the researcher talked with them about the activity: Chata tells the adults that she and the other children are making 'a gate for our people'. She comments that the 'people are standing up' and if they fall off 'in the water, they die when they open they mouth.' She adds that 'It's a party.'

Being ready

For Chata and her sister (recent immigrants) the notion that if the children ('our people') fall off the gate they will drown appeared to be of great significance and the children were working at a complex level of imagination, developing the idea of making a gate in personal, unusual and elaborated ways.

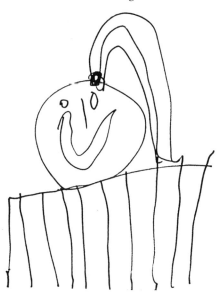

Figure 7.1. Part of Chata's plan for a 'party gate'

- *Persisting with difficulty.* Chata had not made a gate before (she had designed an earlier, more traditional-looking gate, but decided not to make it); this was not a routine activity, it was self-chosen, spontaneous, and unusual.
- *Communication and taking responsibility.* Three of the children had frequently worked together, but Jenny was a new member of the team, and Chata welcomed her and gave her a role.

Being willing

There were two events going on: an imaginative story-line, and a complex construction.

- *Interest and involvement.* The materials at the kindergarten had provided for complexity and sustained interest. The final gate was an elaborate structure with smiling faces attached to the top (faces were drawn on large white shells that they found at the kindergarten, with small feathers attached as hair or hats).
- *Persisting with difficulty.* To an adult's eyes this was a difficult task that involved construction, patterning and measuring. Developing a sustained story-line that linked to the construction was also a challenge.

- *Communication and taking responsibility*. This was a collaborative story-line, and a collaborative construction. It demanded reciprocity.

Being able

- *Communication*. The teachers were also documenting Chata's increasing skill in her second language, as well as in mathematics – in this task, the measuring and patterning – technology, drawing, sociodramatic play and story-telling. We have no notes from the observation about the level of negotiation and group planning during this activity.

Concluding Comments

What these Learning Stories reveal is that the description of critical features of a dispositional domain will be different in different learning places or dispositional milieux. This was very evident in the descriptions of 'taking responsibility'. In the childcare centre looking after the well-being of others and taking responsibility for the programme were highly valued features of the programme. In the kindergarten the teachers were particularly interested in the children sharing ideas and activities, and in group projects. The parents in the cooperative noted episodes of cooperative play; and in the home-based setting those episodes were frequently within elaborate sociodramatic scenarios. One aspect of both communication and taking responsibility of interest to the kaiako in the kōhanga was the different language genre, or 'motherese', that the older children were using as they cared for the younger ones. In the home-based setting, stories about the wider network of friends and family featured strongly, building a community of reference that was wider than the home-based setting. The assessment examples described participation in rather different learning places. At the same time, the children were doing their own describing, as the creative and different gate enterprises (many of which were in no way appropriate for the kindergarten fence) illustrated.

Practitioners were describing learning in *credit* terms. Children's achievements in the five domains of dispositions were described (and documented) because the staff wanted these episodes to occur frequently enough to become inclinations and assumptions about learning. On the whole, being ready was foregrounded, but the adults were also appraising the supporting context as well as funds of knowledge and skills, as the example of Chata building a party gate indicated.

Table 7.1. An analysis of the gate project: being ready, willing and able

Domain of Learning Dispositions	Being Ready	Being Willing	Being Able: Funds of Knowledge	Being Able: Skills
Taking an interest	The children ask questions, join the project, make it their own by designing (and later constructing) gates with personal meaning (the party gate, the electrified gate, for instance). Learners take an interest and make links with prior knowledge.	The children watched the builder plan and design the fence: a gate is clearly needed here. The project has become a key feature of 'what we do here'. The Learning Stories interested the families, and the children had permission to develop their own gate designs.	Funds of knowledge about gates and doors: their materials and their function, analogies with other gates, sources of information about building.	Reading a plan or a diagram, recognising the key features of a drawing or a photograph.
Being involved	Children return to the project day after day; some children work on the same gate over a number of days; some make a succession of gates, solving the same or new problems as they go. Groups of children invite others to join them. Learners get involved over sustained periods of time, and develop creative ideas.	The children are able to be involved, at different levels of complexity, over sustained periods of time. Learning Stories document this involvement. The topic allows children to bring their own ideas and interests to the project.	Safety with carpentry tools, knowledge about plans, carpentry tools, materials. Understanding about different designs and their purposes: a diagonal brace, for instance. Hinges and latches: their design and function.	Nailing, screwing, bracing, joining, measuring, planning, sawing . . . Paying close attention. Designing and constructing symmetry and balance. Developing creative designs (the party gate, for instance).

(continued over)

Table 7.1. (*continued*)   An analysis of the gate project: being ready, willing and able

Domain of Learning Dispositions	Being Ready	Being Willing	Being Able: Funds of Knowledge	Being Able: Skills
Persisting with challenge, difficulty, uncertainty	Children are problem-seeking and problem-solving, recognising error and changing their designs. Learners persist with difficulty and uncertainty and develop creative solutions to problems.	There are many intriguing problems to be solved: designing, strengthening, measuring, hingeing, latching, raising and lowering (the railway gate). Children and adults share ideas for solving problems, often using the Learning Stories displayed on the wall.	Knowledge of a range of interesting problems that might occur and how the community has solved them, e.g. hinges and latches. Solutions often include an understanding of measuring.	Recognising error as part of the pathway to a successful solution. Solving problems by adapting materials at hand (making hinges out of leather strips, for instance).
Expressing an idea, feeling, point of view	Spontaneous discussions of design and function are a feature of the project. Learners express their ideas in a range of ways.	The children could incorporate their own particular 'languages': colour, 2-dimensional drawing, constructing with wood or wires or cardboard tubes, arguing and negotiating. The assessment highlights this.	The work of a carpenter and a draftsperson: demonstrated by the carpenter who built the gate, and a draftsperson who assisted the children to design the final gate.	Skills in verbal and other languages and modes of expression at increasingly complex levels, including drawing and modelling in a range of materials.
Taking responsibility, taking another point of view	Children working in groups negotiate solutions, listen to each other. They share ideas. Learners take responsibility and listen to other points of view.	Staff encourage group projects and the sharing of ideas. Documentation on the wall displays the range of points of view here. Children discuss what should go into their portfolios, and dictate comments to accompany photographs and plans.	Girls can be carpenters too (notions of justice in this context). The value of collaborative opportunities and sharing ideas.	Collaborative skills, appreciating the ideas and skills of others, listening to and considering advice.

8

Discussing

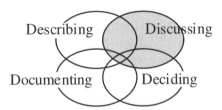

Discussing is the second of the four Ds of assessment using Learning Stories. This chapter is about practitioners discussing the children's assessment and their learning with other staff, with children and with families. Informal and formal assessment discussions help to establish what kind of learning community 'we' (the participants in the child-care centre, in the kindergarten, in the Year 1 classroom) are construct-ing here. The way we discuss with children their behaviour or their actions may not always look like 'assessment', but frequently it in-cludes some powerful judgements about what is interesting and worthwhile, whether persistence is appropriate, and who has the power and responsibility. Discussions also make judgements and as-sessments public. Documenting, the subject of the next chapter, makes assessments public *and permanent*. Assessment is for the early child-hood setting's social community (outside agencies may see these doc-umented assessments as well). So it is important to explore ways in which the making public of assessments enhances and does not weaken or destroy learning dispositions.

Discussions about Learning Stories (between staff, with children and with families) in the five case-study settings had the following major purposes:

- working towards agreement about the constructs;
- transmitting to the children the learning of value here;
- seeking the children's perspectives about their learning;

- including the families;
- deciding what to do next (the subject of Chapter 10).

This chapter explores the first four of these purposes.

Working Towards Agreement about the Constructs

The previous chapter included discussions amongst staff about the categories for Learning Story assessments. At the childcare centre, staff agreed that 'coping with change' was a key aspect of 'taking an interest', and that a central feature of 'taking responsibility' was looking after the other children. Many of the discussions at staff meetings in the childcare centre did not appear to be deliberately designed to agree on these constructs. They were ostensibly about planning, using the Learning Stories as data. Nevertheless, the staff were also establishing a fund of shared understanding about the valued constructs of learning in general, the constructs as they apply to individual children, and the constructs as they apply to the pro-gramme on offer. The following are excerpts from one of their staff discussions.

Discussions about taking an interest and being involved

Early in one of the staff discussions, two-year-old Robert's progress was the topic. At the previous staff meeting a number of Learning Stories on Robert had been discussed and summarised. Robert was introduced in Chapter 2: he had been reluctant to get involved with activities, liked to watch 'messy' finger painting, but would not parti-cipate. After one of the staff had included Robert in the preparation of finger paint, and he did decide to participate, he had continued to be involved in a range of 'messy' play and in the sand pit during the fortnight between the planning and the review. The discussion in-cluded the following comments:

> 'He has more confidence to join in, he makes his own choices.'
> 'He still is, he looks for Julie (one of the staff) always for that first contact. He feels really comfortable with you, eh?'

The staff discussed who were the several staff that Robert liked to check in with when he arrived. '. . . and once he's touched base with one of them he's okay.' A story was told by a member of staff who in the past felt she had not been able to communicate with Robert, but on a more recent occasion he 'chatted away quite happily'. As well as the action of joining in, involvement for Robert meant making his own choices, looking for Julie as a safe starting-off point, and widening his circle of safe adults. This was, implicitly, a discussion of a 'safe' environment for Robert, one in which he felt he could get involved. At the same meeting a side discussion began about the interest of one of the two-year-olds: 'She was funny today, wasn't she?' A story was told, with much laughter, about how at sleep time she wanted to put her shoes on and off, a new skill.

Discussions about persisting with difficulty

The talk turned to Kenny, who the staff felt needed a challenge. One of them commented: 'I think his strength is his sense of humour.' Another: 'Yeah, but how would you work on that?' The staff talked around this for a while and decided that Kenny's sense of humour is linked to a capacity for 'lateral thinking': '(He thinks) I'm going to do it somehow different whether it's right or wrong.'

They decided to extend the challenges in the physical environment, with an emphasis on alternatives and choices. They talked about how they might do this, and one staff member talked about a childcare centre in a nearby town that she had visited. 'We went to a centre down there and it was an old building like this and their area was flat outside, but their challenge was just amazing. Like they had planks going along at one level, and they had it all barked and it was all lovely and well set up . . . and um, just all junk. It was a junk place to climb over.' They reminisced about previous challenge courses and activities that they had constructed outside in the past, and their problems and advantages. Kenny's primary caregiver said, 'Okay, so I've got to extend the challenges in the physical environment. (writing) Redesign challenge course, using planks and ladders, use quadro (outdoor construction units) in different styles.'

The staff discussed plans for transition to the over-twos for Joseph. Jodie (his primary caregiver) was very animated – she *knows* him, and was trying to describe him accurately. At one point she said something like, 'It's so good to talk about it because often you can't find the words and then someone says it, and you think "Yes, that's it".' She had been trying to express the idea that Joseph doesn't problem-solve, and someone chipped in by saying that he doesn't have trial and error *strategies*, just waits for an adult to help. 'Trial and error strategies' had become part of the vocabulary of persisting with difficulty.

Discussions about expressing a point of view and taking responsibility

The discussion then shifted to Billy, and someone said 'Billy was (telling me) this afternoon about where he was going tonight and in the weekend . . . (and he finished up by saying) "oh, it's too hard to explain".' (Laughter) The staff told a story about Rosie taking responsibility:

> Neil scratched him on the leg and he came with Rosie over to me. 'Neil scratched me.' It didn't . . . he had a little mark . . . and I said 'oh, you'll need to go up and get a cold flannel for it. I can't come up with you but,' I said, 'Rosie can you take Billy up?' 'Come on then Billy' (imitating Rosie's voice) and they both put their arms around each other and went walking up the stairs.

Another staff member completes the story: 'She got the cold flannel for him and she put it on his face and . . .' A third staff member adds, 'Yeah, they stopped by the meal table and spoke to me about what had happened.' This story of Rosie taking responsibility for looking after Billy was not written down, but it had now become part of the shared body of stories about the children at the centre, and the staff's shared understanding about 'taking responsibility' here.

Transmitting to Children the Learning of Value Here

The home-based Record Book played a part in formally transmitting to the children the learning of value in the home-based setting: for instance, sharing your crayons, helping the others, giving advice during baking, listening and trying. Informal feedback also transmits to the children expectations about their competence as learners and the dispositions of value, and many Learning Stories include that feedback. Tape recording at the Māori language centre recorded the following story of Tahu (a teacher or kaiako) encouraging Piki at the carpentry table to watch carefully and then to try for himself:

> Tahu: Māu, māu e mahi, he aha ōu whakaaro? (pause) . . . Māu e mahi.

(It is for you, it is for you to do it, what are your thoughts? (pause) . . .
It is for you to do it.)

Mere Skerrett-White comments on the story:

> This whole Learning Story is approximately an hour long. Piki has
> demonstrated skills of perseverance in the task, tolerance, commu-
> nicating, problem-solving, and really the will to continue as he carries
> on working on his vehicle, drawing on his wood with pencil, gluing
> wheels on and so on, in amongst all the interactions with other chil-
> dren and adults.

Part way through the making of his vehicle Piki realises that when he
stands it up on its wheel-base, he has stuck the wheels on one side in
the correct position, down the bottom, but that the wheels on the other
side are in the wrong position, on the top. He spends a short time
examining this. He then pulls one set of wheels off from one side,
selects new wheels and re-glues them (firmly, with a glue gun, carefully watched by Tahu) so that his vehicle has two sets of wheels
which are positioned correctly. Piki then completes the task and
stands his vehicle up. At this point Tahu acknowledges the amount of
effort that has gone into this Learning Story when he turns to ask
other adults to observe.

> One of the other adults: Āe, e rua ngā taha.
> (Yes, it is two-sided.)
> Another adult: Pērā i te waka nē?
> (Just like a vehicle, isn't that so?)

Piki then drives his vehicle over to the other end of the carpentry table
where he sets about painting it.

Seeking the Children's Perspectives about their Learning

Here is part of a discussion between an adult (me) and four-year-old
Harry during the gate project described in some detail in Chapter 7
(we also met Alan making gates in Chapter 3). We are looking at his
portfolio, and the comments he has made on some of the photos.
Harry is able to discuss the difficulties he has had, and he knows that
the teachers (and the researcher) value his perseverance:

> Me: (pointing to one of the photos) You said you'd make it [your
> next gate] a bit smaller so you could do it in one day. How big?

Harry: Well. Alan decided to make a big one but I don't reckon big as
         big as that.
Me: Not as big as Alan's?
Harry: No. He made one a bigger one than my than my big one.
Me: Right. Did he have any difficulty with that?
Harry: Well he didn't he didn't put any ah sides on it. (pause)
         Perhaps he forgot.
Me: Perhaps he forgot.
Harry: Must of forgot . . .
(Harry draws Alan's gate to illustrate, then draws some sides to it.)
Me: Right. So you're using the ruler down the side to put the sides
         on. If you built it what would you do first? Would you do the
         crisscross parts first?
Harry: Well um well I make well I would, well, when I did that
         (gestures to a gate that he made)
Me: Yes, the other one.
Harry: When I did that one (M: Yes) I ah I did the sides first.
Me: Oh, did you. Yes. And was, do you think that was the best
         way?
Harry: It was the best way. Well, it wasn't the hardest well it wasn't
         the hardest bit but the other bit was the hardest (M: Mmhm)
         When I did the nailing.
Me: The nailing was the hardest part. Mm. Mm.

On another occasion, Harry drew his second design for a gate, with a curved top. It included a catch, a diagonal bracing board, and two hinges. He made this second gate at home, bringing it to the kindergarten to try it in the gap in the fence. He described the difficulty of putting the hinges on, and said that if he made another one he 'could make a little one and do it today' (the other gate took several days), and 'I'd decide to put a flat bit like this' (points to a flat-topped gate) 'a bit like Sean's other one . . . the one that he did first'. A further plan is drawn, this time a plan for a wire model. He begins a wire model, but can't figure out how to include the squiggles in the plan: 'I'm fed up. I'll finish it tomorrow.' He does.

Seeking children's perspectives on their learning was particularly apparent when children dictated assessments. Harry and Alan, for instance, had dictated annotation to the photos and designs in their portfolios (see Alan's comments in Chapter 9). In the home-based programme, Jill one day dictated the day's childcare events for her Record Book, highlighting the events as she saw them:

The day according to Jill.
[dictated to mother]

12/6
We went to the gym. We played there. Got some balloons – put them up (she shows me). Threw them up (waving arms above head) hitting and Rabbits' dance, balloon for tail. Georgie blew my balloon up at the gym.
We did lots and lots and lots and lots . . . (the mother has written dots in here to indicate more 'lots and lots') before we went out.
We went to Chartwell [shopping centre] to get some milk. Matthew and me were being sensible but Sarah, Sarah was being like a silly little person and her Mum was getting upset. Matthew and me – we're big sensible people.
We played Teddy Bear games at Georgie's.
[Response from Georgie in the book next day: Not a bad summary.]

Jill has described four events here: one episode at the gym, one at home ('We did lots and lots and lots'), a third at the shopping centre, and a fourth back at Georgie's ('We played Teddy Bear games'). The third story was particularly intriguing. The topic is 'Matthew and me being sensible and grown-up' in comparison with Sarah (Georgie's two-year-old daughter) being 'silly' and 'little'. Georgie is referred to here as 'her Mum' whereas in the other stories she is 'Georgie', incorporating into her story new knowledge that had come up in conversation in the van on the previous day when Matthew had commented 'You've got two names, Georgie and Mum' and they had chatted about sons, grandsons, daughters. Finally, Jill has commented that the adult was 'getting upset' rather than 'getting cross', revealing the capacity that Judy Dunn's research has described of a very young child (Jill was not quite three years old when she dictated this story) to take another's point of view in familiar circumstances. It cannot be discounted that this ability has been developed by the Record Book, i.e. by the documentation itself, which often commented not only on the children's feelings but also on the adult's (in one entry Georgie mentions that the gym teacher Mary is 'sad' that they cannot keep going). The comment by Katherine Nelson about the role of *social sharing* of events in cognitive and language development ('it is only in the light of *social sharing* that both the enduring form of narrative organization, and the perceived value to self and others become apparent'), quoted in Chapter 2, would support such a conclusion. Seeking children's perspectives about their learning, making the goals clear, can run the risk of children becoming self-conscious: that persisting with difficulty, for instance, can become a 'performance' goal (rather than one in which motivation is intrinsic). For Jill, however, the home-based Learning Stories had provided a model of a caring culture in which stories about people looking out for each other are valued, and Jill's Learning Story indicated that she was appropriating at least some aspects of this model.

Including the Families

In the childcare centre the staff were beginning to explore mechanisms whereby families could be more involved in the Learning Story process. Although in this early phase communicating the assessments to families in any systematic way was not a purpose, this was always part of the centre's longer-term plan. The staff had moved a long way in their capacity to write focused observations and use them for planning. There were discussions about the value of sharing the observations with parents. Jane commented about their assessments in the past:

> You know the assessments for a long time that we have been part of don't really (involve the parents). The parents at the end of it, if they're lucky might get to see a result which says, you know, we've assessed your child, and da de da, and this is where they're at. Well, that's no use.

One of the staff had a child at the centre, and she talked about the enjoyment of reading the Learning Stories about her child. Another staff member, Julie, commented that a new parent had come in and asked if they had records on the children, describing the system in a previous centre where there were 'little notebooks and they (the staff) would just jot things in as they happened . . . and they got to keep that when they left and they got to look in that whenever they wanted'. Julie saw the Learning Stories as a similar process, with potentially the same interest for families. She reminisced about how she would have liked to have this kind of record of her own child when she was young, and we talked about videotapes: 'It would be really neat to see what your children are like when you're not there because parents think that their children have been upset for the whole day – when they leave and the child bursts into tears.' Families began to take a great interest in the Learning Stories and the childcare centre later sent out a questionnaire to the families to get their reaction. One parent wrote:

> They are an insightful record into my child's learning and development. They also record 'precious moments' which I miss out on during the day, so they are interesting from that point of view. They also

confirm for me that staff are thinking about holistic learning situations, and that there are programmes in place to monitor my son's progress. They are also a good catalyst for conferencing on the child's progress between parents and staff. I like them. I know they are time-consuming but I think they are very important and worthwhile.

Another parent commented:

Highlighting his strengths and interests to me has allowed me to let him be more independent at home. Allows more conversation at home about what's been happening. Being able to extend at home on what has been happening at the centre. Gives us a sense that we 'belong' here.

The assessment was establishing the wider community of centre and family, even though most of these parents worked full time and had little time to stop for discussion at the beginning or the end of the day.

At the parent cooperative, several of the parents commented that they enjoyed reading other people's stories about their child. Greta, although she wanted to emphasise her view that adults should not intervene in children's development, was valuing the progress her daughter was making in her capacity to discuss things with other adults:

Greta: I think you can actually see what your child's been doing and how they're interacting with others. . . . I think, from a parent's perspective it's really good because . . . you feel it's sort of helping the children, not really developing the children, but, just sort of working with them in their play. . . . It's quite interesting. I've sort of seen, even in the last term how much Lea (her daughter)'s progressed in discussing things with other parents, which is good.

Another parent, Gina, is not specific but she appears to have a renewed respect for her daughter's learning:

Gina: I honestly thought that Lou (her daughter) had outgrown the centre. Um, when I read some of the stories that had been done about her I found out that she is actually learning quite a bit more than I had actually thought.

Rae enjoys the Learning Stories because they value what she values:

Rae: I enjoy it as a parent, reading Learning Stories about my own child. I know my child, but don't know how others see her. As a mother I enjoy reading how other parents see my child. My son at school gets school reports that are achievement orientated, but if I can read a Learning Story about how my three-year-old plays cooperatively, that's really delightful to read. I see how she is when I'm not there, how she reacts without me. Everyone loves a story that's delightful to read. It's really valuable for me to see how others see her – I don't care about her scissor grip or pencil hold, I'm not interested in that. The Learning Stories show that people are taking an interest in your child.

She adds that they are also helpful in reflecting the learning of younger children as well:

Rae: Some of the mothers of younger children were really excited when we eventually wrote Learning Stories about them; we often don't know how to focus on the littlies, the younger ones.

In the previous chapter I commented that one of the parents in the parent cooperative had told a story about a child making an effort to join in with an older group of children dancing, and she had added: 'Having another go, that's persisting isn't it?'

In the case study home-based setting, the Record Book had become a catalyst for discussion and a record of dialogue between Georgie, the home-based caregiver, and the children and the families: documentation and discussion went together. The home-based setting, and the people in it, had become an extended family. The Child Record Book was a three-way communication site, between Georgie, family (usually the mother wrote comments, but fathers, siblings and grandparents all read the book) and child. In the book, Georgie frequently addressed remarks to the child. At the end of the day a parent often read the Record Book with the child as they talked over the events of the day. If and when details of play or talk or achievements were read to the child, he or she received information about what learning both carer and family valued. The day's learning was laid out for the child to recall, revisit, and discuss at home. Likewise, home events were written down for Georgie to cue the child in and enable recall, revisiting, and discussion at the home-based setting. Valued learning was highlighted indirectly by the selection of events and comments in the write-up, but more directly too by: (a) addressing the child directly, (b) praising the child, and (c) cues to the family to ask the child to demonstrate or recall something of particular interest. Here are some examples.

(a) *Direct comments to the child*

25/3 Drawing with Matthew's crayons. Thanks for the lovely sharing Matthew.

28/4 At home Matthew showed us his very clever bike skills, well done.

21/7 Note from Jill's mother. J. is a bit reluctant to share her bike so I hope this doesn't cause more problems than it solves.

22/7 Note from G. Thanks for the lovely bike. They all had a quick ride before kindergarten. Such lovely sharing Jill.

(b) *Indirect comments to the family, praising the child*

12/3 Matthew is good at helping the girls with page turning (one side of the tape for the story 'Dark Dark tales' doesn't have beeps for turning pages).

19/5 Gym. Just missed four fire engines. A faulty alarm in the gym hall, so, had to help Mary (preschool gym coordinator) set up after that delay. More forwards, backwards and trying to turn around while jumping and swinging. Mary commented on Matthew's good listening and trying skills. He always gives everything a good go and usually ends up with a good attempt. Fun trying to jump over a swinging skipping rope.

26/5 Matthew commented to Jill how she needed to mix her baking in a bowl. She then chose a very small bowl. He said, 'get a bigger bowl for that much.' Very logical and practical.

4/6 Lots of alphabet talk at a.m. tea time, not too many that she doesn't know now – so clever – starting school at 3?!!!

(c) *Cues to the family to ask the child to recall or demonstrate*

20/5. Ask her to sing you the song. Jill remembers tunes and words quickly and enjoys singing as part of a group or by herself.

22/5 [Matthew's book] Lunch at the kindergarten. We stayed for the mat time. This week they have been using the I Went To The Zoo book using sign language a lot. Ask Matthew to show you: lion, monkey, turtle, crocodile, zoo and 'I know' signs.

22/5 [Jill's book] Kindergarten – stayed for mat time – they have had the Big Book story I Went To The Zoo using more signing each day. I'm not sure how many signs J. will remember. They have done lion, monkey, turtle, crocodile, elephant – and colours – 'I know', zoo.

Georgie assists the families to help children through exciting events: Matthew taking on a role in a family wedding, and Jill coping with the sale of their house, for instance.

25/3 Matthew is very excited about Stuart's wedding and staying in a motel. . . . Wearing black shoes and clothes from Farmers [a department store]. Have a good weekend, oh nearly forgot, 'you know Georgie, Dale will be dressed up pretty, she be bridesmaid.'

11/8 [Jill's book] Note from mother. Land agents due tomorrow. Jill has started carrying her purse (with money) around in case we see a nice house for us to buy. She was getting upset that someone else may sleep in her bedroom. Note from Georgie: Interesting. Jill only talks about the Lovely Old Troll (Jill's nickname for her grandfather) in nana's new house. Even when I subtly questioned her today, no mention about her house – changed the subject in fact. Thanks for the info. We can chat with her and help her through the sale.

The Record Book was an affectionate and often funny record of a child's two families working and discussing together to provide early childhood care and education, to celebrate achievements and milestones, and to encourage learning. The discussing was very much part of that care and education.

Concluding Comments

This chapter has highlighted the Learning Story process of staff, children and families discussing learning together. This social sharing enriched educators' understanding of learning, of learning dispositions, and of their own interactions with the children. My field notes after attending one of the childcare staff meetings recorded that:

> It is difficult to do justice to the quality and warmth of these discussions. These staff arrived at evening staff meetings, often very tired after a day with young children. Then they began to review and plan with the children's Learning Stories, amusing anecdotes were told to supplement the written stories, side stories were shared, and the exchanges became lively, funny and affectionate. Negative stories were also told, and positive interpretations often given to them by others.

The discussing was collaboratively establishing a learning place in which taking an interest, being involved, persisting with difficulty, expressing your ideas and feelings, and taking responsibility were key features, uniquely defined for this setting. This chapter also outlined how children were finding out what learning is valued here, and the ways in which their perspectives were being sought. The family was getting to know much more about what their child was learning, and in the home-based setting and the parent cooperative they were having a say in this. In other settings, the staff were beginning to puzzle over how families could be more involved in the assessment process. In all the settings, families were enthusiastically reading, and often contributing to, Learning Stories about their children.

9

Documenting

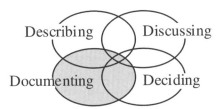

Documenting, the third of the four Ds, is the writing down or recording in some way of learning and assessments. It may include annotated collections of the children's work. This chapter will argue that attention paid to the documenting of Learning Stories sharpens the focus on important features of the children's learning, and provides a powerful support for the authentic assessment of that learning. The documentation provides exemplars for practitioners refining their assessment formats and constructs. A significant issue for practitioners is that documenting takes time, and the time it takes will be balanced against the perceived educational value. This chapter includes some of the practitioners' responses to this issue, noting that when documenting is enjoyable, integrated into everyday practice, useful in contributing to children's learning and in providing feedback for families, then the time required is seen as worthwhile.

When assessments are documented, they become not only public, but permanent, and a number of different audiences now have access to them. There are four potentially different audiences: the children, the practitioners, the family and community agencies. Assessments collected for one audience may be interpreted or judged by another, while the secondary interpreters may not have access to the contextual information or discussion that accompanied the original assessment. Print has a status that cannot easily be altered by discussion. Furthermore, assessments may be accessible to others well beyond their use-by date. At the family and community level, school assessment has usually been summative: summaries are prepared for families, and systems and/or summaries are available so that outside agencies can monitor statutory requirements. Although summative assessments for this purpose have been a characteristic practice in schools, this way of approaching assessment does not need to be adopted without question by providers of early childhood programmes. It may be that evidence from the alternative process of formative assessment which informs the 'inner' two audiences (the children and the practitioners) may provide accurate and realistic accountability to the 'outer' audiences (families and external agencies). Certainly the audiences are different, and assessment for one audience may not be suitable for another. Children are an audience, for instance, and in early childhood and for the first year of school it is unlikely that written assessments will be accessible to them.

The following aspects of the documentation process were topics of interest and debate for the early childhood practitioners in the project:

- reasons for documenting;
- ways in which documenting could become an integral part of the learner-in-action;
- diverse assessment formats.

Reasons for Documenting

A great deal of assessment is not recorded, since it occurs when practitioners are responding to children during a session or a lesson as part of the teaching process: making interpretations and judgements about the child/student's learning, and acting on those interpretations and judgements. This assessment is unplanned, spontaneous, and often initiated by the learner. It is part of good teaching. David Pratt summarises it well:

> In productive learning environments, both students and teachers experiment, try out ideas, take risks, tackle and puzzle over problems, think, reflect, listen, discuss, ask questions, look up information, surprise themselves and each other. Such environments are distinguished by multiple channels of feedback. Participants seek, receive, pay attention to, and respond to messages of inquiry, encouragement, confirmation, and correction. Such feedback is assessment in its broadest sense. At its least formal, and in some ways its best, it is unobtrusively woven into the fabric of classroom activity and interaction. At its most formal, and in some ways its worst, it is separated from the classroom

environment and activities and conducted in ways that are ritualistic and intimidating. (Pratt, 1994, p. 102)

What (if any) of this feedback should we be documenting? As Pauline, in a childcare centre, commented: 'I don't like writing down for the sake of writing down. It's got to be [for] something.' It is helpful to answer this question in terms of the four audiences: community agencies, families, practitioners and children. In 1997 Bronwen Cowie and I set out a table summarising some of the 'why' and 'why not' arguments, for and against documenting, in terms of these four audiences. Table 9.1 is an adaptation of this earlier table.

In the table, arguments *against* documenting focus on the unwarranted status accorded written assessment. Documentation provides a partial account at a particular time, of foregrounded outcomes. It has the capacity to record an increasingly complex pathway of participation in one place, but, especially if the foregrounded outcomes are narrowly conceived, it may not be a reliable indicator of later difficulty or achievement. The documentation should be read as dependent on the context. Families, however, may have expectations that documented assessments predict stable trends, and community agencies may have similar expectations. In Chapter 1, I noted that there is little agreement about the pre-academic skills needed for school success, and in Chapters 2, 3, 4 and 5, I argued for a wider view, that learning *dispositions*, participation repertoires, may be critical. Furthermore, expectations may have a negative influence, as I commented in Chapter 2 when the model of teaching and learning as reciprocal and responsive relationships was outlined. Peter Blatchford and others (1989) found that teacher expectations about new entrants to school (as opposed to the children's actual attainment level) were significantly associated with achievement during the school year: achievement could be predicted from teacher *expectation*, not from student *ability*. Research by Barbara Tizard and Martin Hughes in 1984 indicated that the teachers in nursery school that they observed asked working class children less challenging questions than middle class children, presumably because they expected that the children could not respond to higher levels of challenge. At home, however, working class children were involved in complex and demanding interactions. Sue Bredekamp and Lorrie Shepard (1989, p. 22) maintained that 'parental expectations are the most powerful predictor of children's later school success', and work by Pamela Frome and Jacquelynne Eccles in schools (1998) tells us that parents' perceptions of their children's

Table 9.1. Assessment for four audiences: why document and why not document.

The audience for assessment	Why document?	Why not document?
Community Agencies	For accountability, to ensure that a system of feedback to children and families is in place and children's well-being and learning is being tracked.	External agencies may simply need to have evidence that effective systems are in place, i.e. that (undocumented) feedback is monitored in some way.
Families	To receive feedback about their child's well-being and learning. To inform families about the curriculum and to enable them to participate in its development. To provide families with information about the child's day to share and discuss with the child and other family members.	If assessments are written down, families may interpret short-term assessments as long-term predictions and labels.
Practitioners	To get to know the children: writing down observations sharpens the focus. To get to know the children: written observations can be a catalyst for collaborative discussions: for remembered (undocumented) and shared observations that may confirm or conflict with the written assessment. To share information about learning with different adults who may be working with this child: to share ideas about the way forward and to plan. To establish a learning community with shared values: to reflect on what practitioners notice and value here, and how they respond to the children.	Recorded assessments taken at one particular time may receive unwarranted status. Professional impressions, judgements and interpretations, freely debated and expressed, are not represented and may be inhibited by written records. What is recorded is no longer up for negotiation. Spontaneity may be at risk. Time is taken from adult–child interactions: it is difficult to record and to respond, yet the interaction is often the significant part of the learning.
Children	Self-assessment opportunities: children involved in high status assessment. Children become more aware of what is valued here.	Children can become self-conscious about 'learning', performance oriented. Children cannot read text.

ability and effort predict children's self-concepts of ability and perceptions of task difficulty in mathematics and English better than their grades. Three key audiences (practitioners, parents and children) can be influenced in negative ways by the documentation of early summative judgements when these judgements are deemed to have predictive value.

The arguments for documenting mostly focus on assessment as a *formative* process, contributing to progress and further learning here and now. The experience of practitioners trialling Learning Stories has suggested that if examples of emerging or robust learning dispositions are foregrounded, there are many reasons to document some assessment. Written assessments of this type can provide a catalyst for discussions amongst practitioners that assist them to get to know the children and to plan the way forward. They help practitioners to construct a learning community with shared values, and they extend that community out to the families. They foreground positive expectations and optimism, authentically derived.

Pauline said: 'It makes you take a closer look at that child, doesn't it'; Julie: 'You find out things you kind of knew but never really thought about so you don't really do anything about it, but when you're sitting down observing, things just start clicking.' Lyn made a similar point: 'Well, I think you see more because you're looking at the kids more closely.' During a meeting at the parent cooperative the comment was made that 'there's value in the learning for us in that we are extending ourselves in the way we see children.' Someone perceptively asked, 'Are we evaluating ourselves (in the process)?' Elly: 'Looking at children you're not really homing in on exactly what they're learning and with the help of a sheet of paper and writing down exactly what they were doing you could see. You were more aware of the processes of learning. . . . Challenges, yes and getting involved. All those key words [finding something of interest, becoming involved, etc.] helped to um, to see what you were looking for.'

Ways in which Documenting could Become an Integral Part of the Learner-in-Action

Increasingly, in many settings, the documenting was becoming part of curriculum implementation. The documentation had become an integral part of the learner-in-action. For the families and the centres the stories have become cultural artefacts and literacy events. Children ask for them to be read again and again. For instance, in one centre in which Learning Stories were introduced well after the case study settings, a story about Maddie and Akira is a great favourite. Here it is (abridged). It was accompanied by photographs.

> Maddie spied an orange 'egg' on top of the roof of an outdoor hut at the kindergarten. She rushed off to tell the teacher. She was desperate to get the egg down from the roof. Akira overheard the conversation and joined in, trying to get the egg down from the roof. First they tried to jump and reach it. No luck. Then they climbed onto the wooden seat and tried. The egg was out of reach. Other children came and gave them lots of ideas. Maddie and Akira decided to get a ladder – the egg was still out of reach. More discussion, and they tried the longest plank with cleats on. Again, much discussion and an unsuccessful attempt. At mat time Maddie explained to the children exactly the processes they had gone through to try to rescue the egg. She was passionate about her subject.
>
> The next day, Akira arrived early and successfully managed to get the 'egg' down (the story does not tell how). The 'egg' turned out to be an orange plastic ladle. When Maddie arrived Akira rushed up to her and proclaimed his success. Maddie absolutely refused to believe it was a ladle. She declared that the egg had hatched and the bird had flown away.

As time goes by, it has become an open question as to whether it was really a large orange egg or a plastic ladle, and if the former, what kind of a bird would have hatched from it.

In the kindergarten, the home-based setting and the Māori language centre case study settings the documentation had also become part of the learner-in-action. At the Māori language centre many photographs were taken, to be annotated with short stories and turned into books about each child. The photographs were also mounted on the wall. They provided a language resource, something for the children to talk about, in a setting in which communicating with others in Māori was a primary aim. Similarly, the kindergarten mounted displays of Learning Stories on the wall: children used them to discuss other children's and their own work, and to get ideas for new constructions. Being involved, planning, tackling and persisting with difficulty, and working together were emphasised. These wall displays of the children's work were also a way of outlining the programme for families as they came in to drop off and pick up their children. One of the teachers commented:

> I often see them (the parents) looking at the photos . . . I look up and I think, ooh, that's good. And I think they think it's not just play. Do you

know what I mean? I think they (the parents) feel that they're (the children) actually doing something and learning something. . . . Some of the children, I. and P., they've come in and made a point of showing their parents what they've made.

This perception was confirmed some months later, after a second project (making furniture), when one mother commented that she was 'blown away' by 'the things these kids are learning'. She was reassured that her daughter's new confidence would mean she would do well at school, and she commented that the whole family – including grandparents – had become interested in the work at kindergarten, whereas before the project they had been more interested in the school work of the older brothers.

In the kindergarten documented assessment was also collected in what could be called 'portfolios' for each child. Portfolios have been frequently described as a useful way to assess young children. They can be summative collections, or collections of 'work in progress'. In this case the portfolios included:

- work selected by adults and children, annotated with key aims highlighted;
- dictated comments by the children;
- work photographed using a polaroid camera and children's comments or dictated stories often added; ordinary photographs were also taken;
- transcripts of collaborative exchanges between the children: photocopied and included in each participating child's portfolio;
- photocopies of the photos or of the children's work, so the children could take the original home for discussion with the family.

The children often asked if they could take the photocopy home rather than the original. At a team meeting one of the teachers said:

Today, I wanted to keep Harry's plan, but he wanted to take it home. So I said OK we'll photocopy it so if you come with me I'll show you, so he came and saw it all happening. We had to do two copies because we had to join it up, and then I asked him if he could join it up and he did and I said I'll keep this copy and you can take this one home. And he said after all of that 'no, I want the photocopy.' (Laughter)

We met Alan in Chapter 3. Alan's portfolio included the following Stories:

15/8 First plan for gate. Comment: Alan's first plan.

28/8   Photo of Alan's gate in the nature corner. Comment: Alan tried his gate in the gap in the fence and decided that his gate won't 'reach from the top of the fence to the ground'. He is thinking about making a big one 'the same size as the fence'. He attached it to a post in the nature corner, carefully measuring the gate post first and then sawing it smaller. Bev helped him.

29/8   Photocopy of second plan, with measurements. Comment: 'Alan has measured the gap in the fence to get the right size for his gate.'

2/9   Note: Alan made a cardboard gate model. He worked quietly and independently although there were children all around him. One of the problems was getting the cardboard strips the right length. Another was making and attaching the four hinges.

15/10   Final plan for gate, with measurement. Comment: Alan: 'The lines on the gate go down. You need three hinges. Fence diagonally. There is a lock. The numbers on the top show one metre wide. It's the same high as the fence.'

15/10   Plan for builder with the three hinges and the lock.

Before the project, the teachers had focused their attention on 'need': they shifted this focus to Learning Stories about interest, involvement, challenge ('puzzlement') and collaboration. Because the project often included drawing, the children were included in the documenting.

Diverse Assessment Formats

This focus on assessment as part of the learner-in-action has led the practitioners to take a critical look at the assessment formats. Over the last year or so, practitioners (often with the help of educators in professional development programmes) have adapted and modified their assessment formats to make the process (i) more efficient, (ii) more closely in tune with their everyday practice, and (iii) frequently, more professional looking. Wendy Lee, a professional development facilitator working with practitioners in early childhood on assessment, has commented to me that 'there is excitement in the air'. Some of the Learning Stories look astonishing. Practitioners in centres that can afford it are putting stories onto computer, scanning photos, and using digital cameras. The adaptation and modification of assessment formats began in the trial childcare centre but has now become a feature of a number of centres.

In the beginning, centres used a simple A4 sheet, drawn up with the five domains of dispositions down one side (Figures 9.1 and 9.2). The

Learning Story in Figure 9.1 describes an interaction between a practitioner and a child, a pretend play interaction in the sandpit. Other Learning Stories on the same child record his interactions with peers, and their sociodramatic play centred on Iain's interest in fire engines and fire fighters. Figure 9.2 records Richard's sewing, an activity that assisted him to settle at the beginning of the day. It also records his favourite colour (red) and early literacy skills.

The staff at the childcare case study centre wrote Learning Stories on the A4 Learning Story sheet attached to a clipboard. They chose three or four children a fortnight, and collected Learning Stories together in a folder to summarise on a Planning Sheet at the staff meeting. The primary caregiver for each child supervised this process, but a number of staff wrote observations on each child, in a variety of contexts. Writing observations was initially seen as difficult. Julie pointed out that it was very hard to capture the exact language: 'By the time you've come to write it down you've forgotten what that child has said.' Alternative ways of recording observations were canvassed with the staff. Julie wondered about videoing: keeping a videotape open to record each child's activities in particular for the parents (a centre later began to do this, and the staff there have been puzzling over how to include interpretation and commentary). Pauline thought the writing down was valuable but added 'it would be easier to tape it than to write it. . . . I've played (coached) netball with one and that's how I collected data. I never wrote anything down.' However, they became more confident to write stories down, and were reassured that these stories were to be 'to the point', 'telling', and did not have to be long. A year into the new assessment procedure, they decided that they wanted more cues in the format, and during a staff meeting I assisted them to develop a new format: Figure 9.3. Figure 9.3 records Maria's interest in blocks, patterns and, perhaps, circles. The form includes a smaller space for the story (it can be continued on the other side of the page), and includes 'cues and examples' for each category. The cues are:

- Taking an interest: finding an interest here – a topic, an activity, a role. Recognising the familiar, enjoying the unfamiliar. Coping with change.
- Being involved: paying attention for a sustained period, feeling safe, trusting others. Being playful with others and/or materials.
- Persisting with difficulty: setting and choosing difficult tasks. Using a range of strategies to solve problems when 'stuck' (be specific).

Project for Assessing Children's Experiences

STRANDS IN THE EARLY CHILDHOOD CURRICULUM	DECISION POINTS IN LEARNING STORIES	
BELONGING	FINDING SOMETHING OF INTEREST HERE	✓
WELL-BEING	BEING INVOLVED	✓
EXPLORATION	ENGAGING WITH CHALLENGE AND PERSISTING WHEN DIFFICULTIES ARISE	✓
COMMUNICATION	EXPRESSING A POINT OF VIEW	✓
CONTRIBUTION	TAKING RESPONSIBILITY	✓

LEARNING STORY

Iain started by giving me cups of tea – a plastic tea cup full of sand. I was saying "thank you", "that was lovely" etc. Then he found a big round lid which he told me was a plate. He piled the "plate" with sand and said "Here's your birthday cake" I said "Mmmm, yum that looks delicious", "Has it got candles?" Iain put another pile of sand on top and said "there's the candles", I said "are they lit?" Iain picked up a handful of sand and with the other hand struck a pretend match on the handful of sand – obviously a matchbox! and lit the candles. I said "Are you going to sing Happy Birthday for me?" So he sang Happy Birthday and I blew out the candles.

Name: Iain
Place: Sandpit
Date: 26.8.98
Observer: Priscilla

Figure 9.1. Learning Story assessment format: Iain in the sandpit

<u>LEARNING STORY OBSERVATION SHEET:</u>

Name Richard   Date 7/2/2000
Place Sewing table outside.   Observer Natalie

Belonging	Finding something of interest	Richard didn't want Mum to leave. Natalie suggested some sewing, which he decided might be fun.
Well-Being	Being Involved	Richard asked Natalie for the red wool & then got started on his sewing. He knew to make his needle go up & down through the holes.
Exploration	Engaging with Challenge and persisting when difficulties arise	When he did get stuck he was able to ask Natalie for help & persisted with the activity until complete.
Communication	Expressing a Point of view	He told Natalie that "red was his favourite colour" & it was his brothers birthday so he had to write Happy birthday & draw his brother
Contribution	Taking responsibility	Natalie helped him sound out each letter & he was able to write Happy birthday. Once finished Richard gave his sewing to Natalie for his book.

Jlk Mt. Eden kindergarten 99

Richard

Figure 9.2. Learning Story assessment format: Richard sewing

- Expressing an idea or a feeling: in a range of ways (specify). For example: oral language, gesture, music, art, writing, using numbers and patterns, telling stories.
- Taking responsibility: responding to others, to stories, and imagined events, ensuring that things are fair, self-evaluating, helping others, contributing to the programme.

This format includes what we called a 'short-term review' which summarises what the observer saw as the key point(s) of this story. A cue in this box says: 'Question: What learning did I think went on here (i.e. the main point(s) of the learning story)?' The format also included a box called 'What next?' This was for short-term guidance, and to assist with the planning process. The cues in this box reminded the practitioners of the definition of progress within this approach:

Questions:
How might we encourage this interest, ability, strategy, disposition, story to

- Be more complex.
- Appear in different areas or activities in the programme.

How might we encourage the next 'step' in the Learning Story framework?

Some centres added only a short-term review to the Learning Story format (Figure 9.4). In the example, one of a series about Hamish representing his pet corgi in a number of ways, the story is continued on a separate sheet, so the entire story reads as follows:

Hamish has already sewn one corgi and sculptured a wonderful corgi out of clay. He is very keen to sew another one and has asked me about it for several days. Kindi is so busy – but finally yesterday I said 'Right-oh Hamish – let's get cracking on this corgi project – how about you draw one to use as the pattern.' Off he went and soon returned with the drawing – then it was tidy up time!!! UGH! So I said 'Let's make sure it happens tomorrow!!!!' 'Yes!' he said. Today we both forgot! Until about 11.25 when Hamish remembered. 'Oh no Hamish!!! – It's got to be TOMORROW!!!!' 'Write it down' he said. 'Good idea' – so we went to the office and I wrote 'Hamish's corgi – FIRST THING' in the diary. As we were walking out of the office and on our way to the mat Hamish turned to me – hands on hips and said 'Do you know what I'm going to say to you first thing tomorrow???' 'No' I said. 'LOOK AT YOUR DIARY!' he said – we both had a good laugh together!!

Child's name: ....*Maria*...............
Date: ....*11/10*..............
Observer: ....

		Examples or cues	A LEARNING STORY
belonging mana whenua	**TAKING AN INTEREST**	Finding an interest here - a topic, an activity, a role. Recognising the familiar, enjoying the unfamiliar. Coping with change.	*Gets out half-circle blocks, puts two together to make a circle. Gets*
well-being mana atua	**BEING INVOLVED**	Paying attention for a sustained period, feeling safe, trusting others. Being playful with others and/or materials.	*out longer curved block and tries to add it, then tries to add small half circle.*
exploration mana aotūroa	**PERSISTING WITH DIFFICULTY**	Setting and choosing difficult tasks. Using a range of strategies to solve problems when 'stuck' (be specific).	*Later returns, puts two half circles together, claps her hands.*
communication mana reo	**EXPRESSING AN IDEA OR A FEELING**	In a range of ways (specify). For example: oral language, gesture, music, art, writing, using numbers and patterns, telling stories.	*Piles up small blocks, laughs when they fall. Later, building, carefully fits blocks into a*
contribution mana tangata	**TAKING RESPONSIBILITY**	Responding to others, to stories, and imagined events, ensuring that things are fair, self-evaluating, helping others, contributing to programme.	*rectangular pattern.*

Short Term Review	**What Next?**
Interest in blocks and in fitting them together to make patterns and shapes – returns for second attempt.	*Work with Maria with blocks. Mozaics? Circles? Wheels?*
	Questions: How might we encourage this interest, ability, strategy, disposition, story to
	• Be more complex.
	• Appear in different areas or activities in the programme.
Question: What learning did I think went on here (i.e. the main point(s) of the learning story)?	How might we encourage the next 'step' in the learning story framework?

Hamilton Childcare Services Trust trial 2000

Figure 9.3. Learning Story assessment format: Maria's interest in blocks

Child's name: **Hamish**
Date. **13/sepl/2000**
Observer: **Julie**

Learning Stories

		A LEARNING STORY
belonging mana whenua	**TAKING AN INTEREST**	Hamish has already sewn one corgi and sculptured a wonderful corgie out of clay. He is very keen to sell a-bit one and has asked me about it for several days. Kindi is so busy – but finally yesterday I said "Right-oh Hamish – lets get cracking on this corgi project – how about you draw one to use as the pattern." Off he went and soon returned with the drawing – then it was tidy up time !!! UGH! so I said "Lets make sure it happens Tomorrow !!!" "YES!" he said Today we both forgot! Until about 11-25 when Hamish
well-being mana atua	**BEING INVOLVED**	
exploration mana aoturoa	**PERSISTING WITH DIFFICULTY**	
communication mana reo	**EXPRESSING AN IDEA OR A FEELING**	
contribution mana tangata	**TAKING RESPONSIBILITY**	

PTO →

Short Term Review

There are a number of wonderful things to note about this scenario!

→ Hamishs on-going interest in creating corgis – inspired from this pet which he obviously loves a lot.

→ Hamish is keen to revisit the sewing experience

→ Hamish has a great sense of humour !!!

Question: What learning did I think went on here (i.e. the main point(s) of the learning story)?

Educational Leadership Project 2000

→ Hamish knows clearly how powerful and useful literacy is – writing things down to remember and remembering to revisit them and READ them !

Figure 9.4.   Learning Story assessment format: Hamish

Practitioners in other centres wanted a format that included spaces for photographs, and Wendy Lee designed a range of these. She encouraged those centres with computers and/or scanners and/or digital cameras to write their stories into the computer, complete with illustration. Figure 9.5 is an example. It records part of Ashley's work during a print-making project. Print makers had visited the early

Child:	Ashley	*Learning Stories*
Date:	June 2000	
Observer:	Lesley	

		A Learning Story	
belonging mana whenua	**TAKING AN INTEREST**	Ashley was actively involved at the outset discussion and subsequent sketching stage. Ashley was involved in dialogue re the 'Aunties Insect Show' which she viewed on 30 May.	
well-being mana atua	**BEING INVOLVED**	William was discussing drawing a ladybird, when Ashley said "I'll go and get a book for you, I know where it is". Ashley went away and got the book "Ladybird" by Barrie Watts whose name she copied onto her sketch!	
exploration mana aotūroa	**PERSISTING WITH DIFFICULTY**	Ashley engaged in discussion re whether the print would be printed lengthways or sideways, I introduced horizontal and vertical language.	
communication mana reo	**EXPRESSING AN IDEA OR A FEELING**	Ashley observed me writing number '2' beside her name (I had done this to indicate that she had done 2 prints so far) We talked about the different meanings of two and to and Ashley gave an example of 'to Mummy'.	
contribution mana tangata	**TAKING RESPONSIBILITY**	Ashley worked independently throughout, confidently working through each stage. Ashley initiated an idea using a small block print in the corner, hence the idea of a small block border developed.	

Educational Leadership Project 2000

Figure 9.5. Learning Story assessment format, including photographs of work (continued on page 152)

Short Term Review	What Next?
☆ Ashley showed a long term sustained interest in the printing project.	Ashley had previously been involved in a long term painting project. Maybe we could embark on another printmaking technique i.e. screen printing.
☆ Ashley accessed resources and initiated strategies to both support others and to solve the problem of the broken corner of the polystyrene board.	
☆ Ashley clearly understood the literacy links.	
	Questions: How might we encourage this interest, ability, strategy, disposition, story to
	● Be more complex.
Question: What learning did I think went on here (i.e. the main point(s) of the learning story)?	● Appear in different areas or activities in the programme. How might we encourage the next 'step' in the learning story framework?

Figure 9.5. (continued)   Learning Story assessment format, including photographs of work

childhood centre, taught the children a range of print-making techniques, and over several weeks a group of children experimented with making prints. Figure 9.6 shows some of Ashley's drawings as she experiments with designs for printing.

For many practitioners writing anything down is a chore, but the work of putting the stories onto computer has been exciting. Using computer-generated formats is at the cutting edge of the technology of assessment, and it may be that children will be able to be more closely involved with the process. In the Reggio Emilia programmes, children have used polaroid cameras to record their interests. Digital cameras have the same advantage as polaroid cameras – instant feedback – and children are able to choose which photos reflect key points in the learning episode and therefore should be included in their Learning Stories.

Finally, Wendy designed two formats, one entitled 'The Child's Voice' (Figures 9.7 and 9.8) and one entitled 'Parent's Voice' (Figure 9.9). The Child's Voice included a photo or a series of photos or a drawing and asked the child for the Learning Story. In Figure 9.7 Georgia dictates a story about her drawing; in Figure 9.8 Marshall retells the study of collaboration with another child to complete a jigsaw puzzle. Some centres encouraged family members to write Learning Stories, often as a comment on a photograph or some work done. In

Figure 9.6. Ashley's drawings

Figure 9.9 Darryn's mother has taken a photograph (not included here) of Darryn standing beside the letterbox he made at the early childhood centre. It was set up at the end of the driveway beside the family's letterbox. She adds some comments about it.

Child's name: *Georgia*
Date:
Teacher:

The child's voice

			A LEARNING STORY
belonging mana whenua	TAKING AN INTEREST		
well-being mana atua	BEING INVOLVED		These are the ribs that Matthew my brother taught me
exploration mana aotūroa	PERSISTING WITH DIFFICULTY		that you have. These are the bones of the knees. Those
communication mana reo	EXPRESSING AN IDEA OR A FEELING		are the arms and the legs – and that's the skeleton face. Georgia 17/9
contribution mana tangata	TAKING RESPONSIBILITY		

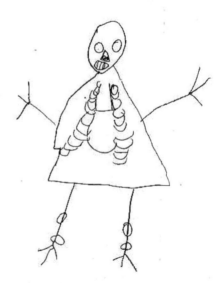

Figure 9.7. The Child's Voice: Georgia's story

Child: Marshall
Date: 25 May 2000
Teacher: Glenys

The child's voice

		A Learning Story	
belonging mana whenua	TAKING AN INTEREST	Glenys was talking to Marshall about the photographs that had been taken of him while he was doing a puzzle. "I'm just finding another one".	
well-being mana atua	BEING INVOLVED	Glenys asks Marshall to tell her about the puzzle. "It was about a fire-engine...... "I think it was C " (child's	
exploration mana aotūroa	PERSISTING WITH DIFFICULTY	name who was working on the puzzle too). "It was helping me cause I couldn't do it by myself".	
communication mana reo	EXPRESSING AN IDEA OR A FEELING	"He did it for me and I did it for him – we did it". "The firemen are driving. One firemen is climbing the ladder – another guy is helping the fireman"	
contribution mana tangata	TAKING RESPONSIBILITY	"I want to do it again" Marshall then went inside to the puzzle area to look for the puzzle.	

Educational Leadership Project 2000

Figure 9.8. The Child's Voice: Marshall tells Glenys about the puzzle

Child's name: Darryn........................

Date: ....

Parent's Voice

		Examples or cues	**A LEARNING STORY**
belonging mana whenua	**TAKING AN INTEREST**	Finding an interest *here* – a topic, an activity, a role. Recognising the familiar, enjoying the unfamiliar. Coping with change.	People have picked up how much better Darryn is at kindergarten and speech therapy and just everywhere.
well-being mana atua	**BEING INVOLVED**	Paying attention for a sustained period, feeling safe, trusting others. Being playful with others and/or materials.	
exploration mana aotūroa	**PERSISTING WITH DIFFICULTY**	Setting and choosing difficult tasks. Using a range of strategies to solve problems when 'stuck' (be specific).	He is doing a lot more things. He's always sawing and helping with things, like he took the wheels off Grant's stock car at the weekend.
communication mana reo	**EXPRESSING AN IDEA OR A FEELING**	In a range of ways (specify). For example: oral language, gesture, music, art, writing, using numbers and patterns, telling stories.	
contribution mana tangata	**TAKING RESPONSIBILITY**	Responding to others, to stories, and imagined events, ensuring that things are fair, self-evaluating, helping others, contributing to programme.	People stop and look at the letterbox. After school all the children are stopping and looking at it.

Figure 9.9.   Parent's Voice: Darryn's mother

Concluding Comments

When the practitioners were developing educational reasons for documenting, ways in which documenting could become an integral part of the learner-in-action, and diverse assessment formats, they were shifting their model of assessment from one in which assessment sits outside learning (Figure 9.10a) to one in which assessment is integral to the enhancement of learning (Figure 9.10b). In Figure 9.10a, assessment happens after an episode of learning and teaching. In Figure 9.10b, on the other hand, assessment is (as David Pratt says at the beginning of this chapter) 'woven into the fabric of classroom activity and interaction'.

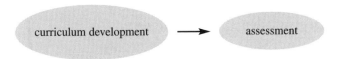

Figure 9.10a. Assessment sits outside learning

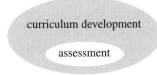

Figure 9.10b. Assessment is integral to the enhancement of learning

This chapter has illustrated the value for the practitioners of documenting Learning Stories. The documentation had become integral to the wider process whereby practitioners got to know the children, planned for their learning, and established a learning community with shared values. Children were included as active participants, and the documenting also provided feedback for families about their children's well-being and learning. This chapter has outlined some of the ways in which assessment formats have been changed to incorporate 'What next?' The next chapter considers more fully that fourth process of assessment: *deciding* what to do next.

10

Deciding

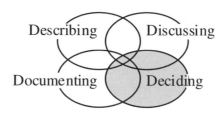

Deciding is the fourth, and final, of the four Ds of assessment. A key process in teaching is deciding what to do next. This includes responding to children's initiatives, taking the initiative, changing the direction, intervening. In many contexts, this is called planning, but *deciding* also includes intuitive and spontaneous responding. The Learning Story formats in the previous chapter included a section called 'What next?': these formats were about *formative* assessment, assessment that is part of the ongoing process of teaching, learning and development. As Mary-Jane Drummond said of Susan Isaacs' observations: 'She did not collect an inert mass of data . . . the data have been set to work, to construct a coherent account of the development of children's intellectual and emotional powers' (1999 p. 4).

Formative assessment keeps track and advises the participants about some of the alternative directions for further development and learning. This chapter, therefore, raises the same question that is raised by the Possible Lines of Development (PLODs) in the Pen Green portfolios: 'what lines of direction are possible?' This chapter also looks at the way the practitioners in the five case study settings were deciding what to do next to enhance the children's learning: for Rosie and Hugo, for a group of under-twos, and for the gate project. The chapter looks at the following contexts for deciding:

- tracking progress and deciding: Rosie and Hugo;
- deciding as responding;
- planning together for learning dispositions and learning places.

Tracking Progress and Deciding: Rosie and Hugo

Taking responsibility for the development and learning of children requires a concept of progress. I have already described development and learning, after Barbara Rogoff and Urie Bronfenbrenner, in general terms as increasing complexity of participation. This chapter is more specific. The cues in the 'What next?' box of the Learning Story format in Figure 9.3 in Chapter 9 asked four questions about progress in terms of increasing complexity of participation. These four questions describe four ways in which increased participation can be tracked: (i) this Learning Story becomes more frequent, (ii) this interest, ability, strategy, disposition, story becomes more complex, (iii) this interest, ability, strategy, disposition, story appears in different areas or activities in the programme, and (iv) the action moves along the sequence in the Learning Story framework, from interest to involvement, from involvement to persistence, from persistence to communication and from communication to responsibility.

Rosie: tracking progress

The four questions in the 'What next?' box frame up a discussion about progress over 10 months at childcare for Rosie (from age just four to 4:10). The observations on Rosie, with their strong component of communication and sociodramatic play, are in Chapter 3.

This Learning Story becomes more frequent
For the action described in a Learning Story to contribute to an inclination, it needs to occur a number of times. A number of stories indicate Rosie's readiness to design sociodramatic story-lines that deal with topics of scary and safe, real and pretend, themes of great interest to her, and then to persuade others to take part. She initially played out these interests with Anna and Louise, and early stories indicate that she was less likely to negotiate than to direct the sequence of events, offering alternatives and giving reasons in order to persuade others to join in.

This interest, ability, strategy, disposition, story becomes more complex
The Learning Stories deepen. Activities will take longer, the challenge and uncertainty will increase, the languages will become more complex, and joint attention episodes will demand more of the participants. The observations of Rosie provide evidence that she is not only practising

old 'bridging' and 'structuring' strategies, she is beginning to try out new ones as well. The language of negotiation is becoming more complex, and the joint attention episodes are demanding more of the participants. In the first observation she is going fishing with Anna, and she directs the sequence of events. In the second observation (going to the Pizza Hut) she also determines the direction of play, and in her final comment she keeps several ideas together to maintain a time sequence to the story-line: she points out to Louise that she can't now pay for the pizzas because she has already gone home. In the third observation (she and Anna disagree about the camera) she appears to weigh up the benefits of keeping Anna happy against the benefits of being the owner of the camera; she gives way on the direction of the play (OK I didn't buyed it). In the fourth observation (trying to persuade Louise to take a role in Peter Pan) she uses her understanding of Louise's favourite role (a mermaid) to try to persuade. In the fifth observation she and Anna are playing Belle and the Beast, and she is now trying to script Anna's thoughts, a complex strategy that refers to what Anna is 'saying to herself' ('You say to yourself "I love Belle eh?" '). In several of these observations, the adult models giving explanations, valuing imagination, and sequencing the play.

This interest, ability, strategy, disposition, story appears in different areas or activities in the programme
The Learning Stories widen. Actions will occur in more than one context or place, with different people and/or in different activities. In observations 6 and 7, Rosie is calling on her negotiating skills in a social activity (riding bikes) and she is expressing her interest in 'scary' characters in drawing. She has shifted her strategies and interests into different activities from her usual sociodramatic play. Her drawings are of scary and friendly creatures, but they also include abstract patterns. An observation of her making a pattern with wool around nails in a piece of wood (not recorded in Chapter 3) may have also been an example of taking that interest in abstract pattern into another domain. One of the later Learning Stories written by Julie documents Rosie caring for the younger children in a routine:

> Rosie 20/11
> Rosie comes into the sleep room. She says: 'Julie, James is awake.' I smile and nod my head. 'Do you want to get up now?' she says to James in a whispering voice. 'Come on, I'll help you, wanna go and play?' She helps James put his shoes on and takes his hand and takes him to the toilet where Jo (another member of staff) takes over.

The action moves along the sequence in the Learning Story framework
The Learning Stories lengthen. Given a particular interest, the child's action moves on to the next step in the learning story sequence. Rosie's sociodramatic play scripts cover all five of the 'steps' in the Learning Story framework: she is taking an interest, being involved, persevering with difficulty, communicating her ideas and taking on another's point of view. There are, however, some stories in which she is taking responsibility in this place, assisting the victims of (scary?) aggression. One of them was me: when I visited the centre and Bruce hit me with a piece of jigsaw, Rosie became the teacher, instructing me to say 'Don't do that Bruce. I don't like it.' In Chapter 8 the staff told a story about Rosie taking responsibility for Billy after he had apparently been hurt by another child. 'She got the cold flannel for him and she put it on his face . . .' She frequently requested the 'scary' Bear Hunt chant as part of the programme.

Rosie: deciding

How were the staff deciding what to do next for Rosie? In this case, a key strategy was to establish a dispositional milieu and to ensure, by assessment, that Rosie was participating. The staff allowed time for interests in sociodramatic play to develop, for story-lines to be played out and scripts established. They introduced stories that might encourage role play (although Beauty and the Beast I think came from home). They provided resources and dress-ups, and occasionally they would take these outside to vary the circumstances and to encourage new players who appeared to be more comfortable with outside play. The adults modelled giving explanations and negotiating (with the children and with each other); they entered the play when they thought it was appropriate and this gave value to imaginative play; they asked questions and made suggestions to make it more complex; they wrote stories about Rosie's participation.

Hugo: tracking progress

Deciding what to do next is usually a combination of setting the scene and deliberate teaching. Hugo is a four-year-old at the same kindergarten as abseiling Timothy and the Story Stones activity. Another regular activity at this kindergarten was the teaching of sign language, often accompanying songs at 'mat' or 'circle' time. When Hugo started kindergarten he was a keen reader, already very accomplished. His parents reported that six months after he started kindergarten, at just over four years of age, he was reading Harry Potter (J. K. Rowling) books at home. He could easily read the picture books on offer at the kindergarten. Hugo's progress at kindergarten was documented with Learning Stories and a web diagram which summarised the key features of the development of his learning. Here is a selection from the Learning Story collection:

24/5:   Year 1: Highly skilled reader (photo of Hugo, on his own, reading in the book corner)

Term 4   Year 1: Reads a story to a group of children (photo)

Term 4   Year 1: Watches children signing. At group time, begins to join in to sign stories and songs.

27/1:   Year 2: Listens in on the edge of a Story Stones session. Adds comments.

18/2:   Totally focused on and listened to story-telling Story Stones session. Does not want to be included in the story.

7/3:   Eager for Story Stones. Enjoys listening to other children's involvement in the stories.

15/3:   Basing sand construction on book 'Livingstone Mouse' (Edwards, 1996). Very engrossed.

7/5:   With two other boys, completes a Treasure Hunt (devised by one of the teachers). Hugo reads the clues out to the others, and while he reflects on them the others race off to find the next clue.

12/6:   Chooses a Stone and takes a part in a Story Stones session.

The Learning Stories also document his oral language, his sense of humour, his developing friendships with other children and his increasing interest in painting and print-making.

The teachers had developed the web diagram by adding the story summaries as they occurred. Another way to illustrate Hugo's progress in one area, language and communication, would be to organise the web in terms of three axes or pathways of progress: stories deepening, widening and lengthening. Figure 10.1 sets this out as a web diagram, with Hugo's love of reading in the centre.

Hugo: deciding

During this period, a number of activities were planned by the teachers.

(i) For the whole group: painting and teaching the children sign language at group time, a feature of the many communication

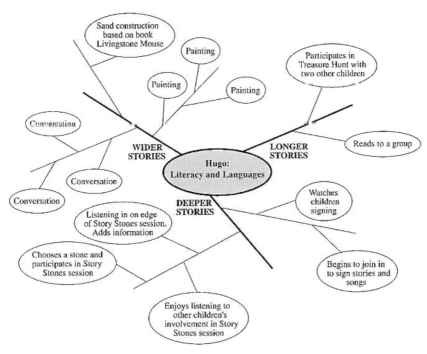

Figure 10.1. Hugo's progress

'genres' at this kindergarten (when the teachers did not know a sign, the children devised one).

(ii) For a number of small groups, freely chosen by the children: the Story Stones.

(iii) An activity for three children especially designed for Hugo to contribute his reading ability in a group: the Treasure Hunt. For a group of three children, including Hugo, one of the teachers wrote and hid clues around the early childhood centre, and the teachers reminisced about the different contributions to the group: Hugo had read out the clues and thought about them while the others solved the problem (finding the next clue). For instance, when the clue was 'near an animal that lives in water', Hugo had reflected out loud about all the animals he knew that live in water, while the other two raced off to the frog tank and shouted out for him to come and read out the next clue.

Hugo had arrived at this early childhood centre eager to read and to decode print, and with the skills and knowledge to do so. The teachers and his family were keen for this enthusiasm to be incorporated in a disposition to communicate in a range of ways in this new setting. They looked for and engineered communication, including reading, in a number of arenas and encouraged its increasing complexity: being the reader in the Treasure Hunt group, participating in story-telling in the context of Story Stones sessions, and learning sign language.

Deciding in Responding

Deciding what to do next is not always documented. Indeed, the processes of describing, discussing and deciding what to do next are usually spontaneous and informal. In the under-twos programme at the childcare centre, for instance, I had observed one of the staff, Jacky, interacting with four children and recorded her responses. In the first five minutes she made the following comments:

(1)	(T. screams when D. approaches his post box) Oh, no screaming.
(2 & 3)	(C. at the top of the slide, looking uncertain) Are you going to go down the slide C.? (asked twice)
(4)	(C. slides down. Looks at Jacky) Oh, well done. Going to go back the other way?
(5)	Here's a few more, T. (gives T. some more pieces for the post box)
(6)	(D. tries to lift a large box) Shall we lift that up and see what's under it? (She helps) Didah! Nothing.
(7)	(D. claps his hands) Yeah: pakipaki! ('clapping')
(8)	(D. approaches T., takes a post box piece. T. squeals) Using your words.
(9)	(D. makes a sound in greeting to Helen who had just arrived) That's Helen.
(10)	(Adult comes in, and T. tries to say her name) That's Jodie.
(11)	(D. climbing up to the slide) Shall I help you? (He shakes his head in reply)
(12)	(C. sings) Happy birthday to you. Is that what you're singing C.?
(13)	(D. at the top of the slide. Looks at Jacky) Are you going to go down there D.?

This tireless feedback, usually undocumented unless it becomes part of a Learning Story, included a number of informal assessments: admiration for C. who had managed the slide, acknowledgements of attempts to communicate, an offer to help that recognised a difficult task ahead, and in almost every comment a message that responsive and reciprocal understandings and communication are valued. We also calculated that at this rate of response (13 in five minutes) an adult might be interpreting a child's meaning and providing feedback or responding 936 times in a six-hour day.

Response style and learning place

This spontaneous *deciding* in responding to children reveals the adults' implicit beliefs about curriculum and pedagogy. In particular, it illustrates the close link between adult responses to children's initiatives and the dispositional domain of taking responsibility. Almost all of Jacky's informal assessments were to do with the task or strategy of interest to both adult and child, or on clarifying the meaning of the child's initiative. They did not include generalised and person-oriented praise (for example: 'good girl', 'I'm very pleased with you', 'you *are* clever'). Her intuition is supported by research evidence. Studies cited in Gail Heyman and Carol Dweck's (1998) discussion of children's thinking about traits, and in Paul Black and Dylan Wiliam's (1998) review of assessment and classroom learning, suggest that praise and evaluation feedback that focuses on traits of the child such as being good or being clever afford 'performance goals' in which children strive to display their goodness or their ability, and avoid difficult tasks in case they make an error and are perceived to be unable. One study cited in Black and Wiliam indicated that feedback interventions that cue individuals to direct attention to the self rather than the task are likely to have negative effects on performance. Another study documented the changing response style of a mathematics teacher over two years: the style developed from evaluative listening (looking for the expected answer) to interpretive listening (seeking information) to listening in which there was co-participation by adult and learner. Episodes of co-participation or joint attention in which adults listen and respond to children, intuitively and rapidly deciding what to do or say next, are rich contexts for learning, enhancing language development as well as strategies for shared interests, respect, involvement, problem-solving and responsibility.

I noted in Chapter 2 that activities can develop their own dispositional milieu, and my research in Jason and Nell's kindergarten indicated some interesting patterns of adult response and assessment in different places, even within the one centre. I compared the adults' comments in two activities. In 58 episodes of screen printing, where adults tended to keep up a supply of evaluative and encouraging comments to keep the children on track, nearly 19% of the teachers' comments were evaluative; in 17 episodes of marble painting this was 12%. The teachers were making informal assessments, providing feedback to the children, between 12% and 19% of the time. However, the type of evaluative comment was markedly different in each of the activities. The adults' evaluative comments were divided into two groups: comments that provided general praise or feedback associated with the self or other people ('your mum will be proud of you') and comments that gave feedback associated with the work or the task. Of all the evaluative comments in screen printing, 33% were general comments, or associated with the self (good girl, busy girl, isn't she clever, good going, fantastic). In marble painting, 92% of the evaluative comments referred to the work or the action (oh that went high, it's like a lot of roads isn't it, what a good idea). In screen printing, 'good girl' appeared in the transcripts 13 times. There were nine boys and nineteen girls participating in screen printing, but 'good boy' was never heard. Screen printing was characterised by performance goals (Danny, whom we met in Chapter 3, was an exception) and adult tutorials; marble painting by collaborative problem-solving and learning goals.

It seems then that response styles can become situated in certain activities. These response styles were not necessarily a possession of a particular teacher: the research indicated that each of the staff used a range of style. Deciding and discussing, when adult comments are evaluative, are forms of assessment that are not usually documented. They can have powerful effects on the classroom as a learning place, on different groups of children within the classroom (girls and boys, for instance), and on individual learners.

Planning Together for Learning Dispositions and Learning Places

It was clear from the examples of Rosie and of Hugo, that *deciding* – spontaneous and formal planning – can be at the individual and the programme level, and these levels can be unobtrusively woven together. Many examples in this book have illustrated the reciprocal and transactional relationship between the individual and the environment, the disposition and the dispositional milieu. Planning in the gate project kindergarten provides one example; planning at the childcare centre for Joseph's transition to the over-twos programme is another.

Planning in the gate project kindergarten

Planning for interest and involvement

In the gate project the teachers kept a record of the children who were involved in the project and they maintained the children's interest and involvement through a series of resources and events:

- interesting tools and materials: clipboards, pens, wire, clay, photos, carpentry tools, measuring tapes, rulers, carpentry aprons;
- discussions with the children;
- visitors: the builder, the draftsperson;
- field trips;
- documentation: photocopying, photographs, stories written;
- in some cases, interest from the families.

At one team meeting one of the teachers commented:

> Do you know what I think, the popular thing about this project is the clipboard. I think every child in the kindergarten has used a clipboard. [She comments on how careful the children are with the pens] And Joe, today they took the tops (of the pens) off and I said give the tops to me and I'll look after them and Joe said 'Oh no, sir, you put it on the end like this' and they knew exactly what to do.

Up until early September their records indicated that the boys were much more involved than the girls; in particular the boys were edging the girls out of the carpentry equipment. They decided to take the children on short walks near the kindergarten to draw and discuss gates, including girls (and boys) who had not been involved in the project so far. They also provided more rulers and measuring tapes, and specifically encouraged the girls to persevere when the boys questioned their right to belong in the carpentry area. By mid-September, 30 children (out of the 44 on the roll, 25 boys and 19 girls) had participated in the project: 17 boys and 13 girls. The teachers estimated that nine out of ten of the older, four-and-a-half-year-olds, were involved. The following notes come from the teachers' journal and from notes taken by the researcher during weekly discussions:

Planning for difficulty

The planning for the project included both children and teachers reflecting on practice.

> Teacher: . . . Because [the project] is done over a much longer period you actually have time to sit and think about perhaps where we have

gone wrong. Children work on their own thing and talk about it with you. [Team meeting 12/9]

At this meeting the teachers expressed disappointment that the children's level of questioning did not appear to have increased. When we discussed whether persevering with difficulty had to include asking questions, the teachers decided that they were interested in evidence of 'puzzlement', and this might not necessarily be reflected in asking questions verbally. At the same time, when they were alert to documenting questions they heard more of them:

> We thought at the beginning that maybe that was something that we were doing wrong [asking too many questions]. The kids weren't able to ask their own questions. We were asking too many questions, but we don't feel that now. Well now I think that, the other day I wrote some down and they were lovely puzzling questions. [Team meeting 12/9]

At the beginning of the project the research team (researcher and teachers) had decided that the gate project had the capacity to raise the following questions:

> Fitting a door/gate to a doorway/gateway (will it fit?)
> Making it swing (will it swing? how are gates hinged?)
> Designing it to fit its purpose (will it do? be strong? keep children out?)
> Latching it firmly (will it hold? how are gates latched?)
> The purpose of gates (why are gates designed the way they are?)

In mid-September the teachers listed the difficulties found and tackled so far:

> Translating plans into gates.
> The rectangular carpenters' pencils provided a problem: they couldn't be sharpened in the usual way. (Tommy 13/8: 'You need to get a rectangle pencil sharpener.')
> The triangular wood provided a problem: difficult to hammer nails into it.
> Designing and attaching hinges.
> Joining (with nails or tape).
> Planning ahead: measuring the nail in relation to the depth of the wood.

In May the next year, after a second project, they listed the following difficult skills:

> Drawing a plan and thinking about it.
> Adding extra pieces on and labelling them (verbally).

Drawing from different perspectives and in three dimensions.
Measurement ('People like D. and I. are able to measure the legs and things like that, I mean, really measure them so they are all the same length.').
Following through a sequence ('Ellen came up to me the day before yesterday and . . . she had all the bits of wood (for a bird house) and she said "this one's for the front, this one at the side, this bit out here is for the bird to stand on . . ." ').
Watching, concentrating, and participating in discussion in the large group.

The research team talked about some possible strategies to increase authentic questions from the children. They decided to model questions themselves, to ask cue questions to the children ('what do we need to do this?' 'what do we need to know?' 'is there a problem here?') and to introduce problems, puzzles and provocations (a strategy they borrowed from the literature on Reggio Emilia programmes). They became very alert to the children's questions, and jotted them down. The following notes were in Tommy's portfolio: 'Listen, how are we going to cut it?' 'How are we going to make it?' 'What are we making, are we making a ring?'

One of the teachers commented that the long-term nature of the project encouraged children to persevere, and return to enterprises they had begun earlier.

And the other thing, some of them have started and haven't finished (projects) but have come back to them the next day. It's been an ongoing project which before, if you're just popping a bit of wood on another bit of wood, it's blah, forgot about. But they'll come back the next day and continue on.

Wall displays highlighted the children anticipating and solving problems. One photo has the caption:

Here (one of the children) is measuring the nail against the wood to ensure that it is long enough to hold the wood together.

A Learning Story in Mel's portfolio: 'Cuts his gate out that he began last week, is not satisfied with two of the pieces of wood that he chose last week as they keep splitting, so he swaps them for new pieces. Pulls off old pieces and joins on the new.' Carol's portfolio includes a photocopy of a picture of a wrought iron gate that had interested her, a drawn plan, and a photocopy of a final wire gate with added paper shapes. A note dictated by Carol on the photocopy of the wire gate: 'I'm making a lock.'

Planning for children to express their ideas

The children approached the project in their own way, and the documentation built into the project alerted the teachers to their special talents. Jenny was particularly interested in the design possibilities of combining triangles and rectangles, and in colour. She was the only child who painted her (triangular) gate. The project encouraged the measurement and number interests of Alan and Natalie; the teachers were interested that Mikey, whose drawing of a gate during a neighbourhood walk was mostly a squiggle, carefully and accurately copied the numbers from the letterboxes. Joe's skilful drawings were a surprise to the research team: he had never drawn at kindergarten before.

> Teacher: I was surprised how good they were, how certain he was of the shape of the gate, and he didn't say anything at all. And what I enjoyed actually was the enthusiasm.

Many children involved the tools that the teachers had introduced for the making of gates in a range of enterprises. Mel made an airport, put the blocks flat on the ground and then checked with the spirit level: 'It's level Annette' he tells the teacher. The introduction of clay interested but did not involve the children; but the introduction of fine wire involved a number of the children for sustained periods, making intricate designs for models of wrought iron gates, and extending this to making jewellery and designs. Two-dimensional wire work photocopied particularly well, and children's work could be accurately recorded for their portfolios. The children devised a number of different kinds of gates: a railway gate, an electrified gate, a party gate. Wall displays were planned to encourage and illustrate the value of discussion. One photo of a child and teacher discussing a plan has the comment:

> Here Sue (the teacher) is discussing with Daisy her plan that she has drawn. Discussions are an important process in our project so children can convey their ideas and feelings and adults can facilitate children's learning, sharing knowledge.

Later in the project the teachers transcribed discussions at mat time, photocopied them, and included them in the children's portfolios. Initially the boys mostly answered the questions and made comments at this group time (21 boys to 4 girls in an early tally). By mid-year the participation levels of the girls at group time was on average the same as the boys. The teachers also tried to include the children 'who are not as quick at calling out answers'.

Planning for co-construction of ideas and enterprises

Although the teachers had planned a project that would encourage the children to collaborate on joint enterprises, it was the co-construction of *ideas* that characterised the activities that emerged from this project, although four girls did collaborate on the 'party gate' (an episode described in Chapter 7). The children were, however, listening and watching each other, discussing each other's ideas (as Harry did when he considered, and rejected, Alan's gate as a possible model to copy), and sometimes helping each other. A Learning Story in Tommy's portfolio:

> 'I could make some wings (for a jointly constructed aeroplane with Mel).' 'I'll cut it for you' (helping a friend). 'How's it going?' asks Tommy. 'I'll show how much times you have to do it.' 'Hey, I've got an idea.' 'I'll cut a long piece out. I need this too, hold that piece please.' 'It's got to be bigger.' 'We made it together, we just cut it together.' Another child: 'We made the same ones.' Tommy: 'It's not the same. It doesn't matter. Hey, we could make one for Tim eh?'

Natalie had watched Alan making his gate with its crisscross design and then made her own, using the same design. She had the same fascination for measuring as Alan and for numbers (she enjoyed writing her phone number, but commented to the teacher that she was having trouble with the 2s). One of her Learning Stories included a photograph of her measuring her gate with a measuring tape, with the comment added 'Natalie is measuring the width of the gate to make sure the opposite sides are the same length.' Another Story included her final plan: she used a ruler and added numbers (mostly 5s and 7s).

As the kindergarten teachers planned for individual children and the programme, they were developing a viewpoint about a good project. It should be:

- interesting and authentic: children will take an interest, the project will make sense, make connections with their lives and those of their community;
- transparent: the intention or meaning of activities associated with the project are readily apparent, children will be able to become deeply involved, at their own level of complexity, over long periods of time;
- challenging: children will be encouraged to engage and persist with challenge, difficulty, uncertainty and puzzlement; in long-term projects, children will become familiar with the kinds of problems and their possible solutions, will return to problems of previous days;

- multi-faceted: children can incorporate and improve their particular talents and 'languages': for colour, design, technology, three-dimensional modelling, reasoning, drawing, social interaction, number and measure, etc.;
- collaborative/accessible: children will collaborate, and 'bounce ideas off each other'.

The project that followed from this gate project, making chairs and tables for a number of purposes, used these guidelines for planning and deciding what to do next. The teachers were alerted to including the girls early in the project, and they also modelled using the more complex tools, especially the drill. Once again, the purpose (to make furniture for a new outside area) was clear; many of the children found an even more attractive purpose, making chairs to take home. Nevertheless their tables, stools and chairs also found homes in useful places around the centre. The children visited a furniture maker and watched a chair being put together. The same carpentry challenges were a feature of this project as well, and while their furniture did not have the imaginative features of the gates, this time around there was a new measure of success: whether the chair could be sat on or the table was reasonably stable: measuring had gained a serious purpose. There were also more collaborative enterprises, perhaps because the designs were less idiosyncratic.

Planning for Joseph's transition to the over-twos programme

I noted in Chapter 8 that in the childcare centre, staff discussions included defining the assessment categories for individual children, establishing a learning culture with shared values, reflecting on practice and getting to know the children. The staff were also planning. In this centre there were two groups, an under-twos and an over-twos, and the transition of children from one area to another was carefully planned. Children visited back and forth for as long as was necessary, and a new primary caregiver took over. At staff meetings, therefore, when the focus child was approaching two years old, the staff were planning for a transition from under-twos to over-twos. The under-twos staff shared their knowledge of the child not only with the next primary caregiver but with all the staff. I wrote the following field notes of the planning discussion about Joseph, a child in the under-twos who was about to go into the over-twos programme.

We talked about Joseph and it was a lively discussion that gave an excellent picture of him. Joseph moves out of the baby (under-twos) room next week and they talked about him, passed around four of his stories. . . . Jules reminded them that they were to 'build on his strengths'. They talked about the way he likes to go into small spaces. . . . Fern described how he was trying to unscrew the table legs when she wanted him to eat lunch, so she played a game to get him to put his hands on the table, then she realised he was trying to unscrew the wing nuts with his feet! (Laughter) Jodie pointed out that persistence with difficulty was certainly a characteristic. It was interesting how the discussion see-sawed from negative to positive. . . . Often the adults put themselves in Joseph's place. It was such a rich mixture of care, sharp analysis, humour, anecdote, exasperation – and a greater understanding came from the discussion.

I asked one of the over-twos staff:

The discussion, to what extent do you reckon it helped, particularly those of you who weren't in the baby room, helped you to know how to react with Joseph?
Reply: It was really good. It was really good knowing, so that we could prepare our environment for it (the transition) . . . we're learning strategies to communicate with Joseph.

At the next staff meeting, the under-twos staff wanted to discuss how Joseph had managed when he had joined the older children's programme in the previous two weeks. The staff discussed the way Joseph had coped with the larger group, and talked about how they would like to have more spaces for children to have quiet moments to themselves. They reviewed Joseph's progress at settling in to the bigger room, and comments were made about how Joseph is 'just so big and you expect more', and has difficulty with taking problems 'a step at a time'. Someone added that Joseph loves water. They talked to and fro on the topic, sharing anecdotes, and concluding that trusting the new environment, being able to go back to the under-twos room for a cuddle with staff there, and finding quiet moments and places will assist with the transition and help Joseph to be interested and involved in the over-twos programme.

Concluding Comments

Using the Learning Stories approach to formative assessment, practitioners were deciding what to do next, and planning, in rich and complex ways: sometimes planning for learning dispositions, sometimes planning for a learning place, usually working towards both of these aims at the same time in the spirit of the learner as a learner-in-

action. Educators planned for Rosie's participation in a caring dispositional milieu, for Hugo's involvement in a communicative and collaborative learning place, for Jenny and Natalie's persistence in carpentry
which had become girl-friendly, for Joseph's transition to a programme in which he would feel that he belonged. Much of the time,
the notion of progress was individual, local and intuitive. These
teachers knew the children well and respected their point of view, and
often they engineered their experiences. Further, the trail of participation was carefully documented, and in some cases progress could be
clearly described in web diagrams. Deciding was also about undocumented responding in responsive and reciprocal exchanges, and although this is not usually considered to be assessment, the view of this
chapter was that response styles are a powerful aspect of assessment
that should be congruent with, and can be informed by, documented
assessments.

11

The Learning Story Journey

In Chapter 1, I set out seven assumptions about assessment that I now find to be problematic. The assumptions were about: the *purpose* for assessment (to check against a short list of skills that describe 'competence' for the next stage of education), *outcomes of interest* (fragmented and context-free school-oriented skills), *focus for intervention* or attention (the deficits), *validity* of assessment data (objective observations of skills, reflected in a checklist, are best), *progress* (hierarchies of skill), *procedures* (checklists) and *value* (surveillance of me as a teacher). This book has argued for alternative assumptions and explored ways in which they have been translated into practice, under the general rubric of 'Learning Stories'. The exploration has tried to weave a connection between theory and practice, and Michael Cole has reminded us that this is not a straightforward matter:

> I have been particularly struck by the impact on my ways of theorizing development that ensued when I climbed down out of the researcher's booth and began to take responsibility, as a teacher, for implementing the theories I was proposing and helping the children I was working with. (1996, p. 261)

I was interested in a set of problematic assumptions; the practitioners I worked with were especially interested in practice: they asked questions like 'How can we help Joseph on Monday?' It has therefore been a journey that a number of educators and I have undertaken together. That journey is still in progress: assessment procedures and frameworks will continue to change while curriculum and assessment remain part of *reciprocal* relationships between staff, children, families and the artefacts that are both on top and on tap in the early childhood setting. This chapter looks back over the data and the argument in the book, framed up by specific versions of the two general questions that were asked in Chapter 1:

- How can the Learning Story approach describe early childhood outcomes in ways that make valuable statements about learning and progress?
- How can the Learning Story approach assess early childhood outcomes in ways that promote and protect learning?

In Chapter 1, I outlined my shift in thinking to an alternative set of assumptions about assessment. The early childhood educators whose work is documented in this book have also changed their minds about many aspects of assessment, and in this chapter I consider some of the features of that change, to hazard some answers to the question:

- How were the educators assisted to shift from a folk model of assessment to an alternative model?

Early Childhood Outcomes

How can the Learning Story approach describe early childhood outcomes in ways that make valuable statements about learning and progress? This book has developed some ideas about the nature of learning, adopting the view of James Wertsch and others that learning is sited in action, in the relationship between the workings of the mind on the one hand and the cultural, historical and institutional setting on the other. Five implications for early childhood outcomes have followed from this socio-cultural position on learning and the learner. Firstly, the learner was described as a learner-in-action, to highlight the close interaction between a learner and a learning place. Secondly, I argued, following Barbara Rogoff, that development and learning are about transformation of participation, and that in the light of that theoretical position and the New Zealand experience five features of participation might be valuable to consider: taking an interest, being involved, persisting with difficulty, communicating with others, and taking responsibility. Thirdly, although Rogoff (1997, p. 279) has argued that the participation view of learning focuses on *process* rather than outcome, I have added (from psychology) the concept of a disposition and (from sociology) the concept of a habitus to argue that learning dispositions about participation describe early childhood outcomes in ways that make valuable statements about learning and progress. Another term for a collection of learning dispositions is a participation or participative repertoire. Barbara Comber's study of children going to school, for instance, concluded that:

Their participative repertoires – including their willingness to display their knowledge and to elicit help – meant that they often received the feedback, advice and teaching they needed at exactly the right time. (2000, pp. 43–4)

Fourthly, returning to the key idea that learning is sited within reciprocal relationships, participation repertoires will include children taking a critical approach to the way the centre sets itself up as a learning place. Roy Nash, writing about Bourdieu's approach, described habitus as a *grammar*. He said that:

> habitus is conceived as a grammar making possible the generation of new forms of expression which may alter the structure of the grammar itself (much as speech made possible by grammar itself transforms grammar) and thus provides the possibility of cultural change. (1993, p. 27)

A language or a grammar is a powerful channelling force, but in these changing times children are meeting several grammars – from home and from the early childhood centre, and even within one early childhood setting – and this provides them with some tools for initiating change. Jason was increasing the level of challenge and teaching the others; Danny had changed the power structure in one of the activities; Rosie was taking a role in running the programme. The fifth and final implication for learning outcomes was that learning dispositions were described as a combination of being ready, being willing and being able to participate in an increasing number of settings, in increasingly complex ways. In the Learning Story framework, being ready (the inclination) is usually foregrounded, but being willing (the situation is appropriate) and being able will be the focus of attention at times.

A major feature to emerge from the above analysis therefore was that learning outcomes in early childhood settings are complex and often unexpected. The examples of children learning in Chapters 3, 4 and 5 were testimony to this; the Learning Story framework mirrors this complexity and provides space for the uncertainty. Elliot Eisner has included the following as one of twelve lessons for the new millennium from experience in the past half-century of US education: 'As objectives and standards become more precise they proliferate and when they proliferate, they swamp teachers' capacities to deal with them' (2000, p. 324). He adds that 'whereas objectives may satisfy some aspects of rationality, their number needs to be few and their level of abstraction needs to be broad'. In the Learning Story framework, outcomes are described as five broad domains of disposition, domains which overlap and interact with each other. In innumerable writings, Eisner has argued that teaching is an art, not a science. The Learning Stories framework has attempted to combine an artistic and responsive view of teaching with an informed and carefully considered view of learning outcomes.

The argument that Learning Stories describe early childhood outcomes in ways that make valuable statements about learning and progress must be followed by the question 'Valuable for whom?' The data from the five case study settings, and from others since then, indicate that the description of learning and progress in Learning Stories can be valuable for teachers, for families and for children. Comments by three teachers at a professional development discussion included:

> 'We are listening to children more; our relationships are more intimate.'
> 'I am much more focused and excited about children's work.'
> 'Learning Stories provided positive outcomes – clear direction and focus has increased staff enthusiasm.'

In an appraisal questionnaire about Learning Stories with another group of practitioners, comments included (under Positive Experiences):

> 'More awareness of group dynamics as well.'
> 'Teachers get to know children better – more in-depth knowledge gained.'
> 'Learning Stories are in context.'
> 'Credit rather than deficit based.'
> 'Gives focus to planning.'
> 'Positive feedback from parents – more interesting for parents.'
> 'Positive documentation to share with parents.'

When the same group of practitioners were asked for Difficulties Experienced, the following comments were made:

> 'Untrained staff do not have the foundation to build on. Important to provide training and support for all staff members.'
> 'The need to explain dispositions.'
> 'Time to build up confidence with new assessment system.'
> 'Doesn't follow steps necessarily.'
> 'Changing systems – staff have invested enormous energy in existing systems, often a dramatic change from deficit (gaps) to credit based.'

It appears that the framework has not been so valuable for untrained practitioners, especially if they have not been part of workshops, and that staff need time, energy and commitment to change from one system to another. The Learning Stories were easy to write about outgoing, confident children; a letter from the supervisor in a child-care centre included the comment:

> We are aware how easy it is to do the L/Stories on children like J. and N. However, we are aware that the more valuable L/Stories will be those that we collect on our quieter, less confident children. We've decided to make a conscious effort to view these children consistently.

The staff in a kindergarten that introduced Learning Stories after the original assessment project asked their parents whether they were valuable. Responses included the following comments from four parents:

> 'As a parent, the Learning Stories have given what is seemingly "play" a new perspective.'
> 'The folders also give us something more to discuss with our children and they let us know how they are progressing and what they are achieving.'
> 'The Learning Stories are an invaluable insight into the skills the children are picking up from their time at kindy. Using the children's dialogue is a refreshing approach and one that parents really appreciate.'
> 'We think the Learning Story folder is wonderful because:
>
> - it allows us to get a picture of what J. is doing at kindy and how well he is adjusting in a structured and learning environment;
> - it is a fantastic record of him;
> - it makes the whole family proud – especially J;
> - it is fun – J. enjoys hearing about himself and explaining the stories about himself;
> - we feel a greater bond with the kindergarten and its teachers because they are taking such an interest in our child, and feel so happy that J. is benefiting so much from this;
> - it means that J.'s Dad (who doesn't often get to see J. at kindy) feels involved in J.'s experiences.'

For these parents, the Learning Stories were valuable for a number of reasons. One major reason was to do with the outcomes they record: adjustment in a learning environment, children's dialogue and skills, achievement and progress, giving 'play' a new perspective. A second reason appears to be the feeling of belonging to the centre community that it gave to the families, especially to those members of the family who were seldom able to visit the centre. These comments are similar to the parents' comments from the case study childcare centre, included in Chapter 9.

Over and above the value for educators and families, however, is the view that participation repertoires are valuable for the children now and in the future. The Learning Story framework argues that by laying the foundations for participation (interest, involvement, persistence, communication and responsibility) in the early years we are setting up structures for lifelong learning. The research cited in Chapter 2 supported this position. In similar critical mode, Iram Siraj-Blatchford maintained that:

> by 'laying the foundations' for racial equality in the early years we are making a major investment for future racial harmony and for the development of a confident and well-informed citizenship. We tend to think only of bigger people as citizens or those worthy of teaching important concepts such as justice and equality, yet it is during the early years that the foundations for these attitudes are laid. (1994, pp. xiii–ix)

And Bronwyn Davies (1989, pp. x–xi) contended that her analysis of the dualistic gender order experienced by preschool children 'opened up the possibility for programs of change that may genuinely work'.

Assessment

How can the Learning Story approach assess early childhood outcomes in ways that promote and protect learning? Assessment has been the theme of the second half of the book, which explored issues about assessing complex and elusive outcomes. David Perkins, Eileen Jay and Shari Tishman have commented:

> Yes, dispositions inevitably include reference to things that are genuinely hard to pin down: motivations, affect, sensitivities, values and the like. But these factors exert no less of an influence on behavior simply because they are hard to define, and we have argued that they must figure prominently in a full account of good thinking (*and learning, and assessment* – my addition). (1993, p. 18)

If, as Pamela Moss (1994, p. 6) suggests, 'what isn't assessed tends to disappear from the curriculum', then we have to find a way to assess educational outcomes that we value. Otherwise, outcomes that can be easily measured will take their place. As I commented in Chapter 1, assessment of things that are easy to pin down do not have a proxy for assessment of complex accumulations of outcome like learning dispositions. Chapters 3, 4 and 5 developed nine guidelines for the assessment of complex outcomes like dispositions, and Chapter 6 followed by outlining one way in which learning dispositions have 'figured prominently' in an assessment procedure: the Learning Story approach. Chapters 7, 8, 9 and 10 looked at ways in which practitioners have tried to ensure that the Learning Story approach continues to promote and protect learning by describing, discussing, documenting and deciding.

Learning Story assessments mirror and protect the complexity of learning by using a narrative approach. A second educational lesson for the new millennium from Elliot Eisner (2000, pp. 350–1) is that 'Educationally meaningful assessment requires data derived from the ongoing context in which students learn.' He points out that teachers get to know students in a variety of contexts in a way that no standardised achievement test can replicate, and he adds that:

> (Teachers) are in a position to interpret the quality of the student's questions, the insight of his or her answers, the degree of engagement they display in doing their work, the quality of their relationship with other students, the level of imagination they attain; these and a host of other personal factors are qualities that teachers can know about. These features, as they emerge in classroom life, ought to be a primary source of data for understanding what students are learning and how far they have come along since the beginning of the school year.
>
> As researchers, we need to design practices in which teachers pay systematic attention to such features and prepare short narratives that would provide a much more replete picture of achievement than a B+ or an 82 on a standardized achievement test.

Eisner's argument is about school assessment, but it is exactly the argument in this book. When the focus of interest is action or activity, 'populated by meaning and intentions' and 'tethered to particular contexts' (Graue and Walsh, 1995, p. 148), then the assessment will be sited in everyday settings and look for the perspective of the learner. It will be interpretive, and ethnographic. A standardised achievement-test or checklist method, with a set of universal standards or performance criteria, loses the *action, activity* or *particular context* that provides the link between the individual and the setting. Learning Stories are a window on the meaning that children are constructing as they participate in 'the richness, complexity, and interdependence of events and actions in the real classroom' (Salomon, 1991, p. 16).

Interpretive or ethnographic approaches to understanding children in early childhood settings have a rich history. The early British tradition of closely observing and then interpreting children's behaviour is best illustrated by Susan Isaacs (1932) and Ann Stallibrass (1974), coming from an Eriksonian or psychoanalytic theoretical framework: behaviour was interpreted in terms of individual emotion, a tradition continued in the United States by Vivian Gussin Paley. The next phase of early childhood observational research in the 1970s and 1980s in the United Kingdom had a more cognitive focus: the Oxfordshire studies of children in English nurseries, notably by Kathy Sylva and David Wood (Sylva, Roy and Painter, 1980; Wood, McMahon and Cranstoun, 1980), and the Barbara Tizard and Martin Hughes (1984) study of working class and middle class girls at home and at nursery school (later given a different reading by Valerie Walkerdine and Helen Lucey in 1989). Studies in the 1980s and early 1990s, frequently American or Australian, were more likely to be about action or activity, located within specific cultural and historical practices and time. Examples include William Corsaro (1985), Sally Lubeck (1985), David Fernie (1988; Fernie *et al.*, 1993), Rebecca Kantor (1988), Marianne Bloch and Anthony Pellegrini (1989), Bronwyn Davies (1989) and J. Amos Hatch (1995). None of these studies specifically investigated the process whereby children are constituted and constitute themselves as *learners*, although Fernie and Kantor and others have focused on the process of 'becoming a student'. More recently, Susan Hill and Barbara Comber and their colleagues, Ann Haas Dyson, Ann Filer, Andrew Pollard, Harry Torrance and John Pryor, and others, have used case studies and narrative approaches to study children learning to be pupils, transitions from early childhood to school and from one classroom to another, and the role of assessment in the process. All of these stories about children in real classrooms and early childhood settings have informed and guided the content of this book.

Narrative frameworks, however, especially in the context of assessment, raise questions about validity. The fact that multiple readings or interpretations are possible raises the major question in interpretive studies, and that is 'how is the data accountable'? In 'positivist' and 'post-positivist' psychometric methods of assessment, conventional criteria of rigour are imposed on the collected data: validity, reliability and objectivity. One looks to the coding (for instance) for consistency across places and observers, and to the role of the task and the observer for neutrality. One seeks appropriate levels of probability in the statistics. In interpretive approaches, however, the local and cultural variables are central to the study, and the assessing teacher is part of those local influences. Questions of accountability and generalisability become serious issues. Measures of validity and reliability are replaced by judgements of 'plausibility' and 'trustability' (Walsh, Tobin and Graue, 1993, p. 472). I refer to the process as 'accountability', which includes both 'plausibility' and 'trustability'. How did the Learning Stories process outlined in Chapters 7, 8, 9 and 10 achieve accountability? There are four major ways in which this ought to be done: keeping the data transparent, ensuring that a range of interpreters have their say, refining the constructs as they appear locally, and being clear about the connection between the learner and the environment.

Keeping the data transparent

The data should be as 'transparent' as possible, so that other staff and families have enough information to track and understand the interpretation presented, and to find alternative readings if they want. Statistics and checklists remove that transparency, but the Learning Stories, although they may be summarised for narrative pattern on a planning sheet, stack up as accessible data. What we might call 'interpretive closure' comes as late as possible in the assessment-teaching process, and the audience can therefore follow the trail. Documenting is a key to this, as was apparent in Chapter 10.

Ensuring that a range of interpreters have their say

In the Learning Story process, several staff collect Learning Stories on any one child, and the stories are shared with others as well as with families. Discussing is an important part of the process, and children have their say as well. Staff debate the interpretation, and try to figure out what to do next: deciding together, or co-constructing a possible direction for development. Alan's teachers were all interested in discussing his learning and his progress, and they included Alan's voice in the portfolio collections of photographs, plans and stories.

Refining the constructs as they appear locally

In the describing part of the process, staff were developing a common view of what the constructs (taking an interest, being involved, persisting with difficulty or uncertainty, expressing ideas or feelings, taking responsibility) look like in this local context, and for any one child. Chapter 7 set this out in some detail. Documenting assists too: documented examples can become exemplars, useful for reference later. Of course, as local validity is increased, so claims of reliability across settings become less plausible. For formative assessment this is not an issue, but any external accountability agents will need to be reassured that local validity processes are in place.

Being clear about the connection between the learner and the environment

The relationship between the person being assessed and the other people and the activities in the environment are key features of the assessment. The meeting in which childcare staff discussed Joseph's Learning Stories and planned for his transition to the over-twos programme was an example. Joseph was seen as a learner-in-relationship, and the staff were ensuring that their understanding of the relationships that had been working well in one place would contribute to the planning for relationships in another.

Shifting from a Folk Model of Assessment

How were the educators assisted to shift from a folk model of assessment to an alternative model? The practitioners who have taken on the Learning Story approach to assessment have made a shift in some of the assumptions outlined in Chapter 1. As one of the practitioners said earlier in this chapter, this has often meant 'a dramatic change from deficit (gaps) to credit based'. One practitioner reported that she had been pushed 'out of comfort zone'. A response to a request for Difficulties Experienced was 'convincing people to change old ways'. What assisted them to do this? Skills-based and deficit assumptions about child development are mirrored in technicist and deficit assumptions about teacher development. It was once believed, as Kiri Gould (1997, p. 1) has pointed out:

> that good professional development opportunities for teachers involved transmitting a well organised, well planned, theoretically sound package of knowledge from the expert (the developer) to the learner (the teacher). Once the teacher had learnt the information thoroughly it was assumed that he or she could go away and put this knowledge into practice. Research has shown, however, that effective professional development is far more complex.

Professional development is also about the social and the personal, often a reconstruction about what it means to be a teacher, as Beverley Bell and John Gilbert (1996) have indicated. The system of which an early childhood setting is a part – the families, the management, the Ministry, the external reviewers – exerts pressures on practitioners that frequently prevent them from changing their practice; folk assumptions can become a 'default setting', supported by families whose memories of assessment at school have informed their expectations of assessment in early childhood. School district test directors in the USA were described by Lorrie Shepard in Chapter 1 as having a consistent implicit learning theory that she called the 'criterion-referenced-testing learning theory'. It included two strong beliefs: that tests (in this case, checklists) and curriculum are synonymous, and that learning is linear and sequential. External reviewers can powerfully convey the view that a 'proper teacher' holds these beliefs too, and translates them into assessment practices. Research also indicates that what has been referred to as the 'ownership' of change is also an important factor (Jane Gilbert, 1993), and in 1994 the contributors to an issue of the *Journal of Staff Development* celebrating 25 years of research into staff development consistently commented on the finding that effective staff development is a process that takes *time* (Gould, 1997, p. 10). Research in New Zealand on professional development put into place to support educators implementing a new early childhood curriculum found that time was important to the success of the programmes, citing six months to a year as the minimum ongoing involvement for facilitators (Foote, Irvine and Turnbull, 1996; Gaffney and Smith, 1997). Long-term professional development programmes include opportunities for discussion, trial and error, and reflection on what is working and what is not, in a safe environment where, I might add, persistence with difficulty and uncertainty is part of the dispositional milieu. In New Zealand, government-funded professional development programmes designed to support the implementation of the early childhood curriculum have frequently been the source of practitioners' learning about the Learning Story approach, and these programmes have often been long term.

On the personal front, many practitioners seized opportunities to explore their assumptions, and to take ownership of the change process. Some Learning Story workshops have focused on where the old assumptions have come from, and participants have reviewed old child development texts and shared experiences of being assessed at school. A National Children's Bureau workshop package on assessment (Drummond, Rouse and Pugh, 1992), designed to surface assumptions and feelings about making judgements and doing assessment, has provided useful workshop ideas. In the assessment project, the researchers, professional developers and educators in early childhood settings took a flexible view of the 'Learning Story' approach. New formats and local definitions emerged, developed by practitioners or from their ideas. On the social front, early childhood educators have a tradition of working collaboratively, discussing ideas and making decisions together. The change process followed that tradition, as the discussions in Chapters 7, 8, 9 and 10 illustrated. On the professional front, it is important for staff to see new practices in action in other settings, so that they can borrow and adapt and reject alternatives. At the end of the assessment project, three videos ('What to assess', 'Why assess' and 'How to assess'; Carr, 1998b) were made in the five case study settings. The examples in real settings have been helpful for educators trying out ideas in their own context; the videos illustrate a diversity of practice. The video package included an accompanying booklet of four workshops. The workshops include overheads of discussion questions, handouts for reflection, quotes for debate and seven short readings. They were designed to encourage debate and discussion. In Chapter 7, I suggested that there were several phases for the introduction of Learning Stories. The first phase was enthusiasm over permission to record and share *positive* experiences. The second phase was to structure those observations, drawing on the specifics of local opportunities and programmes. The development of the formats, in Chapter 10, indicated an increasing interest in what one staff team called 'pinpointing stuff'. The stories became more focused, and change in children's learning over time could be monitored more clearly.

But professional development and change is not just about effective ways of learning how to implement new policies or make changes. It is also about legitimacy and power in the wider system, beyond the early childhood setting (Broadfoot, 1996a, 1996b; Firestone, Fitz and Broadfoot, 1999). The Learning Story practitioners in this book were assisted by a national curriculum framed up by five strands: belonging, well-being, exploration, communication and contribution. This has given legitimacy to the idea of learning as participation. The national curriculum document also calls on a Bronfenbrenner model of learning, emphasising the connection between the learner and the learning environment. The section introducing learning outcomes comments that knowledge, skills and attitudes are closely linked together as working theories and learning dispositions.

Perhaps a key feature has been the acceptance by or inclusion of all the audiences or stakeholders. The later phases of implementing new assessment formats have included a wider network of audiences: arranging for parents to be involved, and consulting children. When the families were interested and appreciative, this encouraged the practitioners. In one centre the practitioners reported that their enthusiasm was considerably boosted by admiration from a parent who was also a primary school teacher. On the whole, external reviewers have taken a 'wait and see' approach to innovative assessment formats; a recent publication included the comment:

> The 'learning stories' approach leads staff to draw connections between their observations and the main dimensions of the early childhood curriculum. Where this is done well it provides good insight into the child as a learner and is useful for programme development. In other cases the links between the records of observation and intended programme are not developed. (Education Review Office, 2000, p. 7)

Other audiences, with less power (colleagues and children), were also important to the practitioners. Finding time as a staff team to work together, to share ideas, was described by practitioners as 'critical'; having no staff meeting time, staff changes and untrained staff were described as difficulties. Consulting with the children was not always easy when the ratios were high, although the case study kindergarten (with 44 children and three teachers) had managed this by their process of using a polaroid camera and seeking comments on photographs and plans. Wall displays of Stories, photographs and drawings provided ready-to-hand opportunities for discussion.

Concluding comments

The original Project for Assessing Children's Experiences contributed only a part of the Learning Story story. This book weaves the work of the project with an analysis of children's learning that underpins a narrative approach, and includes other research. It has been informed by the writers who have gone before and by the many practitioners and professional development facilitators who have now picked up the Learning Story approach to assessment and made it their own. When I asked one early childhood staff team whether they had made any changes to the Learning Story process one of them replied: 'Well, we live a Learning Story here' and they explained that they take on an aspect of practice that interests them, get involved with investigating it, persist with the difficulties, discuss it together, and then take joint responsibility to make changes. They had been exploring a number of different ways to 'house' the Learning Stories, and they had developed a system of robust folders with the children's name down the spine, filed in a bookcase in the centre. After a discussion between one of the staff and one of the children about her achievements in the outside play area, the child went inside and looked through her folder, reporting back that there was no story about her ability to climb to the top of the 'cargo' net, an achievement of a few days earlier that she had greatly valued. They wrote one together. These lively records of learning, enhanced by collaborative describing, documenting, discussing and deciding, have continued to enrich my view of learning outcomes in early childhood. Translating them into assessments stretches our imaginative and practical powers to the limit. Work on formative assessment in early childhood settings is in its infancy. I hope that the ideas, examples, guidelines and processes outlined here will provide a platform for further dialogue and development.

References

Ames, C. (1992) Classrooms: goals, structures, and student motivation. *Journal of Educational Psychology*, 84(3), pp. 61–71.

Astington, J. W. (1993) *The Child's Discovery of the Mind*. Cambridge, Mass.: Harvard University Press.

Athey, C. (1990) *Extending Thought in Young Children – a Parent–Teacher Partnership*. London: Paul Chapman.

Beattie, M. (1995a) New prospects for teacher education: narrative ways of knowing teaching and teacher learning. *Educational Research*, 37(1), pp. 53–70.

Beattie, M. (1995b) The making of a music: the construction and reconstruction of a teacher's personal practical knowledge during inquiry. *Curriculum Inquiry*, 25(2), pp. 133–50.

Bell, B. and Gilbert, J. (1996) *Teacher Development: a Model from Science Education*. London: Falmer.

Black, P. and Wiliam, D. (1998) Assessment and classroom learning. *Assessment in Education*, 5(1), pp. 7–74.

Blatchford, P., Burke, J., Farquhar, C., Plewis, I. and Tizard, B. (1989) Teacher expectations in infant school: associations with attainment and progress. *British Journal of Educational Psychology*, 59, pp. 19–30.

Blenkin, G. and Kelly, A. V. (eds) (1992) *Assessment in Early Childhood Education*. London: Paul Chapman.

Bloch, M. N. and Pellegrini, A. D. (eds) (1989) *The Ecological Context of Children's Play*. Norwood, NJ.: Ablex.

Bourdieu, P. (1990) *In other Words: Essays Towards a Reflexive Sociology*. Stanford: Stanford University Press.

Bourdieu, P. (1984/1993) *Sociology in Question*. 1993 English translation by Richard Nice. London: Sage.

Bredekamp, S. and Rosegrant, T. (1992) Reaching potentials through appropriate curriculum: conceptual frameworks for applying the guidelines. In S. Bredekamp and T. Rosegrant (eds) *Reaching Potentials: Appropriate Curriculum and Assessment for Young Children*. Vol 1. Washington DC: National Association for the Education of Young Children.

Bredekamp, S. and Shepard, L. (1989) How best to protect children from inappropriate school expectations, practices, and policies. *Young Children*, 44(3), pp. 14–34.

Briggs, R. (1978) *The Snowman*. London: Hamish Hamilton.

Broadfoot, P. (1996a) Assessment and learning: power or partnership? In H. Goldstein and T. Lewis (eds) *Assessment: Problems, Developments and Statistical Issues*. Chichester: John Wiley.

Broadfoot, P. (1996b) *Education, Assessment and Society*. Buckingham: Open University Press.

Broberg, A. G., Wessels, H., Lamb, M. E. and Hwang, C. P. (1997) Effects of day care on the development of cognitive abilities in 8-year-olds: a longitudinal study. *Developmental Psychology*, 33(1), pp. 62–9.

Bronfenbrenner, U. (1979) *The Ecology of Human Development*. Cambridge, Mass.: Harvard University Press.

Brown, A. L., Ash, D., Rutherford, M., Nakagawa, K., Gordon, A. and Campione, J. C. (1993) Distributed expertise in the classroom. In G. Salomon (ed.) *Distributed Cognitions: Psychological and Educational Considerations*. Cambridge: Cambridge University Press.

Bruna, Dick (1962) *The Little Bird*. London: Methuen Children's Books.

Bruner, J. (1983) *Child's Talk: Learning to Use Language*. New York: Norton.

Bruner, J. (1986) *Actual Minds: Possible Worlds*. Cambridge, Mass.: Harvard University Press.

Bruner, J. (1990) *Acts of Meaning*. Cambridge, Mass.: Harvard University Press.

Bruner, J. (1996) *The Culture of Education*. Cambridge, Mass.: Harvard University Press.

Carr, M. (1987) A preschool 'drill' for problem-solving. *Investigating*, 3(1), pp. 3–5.

Carr, M. (1997) Persistence when it's difficult: a disposition to learn for early childhood. *Early Childhood Folio*. Wellington: NZCER.

Carr, M. (1998a) *Assessing Children's Experiences in Early Childhood: Final Report to the Ministry of Education*. Wellington: Ministry of Education.

Carr, M. (1998b) *Assessing Children's Experiences in Early Childhood*. Three videos and a Workshop Booklet for Practitioners. Wellington: NZCER.

Carr, M. (2000a) Seeking children's perspectives about their learning. In A. B. Smith and N. J. Taylor (eds) *Children's Voice: Research, Policy and Practice*. Auckland: Addison Wesley Longman.

Carr, M. (2000b) Technological affordance, social practice and learning narratives in an early childhood setting. *International Journal of Technology and Design Education*, 10, pp. 61–79.

Carr, M. (2001) Emerging learning narratives: a perspective from early childhood. In G. Wells and G. Claxton (eds) *Learning for Life in the 21st Century: Sociocultural Perspectives on the Future of Education*. Oxford: Blackwell.

Carr, M., and Claxton, G. (1989) The costs of calculation. *New Zealand Journal of Educational Studies*, 24(2), pp. 129–40.

Carr, M. and Cowie, B. (1997) *Assessment: Why Record*. Position Paper Four. Project for Assessing Children's Experiences. Hamilton: University of Waikato.

Carr, M., and May, H. (1993) Choosing a model. Reflecting on the development process of Te Whariki: national early childhood curriculum guidelines in New Zealand. *International Journal of Early Years Education*, 1(3), pp. 7–21.

Carr, M. and May, H. (1994) Weaving patterns: developing national early childhood curriculum guidelines in Aotearoa-New Zealand. *Australian Journal of Early Childhood*, 19(1) pp. 25–33.

Carr, M. and May, H. (2000) Te Whariki: Curriculum Voices. In H. Penn (ed.) *Theory, Policy and Practice in Early Childhood Services*. Buckingham: Open University Press.

Carr, M., May, H., Podmore, V., Cubey, P., Hatherly, A. and Macartney, B. (2000) *Learning and Teaching Stories: Action Research on Evaluation in Early Childhood*. Final Report to the Ministry of Education. Wellington: New Zealand Council for Educational Research.

Clandinin, D. J. and Connelly, F. M. (1990) Narrative, experience and the study of curriculum. *Cambridge Journal of Education*, 20(3), pp. 241–53.

Claxton, G. (1990) *Teaching to Learn*. London: Cassell.

Cole, M. (1996) *Cultural Psychology: a Once and Future Discipline*. Cambridge, Mass.: Harvard University Press.

Comber, B. (2000) What really counts in early literacy lessons. *Language Arts*, 78(1) pp. 39–49.

Connelly, F. M. and Clandinin, D. J. (1988) *Teachers as Curriculum Planners: Narratives of Experience*. New York: Teachers College Press.

Connelly, F. M. and Clandinin, D. J. (1990) Stories of experience and narrative inquiry. *Educational Researcher*, 19(5 (June–July)), pp. 2–14.

Connelly, F. M. and Clandinin, D. J. (1995) Narrative and education. *Teachers and Teaching: Theory and Practice*, 1(1), pp. 73–85.

Corsaro, W. A. (1985) *Friendship and Peer Culture in the Early Years*. Norwood, NJ: Ablex.

Crnic, K. and Lamberty, G. (1994) Reconsidering school readiness: conceptual and applied perspectives. *Early Education and Development*, 5(2), pp. 91–105.

Cross, S. E. and Marcus, H. R. (1994) Self-schemas, possible selves, and competent performance. *Journal of Educational Psychology*, 86(3), pp. 423–38.

Csikszentmihalyi, M. (1991) *Flow: the Psychology of Optimal Experience*. New York: Harper Collins.

Csikszentmihalyi, M. (1996) *Creativity: Flow and the Psychology of Discovery and Invention*. New York: Harper Collins.

Csikszentmihalyi, M. (1997) *Finding Flow: the Psychology of Engagement with Everyday Life*. New York: Basic Books.

Csikszentmihalyi, M. and Rathunde, K. (1992) The measurement of flow in everyday life: toward a theory of emergent motivation. In J. J. Jacobs (ed.) *Developmental Perspectives of Motivation. Nebraska Symposium on Motivation Vol. 40*. Lincoln: University of Nebraska Press.

Cullen, J. (1991) Young children's learning strategies: continuities and discontinuities. *International Journal of Early Childhood*, 23(1), pp. 44–58.

Dahlberg, G., Moss, P. and Pence, A. (1999) *Beyond Quality in Early Childhood Education and Care: Postmodern Perspectives*. London: Falmer.

Davies, B. (1989) *Frogs and Snails and Feminist Tales: Preschool Children and Gender*. Sydney: Allen and Unwin.

Donaldson, M. (1992) *Human Minds*. London: The Penguin Press.

Drummond, M. J. (1993) *Assessing Children's Learning*. London: David Fulton.

Drummond, M. J. (1999) Comparisons in Early Years Education: history, fact and fiction. CREPE Occasional Paper. University of Warwick, Centre for Research in Elementary and Primary Education.

Drummond, M. J. and Nutbrown, C. (1992) Observing and assessing young children. In G. Pugh (ed.) *Contemporary Issues in the Early Years*. London: Paul Chapman and National Children's Bureau.

Drummond, M. J., Rouse, D. and Pugh, G. (1992) *Making Assessment Work: Values and Principles in Assessing Young Children's Learning*. London and Nottingham: National Children's Bureau and NES Arnold.

Dunn, J. (1993) *Young Children's Close Relationships*. London: Sage.

Dweck, C. S. (1985) Intrinsic motivation, perceived control, and self-evaluation maintenance: an achievement goal analysis. In C. Ames and R. Ames (eds) *Research on Motivation in Education (Vol. 2: The Classroom Milieu)*. San Diego: Academic Press.

Dweck, C. S. (1999) *Self-theories: Impact on Motivation, Personality and Development*. Philadelphia, PA: Taylor & Francis (Psychology Press).

Dweck, C. S. and Reppucci, N. D. (1973) Learned helplessness and reinforcement responsibility in children. *Journal of Personality and Social Psychology*, 54, pp. 109–16.

Dyson, A. H. (1989) *Multiple Worlds of Child Writers: Friends Learning to Write*. New York: Teachers College Press.

Dyson, A. H. (1993) *The Social Worlds of Children Learning to Write in an Urban Primary School*. New York: Teachers College Press.

Dyson, A. H. (1997) Children out of bounds: the power of case studies in expanding visions of literacy development. In J. Flood, S. B. Heath and D. Lapp (eds) *Handbook of Research on Teaching Literacy Through the Communicative and Visual Arts*. New York: Simon & Schuster Macmillan, pp. 167–80.

Education Review Office (2000) *Early Literacy and Numeracy: the Use of Assessment to Improve Programmes for Four to Six Year Olds*. Wellington: Education Review Office.

Edwards, P. (1996) *Livingstone Mouse*. New York: Harper Collins.

Edwards, C., Gandini, L. and Forman, G. (eds) (1993) *The Hundred Languages of Children: the Reggio Emilia Approach to Early Education*. Norwood, NJ: Ablex.

Egan, K. (1993) Narrative and learning: a voyage of implications. *Linguistics and Education*, 5, pp. 119–26.

Egan, K. (1996) The development of understanding. In D. R. Olson and N. Torrance (eds) *The Handbook of Education and Human Development*. London: Blackwell.

Egan, K. (1997) *The Educated Mind: How Cognitive Tools Shape our Understanding*. Chicago: University of Chicago Press.

Eisner, E. (2000) Those who ignore the past . . .: 12 'easy' lessons for the next millenium. *Journal of Curriculum Studies*, 32(2) pp. 343–57.

Fernie, D. E. (1988) Becoming a student: messages from first settings. *Theory into Practice*, XXVII(1), pp. 3–10.

Fernie, D. E., Davies, B., Kantor, R. and McMurray, P. (1993) Becoming a person in the preschool: creating integrated gender, school culture, and peer culture positionings. *Qualitative Studies in Education*, 6(2), pp. 95–110.

Filer, A. (1993) The assessment of classroom language: challenging the rhetoric of 'objectivity'. *International Studies in Sociology of Education*, 3, pp. 183–212.

Filer, A. and Pollard, A. (2000) *The Social World of Pupil Assessment: Processes and Contexts of Primary Schooling*. London: Continuum.

Firestone, W. A., Fitz, J. and Broadfoot, P. (1999) Power, learning and legitimation: assessment implementation across levels in the United States and the United Kingdom. *American Educational Research Journal*, 36(4) pp. 759–93.

Foote, L., Irvine, P. and Turnbull, A. (1996) Professional Development Programmes for Curriculum Implementation in Early Childhood. Paper presented at the New Zealand Council for Educational Research Conference, June.

Forman, G. and Gandini, L. (1995) *An Amusement Park for the Birds* [Videotape]. Amherst, Mass.: Performanetics.

Foucault, M. (1979) *Discipline and Punish*. London: Allen Lane.

Frome, P. M. and Eccles, J. S. (1998) Parents' influence on children's achievement-related perceptions. *Journal of Personality and Social Psychology*, 74(2) pp. 435–52.

Gaffney, M. and Smith, A. B. (1997) An Evaluation of Pilot Early Childhood Professional Development Programmes to Support Curriculum Implementation. Report to the Ministry of Education. Dunedin: Children's Issues Centre.

Gallas, K. (1994) *The Languages of Learning: How Children Talk, Write, Dance, Draw and Sing their Understanding of the World*. New York: Teachers College Press.

Gardner, H. (1983) *Frames of Mind*. 2nd edition. London: Fontana.

Genishi, C. (ed) (1992) *Ways of Assessing Children and Curriculum: Stories of Early Childhood Practice*. New York: Teachers College Press.

Gettinger, M. and Stoiber, K. C. (1998) Critical incident recording: a procedure for monitoring children's performance and maximizing progress in inclusive settings. *Early Childhood Education Journal*, 26(1), pp. 39–46.

Gilbert, Jane (1993) Teacher development: a literature review. In B. Bell (ed.) *I Know About LISP But How Do I Put It Into Practice?* Hamilton, New Zealand: Centre for Science and Mathematics Education Research, University of Waikato.

Gipps, C. (1999) Socio-cultural aspects of assessment. In A. Iran-Nejad and P. D. Pearson (eds) *Review of Research in Education 24*, Washington, AERA, pp. 355–92.

Goodenow, C. (1992) Strengthening the links between educational psychology and the study of social contexts. *Educational Psychologist*, 27(2), pp. 177–96.

Goodnow, J. (1990) The socialization of cognition: what's involved? In J. W. Stigler, R. A. Shweder and G. Herdt (eds) *Cultural Psychology*. Cambridge: Cambridge University Press, pp. 259–86.

Gould, K. E. (1997) *Teacher Professional Development: a Literature Survey*. Position Paper Four. Project for Assessing Children's Experiences. Hamilton: University of Waikato.

Graue, M. E. and Walsh, D. J. (1995) Children in context: interpreting the here and now of children's lives. In J. A. Hatch (ed), *Qualitative Research in Early Childhood Settings*. Westport, Connecticut: Praeger, pp. 135–54.

Gudmundsdottir, S. (1991) Story-maker, story-teller: narrative structures in curriculum. *Journal of Curriculum Studies*, 23(3), pp. 207–18.

Hatch, J. A. (ed.) (1995) *Qualitative Research in Early Childhood Settings*. Westport, Connecticut: Praeger.

Heyman, G. D. and Dweck, C. S. (1998) Children's thinking about traits: implications for judgments of the self and others. *Child Development*, 64(2), pp. 391–403.

Hickey, D. T. (1997) Motivation and contemporary socio-constructivist instructional perspectives. *Educational Psychologist*, 32(3), pp. 175–193.

Hidi, S., Renninger, K. A. and Krapp, A. (1992) The present state of interest research. In S. Hidi, K. A. Renninger and A. Krapp (eds) *The Role of Interest in Learning and Development*. Hillsdale, NJ: Lawrence Erlbaum.

Hill, E. (1985) *Spot at the Farm*. London: William Heinemann.

Hill, S., Comber, B., Louden, W., Rivalland, J. and Reid, J. (1998) *100 Children Go to School: Connections and Disconnections in Literacy Development in the Year Prior to School and the First Year of School*. Canberra, ACT: DEETYA.

Hohmann, M., Banet, B. and Weikart, D. P. (1979) *Young Children in Action: a Manual for Pre-School Educators*. Ypsilanti, MI: High/Scope Education Research Foundation.

Howard, S. and Johnson, B. (1999) Tracking student resilience. *Children Australia* 24(3), pp. 14–23.

Howes, C., Matheson, C. C. and Hamilton, C. E. (1994) Maternal, teacher, and child care history correlates of children's relationships with peers. *Child Development*, 65, pp. 264–73.

Hunt, K. (1999) Respecting the wisdom of a young child in grief. Paper presented at The Third Warwick International Early Years Conference, 12–16 April.

Inagaki, K. (1992) Piagetian and post-Piagetian conceptions of development and their implications for science education in early childhood. *Early Childhood Research Quarterly*, 7(1), pp. 115–33.

Isaacs, S. (1932) *The Nursery Years: the Mind of the Child from Birth to Six Years*. London: Routledge and Kegan Paul.

James, M. and Gipps, C. (1998) Broadening the basis of assessment to prevent the narrowing of learning. *The Curriculum Journal*, 9(3) pp. 285–97.

Jones, E. and Reynolds, G. (1992) *The Play's the Thing: Teachers' Roles in Children's Play*. New York: Teachers College Press.

Kantor, R. (1988) Creating school meaning in preschool curriculum. *Theory into Practice*, XXVII(1), pp. 25–35.

Kantor, R., Green, J., Bradley, M. and Lin, L. (1992) The construction of schooled discourse repertoires: an interactional sociolinguistic perspective on learning to talk in preschool. *Linguistics and Education*, 4, pp. 131–72.

Katz, L. G. (1988) What should young children be doing? *American Educator* (Summer), pp. 29–45.

Katz, L. G. (1993) *Dispositions: Definitions and Implications for Early Childhood Practices*. Perspectives from ERIC/ECCE: a monograph series. Urbana, Illinois: ERIC Clearinghouse on ECCE.

Katz, L. G. (1995) The distinction between self-esteem and narcissism: implications for practice. In L. G. Katz (ed.) *Talks with Teachers of Young Children: a collection*. Norwood, NJ: Ablex.

Kelly, A. V. (1992) Concepts of assessment: an overview. In G. Blenkin and A. V. Kelly (eds) *Assessment in Early Childhood Education*. London: Paul Chapman.

Knupfer, A. M. (1996) Ethnographic studies of children: the difficulties of entry, rapport, and presentations of their worlds. *Qualitative Studies in Education*, 9(2) pp. 135–49.

Krechevsky, M. (1994) *Project Spectrum: Preschool Assessment Handbook*. Cambridge, Mass.: Project Zero at the Harvard University Graduate School of Education.

Laevers, F. (1994) *The Leuven Involvement Scale for Young Children*. Leuven, Belgium: Centre for Experiential Education.

Laevers, F., Vandenbussche, E., Kog, M. and Depondt, L. (n.d.) *A Process-oriented Child Monitoring System for Young Children*. Experiential Education Series, No. 2. Leuven, Belgium: Centre for Experiential Education.

Lather, P. (1993) Fertile obsession: validity after post structuralism. *Sociological Quarterly*, 34(4), pp. 673–93.

Lave, J. and Wenger, E. (1991) *Situated Learning: Legitimate Peripheral Participation*. Cambridge: Cambridge University Press.

Litowitz, B. E. (1993) Deconstruction in the zone of proximal development. In E. A. Forman, N. Minick and C. A. Stone (eds) *Contexts for Learning: Sociocultural Dynamics in Children's Development*. Oxford and London: Oxford University Press.

Litowitz, B. E. (1997) Just say no: responsibility and resistance. In M. Cole, Y. Engeström and O. Vasquez (eds) *Mind, Culture, and Activity: Seminal Papers from the Laboratory of Comparative Human Cognition*. Cambridge: Cambridge University Press.

Lubeck, S. (1985) *Sandbox Society. Early Education in Black and White America: a Comparative Ethnology*. London: Falmer.

Lyle, S. (2000) Narrative understanding: developing a theoretical context for understanding how children make meaning in classroom settings. *Journal of Curriculum Studies* 32(1), pp. 45–63.

Marcus, H. and Nurius, P. (1986) Possible selves. *American Psychologist*, September, pp. 954–69.

Marshall, H. (1992) *Redefining Student Learning: Roots of Educational Change*. Norwood: Ablex.

Merritt, S. and Dyson, A. H. (1992) A social perspective on informal assessment: voices, texts, pictures, and play from a first grade. In C. Genishi (ed.) *Ways of Assessing Children and Curriculum: Stories of Early Childhood Practice*. New York: Teachers College Press.

Middleton, S. and May, H. (1997) *Teachers Talk Teaching 1915–1995: Early Childhood, Schools, and Teachers' Colleges*. Palmerston North: Dunmore.

Moll, L. C., Amanti, C., Neff, D. and Gonzales, N. (1992) Funds of knowledge for teaching: using a qualitative approach to connect homes and classrooms. *Theory into Practice*, 31(2) pp. 132–41.

Monk, G., Winslade, J., Crocket, K. and Epston, D. (eds) (1997) *Narrative Therapy in Practice: the Archaeology of Hope*. San Francisco: Jossey-Bass.

Montessori, M. (1965) *The Montessori Method: Scientific Pedagogy as Applied to Child Education in 'the Children's Houses' with Additions and Revisions by the Author*. Cambridge, Mass.: R. Bentley. Translated from the Italian by A. E. George. Originally published in 1912.

Moore, C. and Dunham, P. J. (eds) (1992) *Joint Attention: Its Origins and Role in Development*. Hillsdale, NJ: Lawrence Erlbaum.

Moss, P. A. (1994) Can there be validity without reliability? *Educational Researcher*, March, pp. 5–12.

Nash, R. (1993) *Succeeding Generations: Family Resources and Access to Education in New Zealand*. Auckland: Oxford University Press.

Nelson, K. (1986) *Event Knowledge: Structure and Function in Development*. NJ: Lawrence Erlbaum.

Nelson, K. (1997) Cognitive change as collaborative construction. In E. Amsel and K. A. Renninger (eds) *Change and Development: Issues of Theory, Method and Application*. Mahwah, NJ and London: Erlbaum.

New Zealand Ministry of Education (1996a) *Te Whāriki. He Whāriki Mātauranga mō– ngā– Mokopuna o Aotearoa: Early Childhood Curriculum*. Wellington: Learning Media.

New Zealand Ministry of Education (1996b) Revised Statement of Desirable Objectives and Practices (DOPs) for Chartered Early Childhood services in New Zealand. *The New Zealand Gazette*, 3 October.

Nisbet, J. and Shucksmith, J. (1986) *Learning Strategies*. London: Routledge and Kegan Paul.

Noddings, N. (1984) *Caring: a Feminine Approach to Ethics and Moral Education*. Berkeley, California: University of California Press.

Noddings, N. (1995) Teaching themes of care. *Phi Delta Kappan*, 76(9), pp. 675–9.

Nsamenang, A. Bame and Lamb, M. E. (1998) Socialization of Nso children in the Bamenda grassfields of northwestern Cameroon. In M. Woodhead, D. Faulkner and K. Littleton (eds) *Cultural Worlds of Early Childhood*. London and New York: Routledge in association with The Open University.

Nutbrown, C. (1994) *Threads of Thinking: Young Children Learning and the Role of Early Education*. London: Paul Chapman.

Olson, D. R and Bruner, J. S. (1996) Folk psychology and folk pedagogy. In D. R. Olson and N. Torrance (eds) *The Handbook of Education and Human Development: New Models of Learning, Teaching and Schooling*. London: Blackwell.

Paley, V. G. (1986) On listening to what the children say. *Harvard Educational Review*. 56(2), pp. 122–31.

Paley, V. G. (1988) *Bad Guys Don't have Birthdays: Fantasy Play at Four*. Cambridge, Mass.: Harvard University Press.

Paley, V. G. (1992) *You Can't Say You Can't Play*. Cambridge, Mass.: Harvard University Press.

Papert, S. (1980) *Mindstorms*. Brighton: Harvester.

Papert, S. (1993) *The Children's Machine: Rethinking School in the Age of the Computer*. Hemel Hempstead: Harvester Wheatsheaf.

Pascal, C., Bertram, A., Ramsden, F., Georgeson, J., Saunders, M. and Mould, C. (1995) *Evaluating and Developing Quality in Early Childhood Settings: a Professional Development Programme*. Effective Early Learning Project. Worcester: Worcester College of Higher Education.

Pascal, C. and Bertram, A. (1998) The AcE project: accounting for life long learning. In L. Abbott and H. Moylett (eds) *Early Childhood Reformed*. London: Falmer.

Perkins, D. (1992) *Smart Schools: Better Thinking and Learning for Every Child*. New York: The Free Press.

Perkins, D. N., Jay, E. and Tishman, S. (1993) Beyond abilities: a dispositional theory of thinking. *Merrill-Parker Quarterly*, 39, 1 January, pp. 1–21.

Piaget, J. (1954) *The Construction of Reality in the Child*. New York: Basic Books.

Pollard, A. (1996) *The Social World of Children's Learning: Case Studies of Pupils from Four to Seven*. London: Cassell.

Pollard, A. and Filer, A. (1999) *The Social World of Pupil Career: Strategic Biographies Through Primary School*. London: Cassell.

Pratt, D. (1994) *Curriculum Planning: a Handbook for Professionals*. Fort Worth: Harcourt Brace.

Resnick, L. B. (1987) *Education and Learning to Think*. Washington, DC: National Academy Press.

Rogoff, B. (1990) *Apprenticeship in Thinking: Cognitive Development in Social Context*. Oxford and New York: Oxford University Press.

Rogoff, B. (1997) Evaluating development in the process of participation: theory, methods, and practice building on each other. In E. Amsel and K. Ann Renninger (eds) *Change and Development: Issues of Theory, Method and Application*. Mahwah, NJ and London: Erlbaum.

Rogoff, B. (1998) Cognition as a collaborative process. In William Damon (ed.) *Handbook of Child Psychology*. Fifth Edition. Vol. 2. Cognition, Perception and Language. (Volume Editors: Deanna Kuhn and Robert S. Siegler.) New York: John Wiley, pp. 679–744.

Rogoff, B., Mistry, J., Goncu, A. and Mosier, C. (1993) *Guided Participation in Cultural Activity by Toddlers and Caregivers*. Monographs of the Society for Research in Child Development Serial No. 236, 58(8).

Rose, Nikolas (1999) *Governing the Soul: the Shaping of the Private Self*. 2nd edition (first edition 1989). London and New York: Free Association Books.

Salomon, G. (1991) Transcending the Qualitative–Quantitative Debate: the analytic and systemic approaches to educational research. *Educational Researcher* (Aug–Sept), pp. 10–18.

Salomon, G. (1993) Editor's introduction. In G. Salomon (ed) *Distributed Cognitions: Psychological and Educational Considerations*. Cambridge: Cambridge University Press.

Schweinhart, L. J. and Weikart, D. P. (1993) *A Summary of Significant Benefits: the High Scope Perry Pre-School Study through Age 27*. Ypsilanti, MI: High Scope.

Sheldon, A. (1992) Conflict talk: sociolinguistic challenges to self-assertion and how young girls meet them. *Merrill-Palmer Quarterly*, 38(1), pp. 95–117.

Shepard, L. A. (1991) Psychometricians' beliefs about learning. *Educational Researcher*, 20(6) pp. 2–16.

Siraj-Blatchford, I. (1994) *The Early Years: Laying the Foundations for Racial Equality*. Stoke-on-Trent: Trentham.

Skerrett-White, M. (1998) Case Study Four: Te Kōhanga Reo Case Study. In M. Carr, *Assessing Children's Experiences in Early Childhood: Final Report to the Ministry of Education*, Part 2: The Case Studies. Wellington: Ministry of Education.

Smiley, P. A. and Dweck, C. S. (1994) Individual differences in achievement goals among young children. *Child Development*, 65, pp. 1723–43.

Smith, A. B. (1992) Early childhood educare: seeking a theoretical framework in Vygotsky's work. *International Journal of Early Years Education*, 1, pp. 47–61.

Smith, A. B. (1999) Quality childcare and joint attention. *International Journal of Early Years Education*, 7(1) pp. 85–98.

Stallibrass, A. (1974) *The Self-Respecting Child: A Study of Children's Play and Development*. London: Thames and Hudson.

Sylva, K. (1994) School influences on children's development. *Journal of Child Psychology and Psychiatry*, 34(1), pp. 135–70.

Sylva, K., Roy, C. and Painter, M. (1980) *Childwatching at Playgroup and Nursery School*. London: Grant McIntyre.

Taylor, P. C. (1998) Constructivism: value added. In B. J. Fraser and K. G. Tobin (eds) *International Handbook of Science Education Part Two*. Dordrecht: Kluwer Academic Publishers.

Thompson, J. B. (1991) Editor's introduction. In P. Bourdieu, *Language and Symbolic Power*. Cambridge, Mass.: Harvard University Press.

Tizard, B. and Hughes, M. (1984) *Young Children Learning*. London: Fontana.

Torrance, H. and Pryor, J. (1998) *Investigating Formative Assessment: Teaching, Learning and Assessment in the Classroom*. Buckingham: Open University Press.

Turkle, S. and Papert, S. (1992) Epistemological pluralism and the revaluation of the concrete. *Journal of Mathematical Behavior*, 11, pp. 3–33.

Vygotsky, L. S. (1978) *Mind in Society: the Development of Higher Psychological Processes*. Edited by M. Cole, V. John-Steiner, S. Scribner and E. Souberman. Translated by A. R. Luria, M. Lopez-Morillas, M. Cole and J. Wertsch. Cambridge, Mass.: Harvard University Press.

Walkerdine, V. and Lucey, H. (1989) *Democracy in the Kitchen: Regulating Mothers and Socialising Daughters*. London: Virago.

Walsh, D. J., Tobin, J. J. and Graue, M. E. (1993) The interpretive voice: qualitative research in early childhood education. In B. Spodek (ed.) *Handbook of Research on the Education of Young Children*. New York: MacMillan.

Weinstein, R. (1989) Perceptions of classroom processes and student motivation: children's views of self-fulfilling prophecies. In C. Ames and R. Ames (eds) *Research on Motivation in Education Volume 3: Goals and Cognitions*. San Diego: Academic Press.

Wellman, H. M. (1990) *The Child's Theory of Mind*. Cambridge, Mass.: The MIT Press.

Wells, G. (1985) *Language Development in the Preschool Years*. Cambridge: Cambridge University Press.

Wertsch, J. V. (1991) *Voices of the Mind: a Sociocultural Approach to Mediated Action*. Cambridge, Mass.: Harvard University Press.

Whalley, M. (1994) *Learning to be Strong: Setting Up a Neighbourhood Service for Under-Fives and their Families*. Sevenoaks, Kent: Hodder & Stoughton Educational.

Wiliam, D. (1994) Assessing authentic tasks: alternatives to mark-schemes. *Nordic Studies in Mathematics Education*, 2(1), pp. 48–67.

Wood, D. J., McMahon, L. and Cranstoun, Y. (1980) *Working with Under-Fives*. London: Grant McIntyre.

Yair, G. (2000) Reforming motivation: how the structure of instruction affects students' learning experiences. *British Educational Research Journal*, 26(2) pp. 191–210.

Yeats, W. B. (1958) *The Collected Poems of W. B. Yeats*. London: MacMillan (first edition, 1933).

Index

Introductory Note.
Alphabetical arrangement is word-by-word.
Added to a page number 'f' denotes a figure or illustration.

198